WHAT ONLINE REVIEWERS ARE SAYING:

Regardless of your denomination or theological orientation, this book is a treasure trove of insight into the Holy Scriptures.
I give it five stars!
Highly recommended!

C. M Mills,
Amazon 'Top 500 Reviewer'

… very well written … puts things in a simple way that everyone can understand.
The illustrations also add a fun touch to it that really brings the writing to life!

Violet Perry,
Just a Bookish Blog and Goodreads Reviewer

Mr. Mansbridge shares in every way my preferred approach to understanding the Bible … [it is a] wonderful manual … ideal as a text in a small group dedicated to honing one's skills in interpretation.

B. Marold,
Amazon 'Hall of Fame Reviewer'

WHAT MINISTRY SCHOOL LEADERS ARE SAYING:

Chad Mansbridge has provided an invaluable service ... rich and practical ... straightforward and engaging ... an excellent teaching resource for an introduction to biblical interpretation.

Bruce W. Gore, *ret. Adjunct Professor of Theology, Whitworth University, USA*

... accessible, memorable and applicable to all of us ... I recommend this work to anyone who wants to confidently read the Scriptures in a more thorough and meaningful way.

Dr. Phillip Barnard, *fmr. Senior Lecturer, Hillsong Church Ministry School, UK*

... an excellent new publication ... drawing on time-honoured principles, he offers plenty of examples of original thinking, creative illustration and contemporary application ... a book for Christians both new and old ... Chad has hit the mark!

Dr. Barry Chant, *Founding President, Tabor College, Australia*

... easy to understand ... great principles ... This book should be read by every believer who wants to understand their Bible.

Susan Hoover, *Director, World Impact Bible Institute, Indonesia*

WHAT LOCAL CHURCH PASTORS ARE SAYING:

... relatable, conversational and often humorous ... an easy, accessible and enjoyable read ... a great introductory resource for anyone wanting to develop their Bible interpretive skills.

Catherine Hoekendijk, *Harmony Church, New Zealand*

... approachable and engaging ... peels back the inaccessibility that's commonly associated with Bible hermeneutics, and instead reveals its dynamic power, beauty, simplicity and relevance for the world today.

Jocel & Mylene Evangelista, *New Life Main, Philippines*

YOU CAN HANDLE THE TRUTH

MAKING SENSE OF THE BIBLE IN 3 SIMPLE STEPS

CHAD M. MANSBRIDGE

with illustrations by Louis Decrevel

LIVING
LETTERS
PUBLISHING

For my kids and theirs; and their kids and theirs.

May the Eternal Word of our Father
take His place in your hearts and lives.

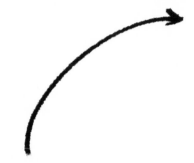

Contents

Therefore, since through God's mercy we have this ministry, we do not lose heart. Rather, we have renounced secret and shameful ways; we do not use deception, nor do we distort the word of God. On the contrary, by **setting forth the truth plainly** we commend ourselves to everyone's conscience in the sight of God.

2 Corinthians 4:1–2

DEAR PASTOR

To my fellow pastors, ministry leaders and next-generation mentors: when you and I said 'yes' to God's call to ministry, we embraced a truly noble task. To love, lead and feed God's people—that is, to shepherd them—is both a great privilege and a grave responsibility, in that it brings together a stewardship of the planet's most precious commodities: the Gospel of Christ and the lives of those for whom He died.

As Christian leaders, one of our fundamental duties is to proclaim God's Word. Technological advancements of recent decades have provided us with many means to do this, enabling a reach and range of communication of which previous generations could only dream. The so-called information age has changed everything, yet this blessing has not come without challenges. Today, more than ever before, we are working with a generation of believers who desperately need help *to filter out the noise and hear God's voice for themselves.* Our task is not merely to teach the Scriptures, but to train others in how to hear, understand and apply its truth, personally and properly.

You Can Handle the Truth is a comprehensive, step-by-step guide to the field of biblical interpretation (i.e., hermeneutics). It is designed for those who wish to increase their confidence and competency in handling the Scriptures well—to equip everyday believers with the tools to read and heed God's Word.

The book follows a simple three-step structure, which I frame around three key questions: *What does it say? What does it mean? What does it matter?* In Step 1, we take a brief look at the issue of translation before delving into practical approaches to reading the Bible. Step 2 is the most detailed part of the book. Here, we address the critical concern of exegesis—discovering the author's intended meaning. Literary genre, grammar, covenant, culture and the Bible's metanarrative all feature strongly in this part of the process. In Step 3, we close by considering the implications of biblical truth to our lives today, and how we should apply it. Or rather, how we should go about applying our lives *to it*.

Its purpose is to present long-established principles of biblical interpretation to a new generation of Bible students. My hope is that the reader finds the content simple but substantive, principled but practical, memorable and shareable. That those you serve are equipped and encouraged to take hold of God's Word and bring themselves to personal manifestation of its powerful realities.

In short, this book is my humble attempt to help you help others, and themselves, to hear God.

Together for His cause,

Chad M. Mansbridge

DEAR READER

I would stake a guess that most church-going Christians are well aware that we should read our Bibles. Most Christians understand that we should take the Bible's teaching seriously and practice what it preaches. But there's a big difference between knowing that we *should* do something and knowing with confidence that we *can*. Everyone knows that they should exercise regularly, eat well and follow a comprehensive financial plan, but very few do. Being told *why* we should do such things is often not enough. For many of us, the motivation and confidence required to engage with such disciplines comes only when we have first been shown *how*.

The message of this book is simple: you *can* handle the truth! As a follower of Christ presumably you have heard already many good reasons as to why you should read, understand and apply God's Word. I agree—yes, you *should*. But now it's time to discover *how*.

> Do your best to present yourself to God as one approved, a worker who does not need to be ashamed and who **correctly handles the word of truth**. (2 Tim. 2:15)

The purpose of this book is to equip everyday believers to handle the Scriptures well. It has been written with the express intent of ministering to your *head*, *heart* and *hands*—to effect positive change in how you think, feel and behave towards the Bible.

First and foremost, I want to see your love for God and His Word reach higher heights and deeper depths. I want you to take the scroll and devour it, taste it and see that the Lord is good: 'When I discovered your words, I devoured them. They are my joy and my heart's delight' (Jer. 15:16 NLT).

Second, like the apostle Peter, I write to 'stimulate you to wholesome thinking' (2 Peter 3:1). I am a firm believer that good teaching solidifies certainty and stirs curiosity. Sound biblical exposition should leave the hearer with a greater sense of clarity and confidence in their scriptural convictions. Additionally, it should simultaneously stimulate their thoughts, evoke questions and inspire a desire to enquire. The role of the educator is to teach people *how* to think, not just what to think, and to encourage the pupil to seek out truth for themselves. From the outset, let me be clear that this is one of my express intentions: I want to start you *thinking*.

Last, but certainly not least, I want to equip you with practical tools so you can handle the Bible well, applying long-established rules of biblical interpretation to your reading, study, application and communication of God's Word. In regard to its fundamental principles, this book contains nothing new. In fact, you should be concerned if I claimed it did! As to content and the way it is presented, my hope is that you find it fresh, user-friendly and even a little fun.

Whether you are new and relatively unfamiliar with the teachings of the Bible, a seasoned reader or even an experienced preacher-teacher, I'm thrilled that you have decided to take this journey with me. Together, we will grow in our confidence and competency in correctly handling the Word of Truth.

Let's go.

CHAPTER 1

Introductions

Soon after I was born, on the day I was 'dedicated' at my parents' church, an elderly lady handed my folks the following portion of Scripture, sensing the truths it contained would prove particularly pertinent to my life and personal walk with the Lord. While I have no recollection of this individual and limited knowledge of her life, this passage has become very dear to me for the hope and prophetic encouragement I have found in its words:

> **The Lord will guide you always**; he will satisfy your needs in a sun-scorched land and will strengthen your frame. You will be like a well-watered garden, like a spring whose waters never fail. Your people will rebuild the ancient ruins and will raise up the age-old foundations; you will be called Repairer of Broken Walls, Restorer of Streets with Dwellings. (Isa. 58:11–12)

This Scripture, and many others like it, helped convince me that God is committed to leading and guiding His people. Our God speaks. Our God is dedicated to making His will, wisdom and ways known in clear and comprehensible ways, that those who hear and heed His voice find paths of peace and prosperity, purpose and productivity. Wrote the psalmist, 'Your word is a lamp for my feet, a light on my path' (Ps. 119:105).

Over the years, I've learnt that there are multiple ways the Good Shepherd guides His sheep, and many ways His Word is heard. While the modern Christian world may be split regarding the veracity of angelic visitations, dreams, heavenly encounters, prophetic utterances and the like, it seems we can all agree that God is committed to guiding us through His written Word—the Holy Scriptures.

Through my teenage and young adult years, I began to cultivate a deep passion for the Bible. It began when my parents sent me on a Christian youth camp over summer. Operated by a non-denominational ministry group, the event attracted high-school kids from all sorts of church expressions: liturgical, evangelical, cessational and Pentecostal. At the time, these terms were all foreign to me (as they may be to you!) and apparently I was one of the 'Pentecostal kids' … or so I was told. News to me.

Rubbing shoulders with Christians my own age from notably different backgrounds and belief systems benefitted me immensely. I met some who believed God no longer works miracles today, that praying in tongues was 'of the devil' and that God stopped speaking the moment John wrote 'Amen' at the end of his Revelation (22:21). Again, news to me. But exposure to such varied views only stirred my curiosity, inspiring me to seek out the Scriptures and determine *what* I believed and *why*.

My love for the Bible continued to grow as I entered adulthood. I relocated to the city for further study and joined an evangelical Christian student group at my university, again allowing me to befriend believers from many different backgrounds and traditions. I plugged in to a new church that appealed to me, partly because of its emphasis on the working of the Spirit and the weightiness of Scripture. It was during these years that I received a clear call to ministry. Full disclosure: I never attended seminary or Bible college. I do not have a doctorate in theology, diploma in ministry, certificate in Christian studies or any such thing. I graduated university, certainly, but my studies were limited to philosophy and law. My 'pastoral training' was an entirely local church-based, rubber-hits-the-road, on-the-job, hands-on, do-or-die enterprise.

Local Church Planting, Pastoring and Preaching

Pioneering a church at age 23 brought the serious responsibility of consistent Bible study and sermon preparation. I dug into the Word like never before, and it was soon apparent that a significant number of people found benefit and encouragement in my preaching and teaching ministry. Our church grew and I received invites to minister elsewhere. People began requesting our material and, especially after publishing my first book, my international profile and demand for my ministry increased around the world. It turns out there are plenty of people who share a similar love and hunger for His Word!

As it currently stands, I have two great preaching passions. The first is simple: Jesus. '[We] preach Christ crucified', said Paul, for 'the message of the cross is ... the power of God' (1 Cor. 1:17–25). When it comes to proclaiming His Word, I am, first and foremost, a messenger of His Gospel: *the Good News that the person of Jesus makes it possible for all people to participate in the presence of God and the provisions of God, both now and for all eternity.* Good tidings of great joy, indeed!

My second passion is healthy biblical interpretation. The church from which we were released into pastoral ministry taught me that the role of the teacher is not simply to explain the Bible, but to equip His people to handle it for themselves (Eph. 4:11–12). As the old saying goes, 'Give a man a fish and you feed him for a day. Teach a man to fish and you feed him for a lifetime'. I stepped into pastoral ministry in response to God's call, but also because I wanted to help people, to help others know and enjoy Christ as I did. Developing an accurate and working knowledge of the Scriptures is key to this. Helping others *help themselves* to feed on, and find freedom through, His Word became my holy ambition.

I have provided you this personal background to make this point: the book you are holding deals with one of the most complex concerns to the Christian community. How are we to properly understand, interpret and apply God's precious, yet powerful, written Word? This discussion is nothing new. For over 2,000 years, the best minds in Christian and Jewish scholarship have developed interpretive approaches, theories, courses, papers, books, studies and seminars in this quest. I am certainly not the first to be passionate about this important issue.

Yet this book is distinctly different from most in its field: it was written by an ordinary believer-come-Bible preacher. I am not an academic, scholar, professor or doctor. I have no degrees on my wall or letters after my name. I do not read Hebrew or Greek, nor do I consider myself a theologian in the strict sense of the term. I am a local church pastor, charged with communicating God's Word to everyday people like myself. I approached the production of this book in the same way that I prepare my sermons—striving to simplify the complex, and distil highly detailed truths into memorable tools and repeatable techniques for the typical, run-of-the-mill follower of Christ. This brings me to you:

> **Timothy, my son,** I am giving you this command in keeping with the prophecies once made about you, so that by recalling them you may fight the battle well, holding on to faith and a good conscience … be strong in the grace that is in Christ Jesus. And the things you have heard me say in the presence of many witnesses entrust to reliable men who will also be qualified to teach others. (1 Tim. 1:18–19; 2 Tim. 2:2)

This book is written for Timothys and, for my female readers, Tammys. Tim and Tams … it's an Australian thing. Just go with it. My intent is to encourage and equip everyday people to handle the Bible personally, properly and productively. If you consider yourself a student of the Scripture, committed to following the guidance of God over your life, this is for you.

TAM

TIM

With that said, it is also for budding Bible teachers. My hope is that you will take from its pages *tools and techniques* with which you can help others. That, like Timothy, you can teach others who can teach others. They say imitation is the sincerest form of flattery. If you find anything useful in the pages that follow, I would be delighted if you were to repeat it to others.

The gift of God's Word is too good to keep to ourselves!

Training Timothy

> I hope in the Lord Jesus to send Timothy to you soon, that I also may be cheered when I receive news about you. I have no one else like him, who will show genuine concern for your welfare. For everyone looks out for their own interests, not those of Jesus Christ. But you know that **Timothy has proved himself, because as a son with his father he has served with me in the work of the gospel**. (Phil. 2:19–22)

Throughout this book, we will examine some of the apostle Paul's encouragements to his spiritual son Timothy as it relates to his developing preaching and teaching ministry. But first, let's cover some background on these two individuals.

Acts 16–18 records highlights from Paul's second apostolic journey of approximately three-and-a-half years around 49–53 AD. From his ministry base in Antioch, accompanied this time by Silas, a respected prophet from the Jerusalem church, Paul returns to the Lycaonian towns of Lystra and Derbe in the Roman province of Galatia, in modern-day Turkey. Here, he meets a young man named Timothy who, partly because of his positive reputation among believers in that region, is invited to travel with the apostle (Acts 16:1–3).

The young believer gladly accepts Paul's offer: thus, beginning what is arguably the most successful mentoring relationship of the great apostle's life and ministry. During this exciting expedition, Timothy would learn many invaluable lessons from the seasoned teacher.

First, he would witness Paul faithfully respond to the leading of Holy Spirit. Whether by overt and dramatic manifestations, such as his visions of Christ, the Macedonian man and the supernatural earthquake that shook the prison foundations; or discreet promptings, like the inner disturbance he experienced when a slave girl joined his entourage in Philippi, time and again, Timothy would learn the value of being sensitive to the personal leading of the *Spirit*.[1]

Second, Timothy would witness Paul partnering with fellow ministers such as Silas, to strengthen existing churches and build new ones. He would listen as Paul communicated not only the revelation he had personally received from Christ, but also that given to his apostolic contemporaries in Jerusalem. He would watch Paul work as a tent-maker alongside Italian refugees in Corinth, and time and again, receive hospitality and financial support from fellow believers. In all this, Timothy would learn the value of team, of working and walking together with fellow *saints*.[2]

Finally, Timothy would watch, listen and learn as Paul masterfully unpacked the glorious truth of Christ from the Holy *Scriptures*. In Philippi, Paul would communicate the Gospel to the families of both Jewish businesswomen and Greek jailers. In Thessalonica, Berea, Athens, Corinth and Ephesus, Paul would teach in the synagogues, reasoning, explaining and proving from the Hebrew Scriptures information concerning their promised Messiah.

Make no mistake: while Paul's preaching and teaching in these contexts was no doubt undertaken with great passion, and accompanied by supernatural signs, wonders and miracles, he also communicated with great clarity and intellectual aptitude. The language in Acts is very clear on this:

> As was his custom, Paul went into the synagogue, and on three Sabbath days **he reasoned with them from the Scriptures, explaining and proving** that the Messiah had to suffer ... **philosophers began to debate with him** ... **he reasoned** in the synagogue, **trying to persuade** Jews and Greeks ... Paul stayed in Corinth for a year and a half, **teaching them the word of God.** (Acts 17:2–3, 18; 18:4, 11)

By accompanying Paul on this exciting apostolic venture, we can be certain young Timothy gleaned many lifelong lessons from his ministry mentor-come-spiritual father. Yet, it is three that stand out to me the most: Timothy was trained how to be sensitive to the *Spirit*, partner with the *saints*, and correctly and intelligently handle the *Scriptures*.

Over a decade later, with Timothy now a prominent and leading figure in the Ephesian church, these three lessons would be repeated and reinforced as Paul wrote to his son.

Lessons that you and I would do well to heed today.

CHAPTER 2

Handle with Care!

As I urged you when I went into Macedonia, stay there in Ephesus so that you may command certain people not to teach false doctrines any longer or to devote themselves to myths and endless genealogies. Such things promote controversial speculations rather than advancing God's work—which is by faith. The goal of this command is love, which comes from a pure heart and a good conscience and a sincere faith. Some have departed from these and have turned to meaningless talk. They want to be teachers of the law, but they do not know what they are talking about or what they so confidently affirm. **We know that the law is good if one uses it properly**. (1 Tim. 1:3–8)

Amid his opening remarks in this first letter, Paul makes a remarkable point: 'We know that the law is good when used correctly' (1 Tim. 1:8 NLT). By 'the law', Paul is either referring to the Ten Commandments, given at Sinai (Ex. 20); the Torah, the 'books of Moses' (Genesis–Deuteronomy); or the Tanakh,[3] the entire Hebrew Bible or Old Testament (Genesis–Malachi). Regardless, his general point is clear enough: the Scripture is good.

As he would later assert, 'All Scripture is God-breathed and useful', and all Scripture is worthy of Timothy devoting himself to reading, teaching and preaching in and out of season (2 Tim. 3:16; 1 Tim. 4:13). This sentiment is embraced and echoed by all good preachers everywhere. From the books of Moses, to the last of Israel's Prophets, from the four Gospels, to the closing chapters of Revelation: *all Scripture is good.*

However, it needs to be used properly.

You see, there is a proper and an improper way to handle God's Word. There is a right and a wrong way to use the Bible. We need look no further than Jesus' wilderness temptation to witness this:

> Then the devil took him to the holy city and had him stand on the highest point of the temple. 'If you are the Son of God,' he said, 'throw yourself down. For it is written: "He will command his angels concerning you, and they will lift you up in their hands, so that you will not strike your foot against a stone."' Jesus answered him, 'It is also written: "Do not put the Lord your God to the test."' (Matt. 4:5–7)

The devil may have been accurate in his citing of the Scriptures, but he was clearly off base in his summary and conclusions; demonstrating that one may have God's words right but handle them all wrong.

What Helps May Harm

While God certainly intends for His Scripture to help people, it can bring harm because God's Word is not only a good thing, it is a very *powerful* thing:

> '**Is not my word like fire**', declares the Lord, '**and like a hammer** that breaks a rock in pieces?'. (Jer. 23:29)

Fire is essential to our survival. Throughout human history, its power has been used to prepare our food and provide warmth to our families. We use fire to celebrate the things we value and eliminate the things we don't. We use fire to drive our machinery and increase our productivity. Fire is *good*.

However, it can also do incredible damage. The very thing that so often helps us can harm us, especially when it is mishandled. Sadly, many a burns victim and, particularly in a place like Australia, those who suffer loss from large-scale bushfires (i.e., wildfires) are testament to this. You see, fire is not only good, it is *powerful* and powerful things must be handled with care.

Similarly, like a hammer in a worker's hand, the Scripture can be used to both build and break things. Hitting the nail on the head is one thing; hitting yourself in the head is another! Likewise, how one handles the Word of Truth will lead to either constructive or destructive outcomes. God's Word has the power to both heal you and hurt you, depending on how you use it.

Paul's warning to Timothy is simple; in Ephesus, certain men were teaching false, meaningless and damaging doctrine. They were doing so by appealing to the Scripture.

While the Scriptures these teachers quoted were true, the conclusions they reached were false. By mishandling the Bible, these men were misleading their listeners, and Timothy was instructed to take note and act accordingly to refute them.

Years later, in what many believe to be the apostle's final epistle, Paul encouraged Timothy to not fall into the same trap as these men:

> Do your best to present yourself to God as one approved, **a worker who does not need to be ashamed and who correctly handles the word of truth**. Avoid godless chatter, because those who indulge in it will become more and more ungodly. (2 Tim. 2:15–16)

Again, the same point is made. There is a correct way—and thus, an incorrect way—to approach, apprehend and apply the Bible. While the content of the

Scriptures is true, the conclusions we reach may not be true. Therefore, great care and consideration must be employed as we commit ourselves to correctly handle God's Word.

Tim the Tool Man

I won't lie to you; I'm not the handiest handyman to have around. At church building projects, it is more common to see me with a clipboard or list of coffee orders in my hand than a power-tool. Like Jesus, I'm a preacher and the son of a tradesman, but, unlike the apostle Paul, I could not make a living from doing both. Let's just say I'm a more competent communicator than I am a carpenter.

Having said that, like any red-blooded male, I feel right at home browsing the aisles of my local hardware store and, as a result, possess a cupboard full of tools, tins, kits and bits. I may not be a natural when it comes to hands-on construction tasks, but with the right tools in one hand and step-by-step instructions in the other, I can assemble almost anything. It must be all those hours spent playing with LEGO® bricks as a kid. But enough about me—back to our title text:

> Be diligent to present yourself approved to God, a **worker** who does not need to be ashamed, **rightly dividing the word of truth**. (2 Tim. 2:15 NKJV)

As a self-proclaimed 'master builder' (1 Cor. 3:10 ESV), Paul was leaving his co-labouring apprentice with no room for doubt; correctly handling the Scriptures requires *work*. Rightly dividing the Word of Truth is a job that must be approached with informed intentionality and the willingness to apply oneself to the task at hand.

Yes, there is work to be done. The Bible comes to us with 'some assembly required'. But let me encourage you again—you *can* do this.

Please don't allow the apparent complexity or weightiness of biblical interpretation to overwhelm you. While Paul himself was a career theologian and thoroughly educated Bible teacher, schooled in the Hebrew Scriptures by the most highly acclaimed of Israel's rabbis and scholars, young Timothy had no formal training.

Instead, Timothy's Bible knowledge developed as he grew up in a household of faith, attended a Bible-believing community, learnt from mature ministers and applied himself personally to scriptural study and application.

If Timothy could succeed in handling the Scriptures well, you can too! So, let's get started.

Getting Started

As we make a start on unboxing our Bible we need first to establish some preliminaries. In this section, we introduce the step-by-step *process* every good worker must follow to successfully construct a God-honouring, accurate and workable understanding of the Scriptures. In broad terms, this process, together with its guiding principles and practices, is known as *hermeneutics*. The bulk of this book is dedicated to coaching you in the three essential steps of the hermeneutical process, as demonstrated in Nehemiah 8.

Before then, however, our first task is to familiarise ourselves with the *tools* we have been provided. God has not left us to helplessly fend for ourselves in this work, but rather has committed to equip us with all we'll ever need for doing His will (Heb. 13:20–21). There are three such toolkits available to you, each one packed full of helpful aids and ways to get the job done, and each one corresponding to the three life lessons Timothy gained when he accompanied Paul on his apostolic travels as discussed in our opening

chapter: sensitivity to the *Spirit*, partnership with the *saints* and intelligent treatment of the *Scriptures*.

These three disciplines are also the three main mechanisms by which we can all correctly handle the Word of Truth today:

> The Spirit
>
> The Saints
>
> The Science of Hermeneutics

These are your three toolkits, each fully equipped with all you'll ever need to get the job done. Let's unpack them, shall we?

CHAPTER 3

The Spirit

You then, my son, be strong in the grace that is in Christ Jesus. And the things you have heard me say in the presence of many witnesses entrust to reliable people who will also be qualified to teach others. Join with me in suffering, like a good soldier of Christ Jesus. No one serving as a soldier gets entangled in civilian affairs, but rather tries to please his commanding officer. Similarly, anyone who competes as an athlete does not receive the victor's crown except by competing according to the rules. The hardworking farmer should be the first to receive a share of the crops. **Reflect on what I am saying, for the Lord will give you insight into all this**. (2 Tim. 2:1–7)

While he may not have realised it at the time, as Timothy read these words, he was actually reading Scripture! The encouragement to be strong in the grace of Christ, to mentor those who would mentor others and to somehow give himself to the lifestyle of a soldier, athlete and farmer, were all God-breathed revelations expressed through the pen and personality of the apostle Paul.

However, it wasn't enough that Timothy simply read these instructions or settled for a purely cognitive comprehension of the words, phrases and metaphors in the text. For Timothy to correctly handle the Word of Truth that was before him, he had to stop and *reflect*, allowing the Spirit of God Himself to minister to his heart and mind regarding those written words.

It is the same for us today. The Bible is a spiritual book, and it takes a work of the Spirit to adequately understand it. Before opening your Bible, I would encourage you to first open your heart and expect the Good Teacher Himself to personally tutor you. After all, it is the only book for which the author Himself is present with you, every time you read it.

The Lord Gives Understanding

The word Paul uses here for 'insight' (Greek: *synesis*) literally means to *put it all together* and is repeated in Colossians, in which Paul writes: '[we] do not cease to pray for you, and to desire that ye might be filled with the knowledge of his will in all wisdom and **spiritual understanding**' (Col. 1:9 KJV).

According to Luke's Gospel, it is this form of understanding that Jesus possessed as a 12-year-old boy that amazed the temple-goers in Jerusalem. It is this special type of insight He later brought to Cleopas and his companion on the Emmaus road on the day of His resurrection (Luke 2:47; 24:27–32).

When He happened upon them, these two unsuspecting disciples were discussing their disappointment at the death of their Lord and dismay at the apparent disappearance of His body. Kept from recognising Him at first, Jesus explained to them that the Hebrew Scriptures, both the Law and the Prophets, foretold these very things.

However, as accurate and informative as His teaching must have been, it was not enough for these despondent disciples to simply have their minds engaged with biblical facts. These travellers required a *spiritual encounter* that affected their inner selves.

In response to what they later described as a *burning sensation in their hearts*, the couple invited and persuaded Jesus to eat with them. A shift had taken place. On the road, their focus was the message; at the table, they turned their attention to the man Himself. Suddenly and unexpectedly, everything fell into place for them as 'their eyes were opened and they recognized him' (Luke 24:13–35).

Make no mistake; these two Jewish disciples knew what the Scriptures said. Through their own study and teachings from their family, community, schooling and synagogue, their knowledge of the Scriptures was quite comprehensive, at least from an academic and intellectual perspective.

Yet despite their biblical knowledge, it took an encounter with the Resurrected Christ Himself, and a spiritual work of God in their internal worlds, for them to truly understand the message and meaning of the Scriptures: 'Were not our hearts burning within us while he talked with us on the road and opened the Scriptures to us?' (Luke 24:32).[4]

Engaging the Spirit of Truth

Prior to His death—again, while sharing a meal with friends—Jesus promised that while He would be physically removed from the disciples, He would nevertheless send a helper to accompany and empower them to continue the work He had begun. Jesus described this helper as, 'another advocate ... the Spirit of truth ... the Holy Spirit ... [who] will **teach you all things** and will remind you of everything I have said to you ... [and who] will testify about me ... [and] **guide you into all the truth**' (John 14:16–17, 26; 15:26; 16:13).

Jesus even claimed that while He desired to share more with His friends, He knew they were not yet ready and could *not yet handle it*. In other words, Jesus deliberately withheld certain truths from His disciples, knowing Holy Spirit would be the One to teach them when the time was right (John 16:12–13). Throughout the book of Acts, we see Holy Spirit do exactly as Jesus had promised.

While Peter had read the prophetic texts declaring that the work of the Messiah would be for both Jew and Gentile (e.g., Isa. 49:6), and had personally heard the commission from Jesus' own lips to go into all the world as a witness to all people (e.g., Matt. 28:19), it nevertheless took a heavenly vision during a Spirit-induced trance for this apostle to put the pieces together and admit that, 'All the prophets testify about him that **everyone who believes** in him receives forgiveness through his name' (Acts 10:43).

While Paul (Saul of Tarsus)[5] had spent many years of his life training as a Pharisee, becoming academically acquainted with the Hebrew Scripture, it took a supernatural encounter with the manifest presence of Christ, a filling of Holy Spirit through the hands of Ananias, and time alone receiving heavenly revelation for him to piece together its messianic message.

Prior to Acts 9, Paul was simply another religious leader who read, studied, recited and taught the Scriptures, but did not *know* the Scriptures. Like the Sadducees Jesus confronted in Jerusalem, Paul was in error because he did not truly 'know the Scriptures or the power of God' (Matt. 22:29).

Before his Damascus road encounter, Paul's inadequate understanding led him to conclude that he should do everything in his power to demean the name of Jesus and destroy His followers (Acts 22:3–5; 26:9–11). But after receiving and responding to Holy Spirit, everything changed. Paul became Christianity's greatest champion, and the Scriptures he once used to oppose Jesus became the very same Scriptures he used to endorse Him:

> I too was convinced that I ought to do all I could to oppose the name of Jesus of Nazareth … And now I stand on trial because of my hope in the promise that God made to our fathers … **I am saying nothing beyond what the prophets and Moses said would happen**: that the Christ would suffer, and as the first to rise from the dead, would proclaim light to our people and to the Gentiles. (Acts 26:1–23)

The Scriptures themselves never changed, but Paul's understanding of them did, thanks to an encounter with the person of Christ, the heart of the Father and the Spirit of Truth. As he would later write to the church in Corinth:

> [What] no human mind has conceived … **God has revealed to us by his Spirit** … no one knows the thoughts of God except the Spirit of God … **[we have received] the Spirit who is from God, so that we may understand** what God has freely given us … because they are discerned only through the Spirit. (1 Cor. 2:9–14)

Says John:

> But you have an anointing from the Holy One, and all of you know

the truth … As for you, the anointing you received from him remains in you, and you do not need anyone to teach you. But as **his anointing teaches you about all things** and as that anointing is real, not counterfeit—just as it has taught you, remain in him. (1 John 2:20–27)

My point is this: the Bible is a spiritual book containing spiritual thoughts; thus, it requires receiving the Spirit of God to correctly discern and accurately apply its truth.

Your Personal Tutor

Occasionally, I hear Christians refer to the Bible as our 'Manual for Life', a divine instruction book, if you like, to a fulfilling, fruitful and God-honouring existence.[6] As imperfect as it may be, I am willing to accept this analogy *but only on one condition*. If the Bible is to be viewed as our manual, we must acknowledge that together with the Book, God has also given us a personal Tutor.

Yes, God has given us the Scriptures, but, more importantly, He has given us *Himself*. His very personal and powerful presence. Without an authentic, intimate and ongoing relationship with the Spirit of God Himself, there is no hope of walking in a true, thorough and life-giving understanding of His Word.[7] Ultimately, the whole purpose of the Scriptures is to help us know Him!

By all means, do whatever you can to increase your understanding of the Bible, but please remember God is not Father, Son and Holy Scriptures. He is Father, Son and Holy Spirit. We have the Book that we may know the Author.

Says John of his Gospel, 'But these are written that you may believe that Jesus is the Messiah, the Son of God, and that by believing you may **have life** in his name'. To a crowd of worshippers, Jesus claimed, 'You study the Scriptures diligently because you think that in them you have eternal life. These are the very Scriptures that testify about me, yet you refuse to **come to me to have life**' (John 20:31; 5:39–40).

Eternal life is not experienced by familiarity with the Scripture, but by knowing and trusting the Son whom that Scripture reveals (John 17:37). I do not know how you have come to be reading this book today but before we move on, I encourage you to stop and ask God to reveal Himself to you—to make His reality known to you.

God's invisible presence is not far from any of us. His Spirit is with you right now; His desire is to lead you into a knowledge of what is true, and into a genuine relationship with a God who deeply loves and cares for you.

 Timothy, Tammy... stop. Reflect on what I am saying, so the Lord Himself can give you insight into all this.

CHAPTER 4

The Saints

> You, however, **know all about my teaching, my way of life,
> my purpose, faith, patience, love, endurance, persecutions,
> sufferings**—what kinds of things happened to me in Antioch,
> Iconium and Lystra, the persecutions I endured. Yet the Lord rescued
> me from all of them. In fact, everyone who wants to live a godly life
> in Christ Jesus will be persecuted, while evildoers and impostors will
> go from bad to worse, deceiving and being deceived. But as for you,
> continue in what you have learned and have become convinced of,
> **because you know those from whom you learned it**, and how from
> infancy you have known the Holy Scriptures, which are able to make
> you wise for salvation through faith in Christ Jesus. (2 Tim. 3:10–15)

As a young man, Timothy greatly expanded his understanding of Scripture
through his exposure to Paul's preaching and teaching. But how could it
be said that Timothy knew the Holy Scriptures from his *infancy*? Simple.
Timothy had a mother and grandmother who instructed him, and—some
suggest[8]—exposed him to the synagogue throughout his childhood, where
the Hebrew Bible was read aloud, taught and discussed (Acts 16:1–2; 2 Tim.
1:5).

At the time he received this second epistle, Timothy was likely well into his
thirties. By now, he had years of ministry experience behind him, and—while
still recognised as a 'dear son' to Paul—was an established and influential
leader in his own right (2 Tim. 1:2).

Over time, Timothy learnt and became convinced of many powerful truths from God's Word. Paul urged him to persevere in these lessons and to do so confidently, based on his intimate knowledge of *the life-testimony of those who had instructed him.*

Yes—the Bible is a spiritual book, and so we need the Spirit to help us understand it. But the Bible is also a community book, so God gives us the *saints* to teach us what we could never discover on our own.[9]

With a Little Help from My Friends

> Meanwhile a Jew named Apollos, a native of Alexandria, came to Ephesus. **He was a learned man, with a thorough knowledge of the Scriptures.** He had been instructed in the way of the Lord, and he spoke with great fervor and taught about Jesus accurately, though he knew only the baptism of John. He began to speak boldly in the synagogue. When Priscilla and Aquila heard him, they invited him to their home and **explained to him the way of God more adequately.** (Acts 18:24–26)[10]

I trust the implications of that last passage did not go unnoticed. The impassioned preacher, Apollos, was already well versed in the Scriptures when he arrived in Ephesus. However, his understanding of Jesus' work was notably deficient—this eloquent and learned man had room to grow. This he did, thanks to the input of tent-making tradespeople from Rome (Acts 18:2–3, 18–19).

It was also Ephesus in which young Timothy would one day take a leading role under the ongoing mentorship of the apostle Paul. In this community, Timothy was tasked with appointing faithful leaders and confronting false teachers, communicating God's Word to both believers and unbelievers, instructing Christians in matters of prayer and propriety, and guiding the stewardship of church funds towards those in need and those who feed.

Yet Timothy was clearly not the only reputable preacher in town. Paul describes how several Ephesian elders were specifically called to 'labor in preaching and teaching'. So important was this calling, so valuable the work of teaching the Scriptures, the apostle insisted these preaching pastors be paid well, and therefore, be empowered to succeed in their task (1 Tim. 5:17–18 ESV).[11]

While every believer in Christ has access to the Spirit as our ever-present teacher and personal tutor, God has ordained it so *that we also learn from others*, including pastors, parents, professionals, pupils and peers.

Paul's open letter to the Ephesian church claims similarly. While all believers have received the same grace for salvation, each believer has received a specific grace for service. While all believers belong to the same body, each believer has a unique part to play and contribution to make (Eph. 2:3–9; 4:4–16).

Together, '**we** [plural] **are God's masterpiece**'—a multicoloured, multidimensional work of art displaying the multicoloured, multidimensional nature of our Maker (Eph. 2:10 NLT). God is multifaceted and beautifully complex. His Scriptures are multifaceted and beautifully complex. And it takes a multifaceted community to experience, explain and exhibit the full beauty of that complexity: 'So now **through the church the multifaceted wisdom of God** [in all its countless aspects] **might now be made known**' (Eph. 3:10 AMP).

By recognising, receiving and responding to the manifold ministry of Christ's apostles, prophets, evangelists, pastors and teachers, all the saints will come to 'unity in the faith and in the knowledge of the Son of God', no longer 'blown here and there by every wind of teaching', but grounded and growing in the truth of God's Eternal Word (Eph. 4:11–16).

The Father has created you for community. Surround yourself with Spirit-sensitive, Bible-believing saints—men, women and children who are distinctly different from you. Fill your bookshelf and audio devices with the works of Bible teachers living and dead, local and foreign, devotional and academic, reputable and controversial.

Learn from them. Listen to them. Because they will see truth in the Scripture that you yourself may never discover without the help of their perspective.

Do You See What I See?

Time for a story.

Some years back, my family and I were spending a glorious summer's day at one of our favourite beaches. My wife, Jaye, and I were lazing about in the sun while our kids played in the sand nearby. At some stage, I glanced south towards the cliffs, a good distance away and noticed close to a dozen wind turbines on the clifftop.

'Hey kids, take a look at the windmills!', I said. Upon offering a disinterested glance, they swiftly replied, 'There's nothing there, Dad', and returned to their play. 'Come on, look properly kids. There's at least ten massive wind turbines up high on that cliff top.'

This time in response to my appeal, Jaye looked up from her magazine, squinted in the direction of the cliffs and responded, 'Chad, you're imagining things. The kids are right; there's nothing there'. I couldn't believe it. First my kids and now my wife—what was their problem?

'What are you talking about, nothing there?' I began counting out loud as I pleaded my case. 'There's at least eight, nine, ten … possibly twelve massive, white turbines moving in the wind on top of that cliff. Look!'

'Sure, darling.'

I quietly contemplated how my wife and three kids could not see something that stood out as plain as day to me. We were all in the same locality, with the same line of sight. I obviously held no advantage insofar as distance or strength of vision was concerned. Why was their perspective so different?

Then it occurred to me. I was the only one wearing sunglasses. I removed them, glanced back up at the clifftop, and suddenly those wind turbines disappeared from my sight.

I had been wearing polarised lenses. My sunglasses were designed to filter out horizontal light waves from my vision, and in doing so, enabled me to see something otherwise invisible to the naked eye. After convincing Jaye to look again (this time with my sunglasses on), she too could easily count up to a dozen white wind turbines. The turbines were always there, but it required the assistance of polarised lenses to see them.

The same is true with the Bible. Sometimes an individual will see a truth in the Scripture you have not, and would not otherwise understand or even notice. Whether by their natural peculiarities, personalities and persuasions, or by a supernatural calling, anointing and grace-gifting, other people will see things in the Scripture that you will never discover on your own. I am convinced God planned it this way.

Over my Christian experience, there have been many moments when I have read an author or heard a teacher reveal something in a passage of Scripture I have read hundreds of times, but have never myself seen. Conversely, I can recall numerous occasions in which seasoned pastors and preachers have approached me to tell how I had helped them discover a perspective on biblical truth that had never occurred to them before.

The point is, no matter how well researched or revelatory you or your favourite Bible teacher may be, no single person or preacher on the planet can profess a full and flawless understanding of the Holy Scriptures! The Bible is a community book; it is designed to be learnt and lived out in community. By all means, study the Scriptures *for* yourself, but it's not enough to study the Scriptures *by* yourself.

To assist you in correctly handling the Word of Truth, God has given you the saints.[12]

CHAPTER 5

The Science of Hermeneutics

All Scripture is God-breathed and is useful for teaching, rebuking, correcting and training in righteousness, so that the servant of God may be thoroughly equipped for every good work. In the presence of God and of Christ Jesus, who will judge the living and the dead, and in view of his appearing and his kingdom, I give you this charge: preach the word; be prepared in season and out of season; correct, rebuke and encourage—with great patience and careful instruction. For the time will come when people will not put up with sound doctrine. Instead, to suit their own desires, they will gather around them a great number of teachers to say what their itching ears want to hear. They will turn their ears away from the truth and turn aside to myths. **But you, keep your head in all situations**, endure hardship, do the work of an evangelist, discharge all the duties of your ministry. (2 Tim. 3:16–4:5)

The Bible is a spiritual book, so we need to read it with the Spirit—our personal tutor and ever-present teacher. The Bible is a community book, so God gave us the saints—that we may come to a fuller understanding and appreciation of its multifaceted truth. However, the Bible is also an intelligent book and we need to read it with our brains engaged.

The Bible is a history book and is to be approached with a sober, clear and mature mind that employs the scientific process of *healthy hermeneutics*.

Healthy Herman, Who?

'Hermeneutics' is the broad term that describes the principles and processes by which we interpret the Scripture. And 'healthy hermeneutics' (my term) involves doing so intelligently.

The word itself has Greek origins, variations of which can be found in the pages of the New Testament, in which it is commonly rendered 'interpretation' (1 Cor. 12:10; 14:26; Heb. 7:2). Hermeneutics is a derivative of *Hermès*, a common Greek name (Rom. 16:14) and one given to Paul during his first visit to Lystra:

> When the crowd saw what Paul had done, they shouted in the Lycaonian language, 'The gods have come down to us in human form!' Barnabas they called Zeus, and **Paul they called Hermès because he was the chief speaker**. (Acts 14:11–12)

In Greek mythology, Hermès was the son of Zeus and messenger of the gods. He was tasked with heralding the communication of the deities to mortals, thereby interpreting their divine messages. Some credit him with the invention of speech itself. Nothing like a touch of pagan mythology to guide us in our spiritual development, is there?

Arguably, our greatest challenge as students of the Scripture is in learning how to take its *heavenly revelation* to *hands-on application*, in which we accurately assess *modern-day implications* from *age-old inspiration*.

As we have just read, all Scripture is divinely inspired and useful for the people of God. Believers around the world agree with this principle, yet we clearly do not agree on all points of doctrine. When it comes to drawing conclusions from the text as to how it relates in practical terms to the world and church today, Christians are far from united on many issues. We may all have the same text, but we clearly do not all employ the same interpretive rules when reading it. We may agree on the facts of revelation and inspiration, but differ greatly in describing the Bible's implications and modern-day applications.

In the same way Paul and Timothy faced false teachers in first-century Ephesus, today, those who employ a faulty hermeneutic often emerge with distorted and, in the worst cases, dangerous, destructive and even demonic doctrines that 'bring the way of truth into disrepute' (2 Peter 2:1–2; 1 Tim. 4:1).

Our responsibility is to apply healthy hermeneutics to the Scripture's ancient and unchanging content, and thereby reach correct contemporary conclusions. Doing so protects our hearers, honours the text and ultimately brings glory to the Divine Author who inspired it.

Simply put, *healthy hermeneutics is both the art and science of intelligent interpretation*[13]—the process that bridges the gap between historical information and the here-and-now implications.

Hermeneutics: How We Understand Literature

Hermeneutics does not just apply to our reading of the Bible. In fact, we employ hermeneutical principles almost every time we approach *any form of literature*. Be it a classic children's fable, a live newsfeed on our smartphones, digits on a street sign or in the back end of a computer program, a stone inscription at an ancient temple or a twitter hashtag by a Hollywood celebrity, we apply rules of interpretation every time literature is presented to us, whether we are conscious of it or not.

When handed a menu in a restaurant, you instantly apply hermeneutics as you peruse its content. As soon as you see words presented in the form of a list, you understand that you are reading the name and description of real-life meals. No matter how unfamiliar or even 'un-food-like' those words may seem, you are convinced that what you are reading is indeed a list of meals and that the numbers corresponding to each item indicate the money you must pay to receive them. After all, you are in a restaurant and the document is labelled 'menu'. The context demands the application of certain interpretive rules, and somehow you have come to learn these rules (consciously or subconsciously) through years of experience with similar situations.

YOU CAN HANDLE THE TRUTH

When reading a web-based traffic map, you apply hermeneutical rules to understand its content. When your screen shows a bright red line through the main road you wish to travel down, you don't take that literally! You don't interpret that to mean somebody has literally painted that road red. 'Yesterday it was a dark grey bitumen road, but now my app is showing me it's been painted red!' No! That is not healthy hermeneutics.

A correct interpretive method understands that the bright red on the screen indicates heavy or slow-moving traffic at that time. This is how the creators of that program *want you* to understand it. Once you properly understand their intended meaning—the message they intend to communicate by displaying a red line—you may then appropriately respond to that information.

The autobiography of a world leader is to be approached differently than is a J. R. R. Tolkien fantasy trilogy, and we open the book knowing this. We appreciate there is a difference between fiction and non-fiction literature. A National Geographic documentary on the lives of Zimbabwe's big cat population is to be approached differently than is Disney's *Lion King* movies—one exists to educate, the other to entertain—and we watch the programs with this understanding.

No matter what form or fashion it may take, whenever information is presented to us it is imperative that we apply healthy hermeneutical rules appropriate to the type of literature in question. The Bible is no exception.

When it comes to correctly handing the Scripture, we need to keep our heads, and intentionally and intelligently employ the principles of healthy hermeneutics.

The remainder of this book is dedicated to training you in that process. My intention is to share what I consider the most important principles in healthy hermeneutics, and to do so simply, so that not only will you grow personally in your ability to handle the Scriptures, you will also be able to relay these lessons to your fellow Bible students.

That, like Timothy, you also can 'teach others to teach others'.

Your Three Toolkits—Closing Comments

Before we move on, let's sum up the lessons learnt in these last three chapters.

As we approach the Scriptures, to correctly handle the Word of Truth, we are to do so with the presence of the *Spirit*, in partnership with the *saints*, by practising the *science* of healthy hermeneutics.

Timothy, Tammy, let me assure you of this: with your heart committed to the Counsellor, your hands connected in community and your head concentrated and clear … you *can* handle the truth!

CHAPTER 6

Your Three-Step Process

Then David gave his son Solomon the plans for the portico of the temple … **He gave him instructions** for the divisions of the priests and Levites, and for all the work of serving in the temple of the Lord … 'All this,' David said, 'I have in writing as a result of the Lord's hand on me, and **he enabled me to understand all the details of the plan.**' (1 Chron. 28:11–19)

I appreciate that you may have a natural aversion to following directions. Perhaps you avoid manuals, instruction books and those pesky policy and procedure documents. After all, you can figure it out as you go along, right?

The truth is, when it comes to constructing anything of significant value, weight, size or complexity, a plan is essential. What could be more important than building a God-honouring, accurate and workable understanding of the Holy Scriptures?

Be diligent in these matters; give yourself wholly to them, so that everyone may see your progress. **Watch your life and doctrine closely**. Persevere in them, because if you do, you will save both yourself and your hearers. (1 Tim. 4:15–16)

Again, let's keep this simple.

Correctly handling the Word of Truth requires us to succinctly and successfully answer the following three questions of the Scripture: *What does it say? What does it mean? What does it matter?* If the three 'Rs' of a good education are *reading, writing* and *'rithmatic,* then for healthy hermeneutics they are *read, reflect* and *respond.*

A principal example of this process is at the restoration of Jerusalem's walls in the book of Nehemiah. Let's do a quick Bible study before delving a little deeper.

Step 1: What Does it Say?

> They read out of the book of the law of God, **translating [it]** … (Neh. 8:8a CSB)

Gathered in the public square by the newly repaired Water Gate of Jerusalem, an assembly of post-exile worshippers listened intently as Ezra stood high on a platform and read aloud the Torah in its original Hebrew. Accompanying him were 13 Levites—those from Israel's priestly tribe—who proceeded to *translate* the written words, thereby making it clear to listeners.

You see, the audience at this public reading was predominantly Aramaic speaking, having just spent the best part of a century living in the Babylonian and Persian empires. Much like you and me, this group needed a little help from language experts to know what the Scriptures *actually said.* Reading an accurate translation of the Bible in a language familiar to you is essentially the first step in our process. On to Step 2.

Step 2: What Does it Mean?

> They read out of the book of the law of God, translating **and giving the meaning** so that the people could understand what was read. (Neh. 8:8 CSB)

Understanding what the Bible *says* is relatively straightforward, but understanding what the Bible *means* can be something else entirely. And these Levites knew it. Ezra and his team were fully aware that before people could appropriately act upon God's Word, they needed to understand both what it *said* and what it *meant*.

The task of discovering and discerning a text's meaning is commonly known as *exegesis*. For the worker who correctly handles the Word of Truth, this is a core component of our trade and its importance must never be overlooked or underestimated. I would argue that most of our work, some 70% or more, belongs here in answering this second critical question. Having read the text, we are now required to reflect, research and reason our way to discover its meaning. I will say much more about exegesis later.

Step 3: What Does it Matter?

> Nehemiah the governor, Ezra the priest and scribe, and the Levites who were instructing the people said to all of them, 'This day is holy to the Lord your God. Do not mourn or weep.' For all the people were weeping as they heard the words of the law. Then he said to them, 'Go and eat what is rich, drink what is sweet, and send portions to those who have nothing prepared, since today is holy to our Lord. **Do not grieve, because the joy of the Lord is your strength**'. (Neh. 8:9–10 CSB)

Having heard the Word and understood its meaning, Ezra's audience was fully aware that the divine truths recorded in their past held implications and applications for their present situation. Though the Torah contained words originally spoken to a community many generations removed from theirs, the meaning of the ancient message *mattered to them*, and somehow demanded a response.

With some correction, clarity and coaching from Nehemiah, Ezra and their Levite contemporaries, the people eventually embraced the true implications of the revelation, as it applied to them then and there, and responded accordingly. Thus, the process was complete.

The three big questions had been answered: *What does it say? What does it mean? What does it matter?* Lesson completed. Easy stuff.

This basic three-part process is the framework for the rest of this book. In the chapters and pages that follow, we will investigate each step in detail, using a mix of principled explanation and practical examples.[14]

 Buckle in, Tammy, it's going to be quite a ride. Together with my commitment to simplicity, I also have a few surprises in store. Not everything is as straightforward as it seems.

Nevertheless, by following this simple sequence of inquiry and implementing the practical tools and rules discussed in this book, I am convinced you will not only avoid many of the pitfalls of poor Bible interpretation, you will also increase your competency and confidence as both a student and minister of God's Word.

Be encouraged. No matter how complicated, convoluted or confusing certain Scripture may seem at times, God has provided the means necessary for you to enjoy a healthy understanding of His Word, and to correctly communicate it to others.

I'll say it again—you *can* handle the truth!

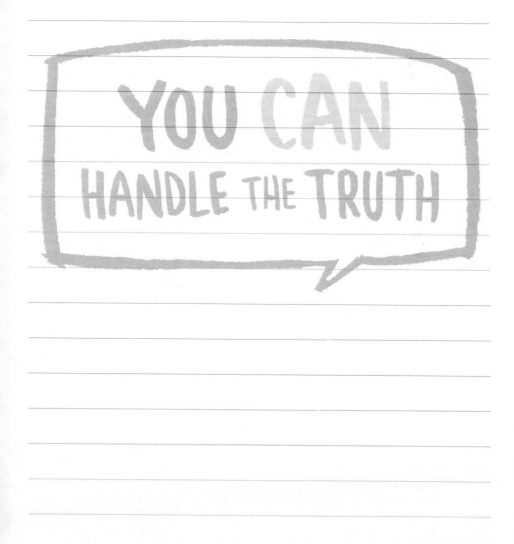

Step 1

What Does it Say?

The first step in our three-part process is all about addressing the question, *what does the Bible say?* How we go about answering this is a bit of a no-brainer. We simply have to *read it*. Off to an easy start, aren't we?

> Study this Book of Instruction continually. Meditate on it day and night so you will be sure to obey everything written in it. Only then will you prosper and succeed in all you do ... Joshua then **read to them** all the blessings and curses Moses had written in the Book of Instruction. Every word of every command that Moses had ever given **was read** to the entire assembly of Israel, including the women and children and the foreigners who lived among them. (Josh. 1:8; 8:34–35 NLT)

In Step 1, I will encourage you to acquire a selection of Bibles from which to read and study. Let me say upfront that the Bible of which I speak is the Protestant Bible, with its canon of 66 books from Genesis to Malachi,

OBSERVE WHAT IT SAYS

Matthew to Revelation.[15] Discovering how the original compositions of the ancient authors were transmitted through the ages to become the modern text we have today; how particular books were received as authoritative within the community of faith; how this particular Bible varies from others (such as the Catholic, Eastern Orthodox or Mormon varieties); and issues surrounding textual variance between manuscripts, all make for fascinating study—and are beyond the scope of this book.[16] We limit our discussion to the question of which *translations* of the Bible we should read.

We will then move on to some helpful hints and tips regarding *how* we should read the Bible. When it comes to successful relationships, communication is key. We all know what it's like to have an audience exercise poor listening skills and hear something different to our actual message. Similarly, how we listen to the Bible (or how we go about reading it) is all-important. In many ways, the strength of our relationship with God depends on it.

Four Must-Have Bibles

During that time the devil came and said to him, 'If you are the Son of God, tell these stones to become loaves of bread.' But Jesus told him, 'No! **The Scriptures say**, "People do not live by bread alone, but by every word that comes from the mouth of God"' ... Jesus responded, '**The Scriptures also say**, "You must not test the Lord your God" ... Get out of here, Satan,' Jesus told him. '**For the Scriptures say**, "You must worship the Lord your God and serve only him"'. (Matt. 4:3–10 NLT)

For the most part, establishing what the Bible says is pretty straightforward. While originally written in ancient Hebrew and Greek (with the occasional Aramaic), over the centuries, there has been great progress in presenting the Scriptures in every major language of the modern world. The goal of translation is to communicate the unchanging message of the Scripture in a language that makes sense to a particular audience.[17]

As an English speaker, I count myself among the most privileged of Bible students, in that it is for my native tongue that arguably the most study and scrutiny, time and resourcing has been given to the task of translation. Browse the shelves of any Christian bookstore and you'll see the vast variety of English language options available, together with a horde of acronyms. Be it the ASV, NIV, CEV, ESV, NRSV and KJV, the CSB, GNB, HCSB and NASB or the AMP, TPT, NLT and MSG; there's an abbreviation to suit every Bible reader!

Let's keep this simple, Timothy.

My proposal to you is this—every serious Bible student should have ready access to at least four different Bibles: something old, something new, something borrowed, something blue.

Something Old

Your *something-old* Bible is the one you are most acquainted with. It's not necessarily your favourite translation, but it is your most familiar. Let me explain.

At age 16, I was given a blue, leather-bound, New International Version (NIV) Study Bible from my folks as a Christmas gift. This was my first 'adult' Bible and fast became my *sola Scriptura*.

Throughout my teenage and young adult years, I used it for my personal readings, took it to church, camps and conferences, highlighted passages, underlined and circled key words, and filled its empty space with notes, cross-references and useful anecdotes. When we pioneered our church and I began my preaching ministry at age 23, prophetic promises, sermon outlines and sticky notes were added to my editorial mosaic.

Despite the fact that I've become aware of many of this version's faults and failings (some of which were addressed in the 2011 edition) and have even attempted to switch to other translations in the past, like it or not, my brain has been trained in the flow and form of this particular Bible.

When I quote verses from memory, they're from the 1984 NIV. While at times I struggle to recount the precise chapter and verse of a particular passage, more often than not I can picture its placement on the printed page and locate it quite readily that way. Today, I still take this Bible with me on ministry trips and to prayer meetings. In these contexts, should I be called upon to spontaneously contribute, it is my ragged, but now rebound, 1984 NIV Study Bible that I want on hand.

Note that it is the NIV's rendering of 2 Timothy 2:15 after which this book is named: 'Do your best to present yourself to God as one approved, a worker who does not need to be ashamed and who correctly **handles the word of truth**'.

While I now have many Bibles on my bookshelf and countless more available in digital format, I'd rather have one edition with which I am thoroughly acquainted than a dozen versions with which I am only partially familiar. When fronting up to a battle, it is better to have one 'old-faithful' sword at the ready than a cabinet full of weapons with which you are unaccustomed and awkward.

Timothy, I encourage you to have a Bible like this. If you are a young believer, and do not yet have a well-worn Bible of your own, ask some trusted voices within your church community to suggest a 'go-to' translation for you—ideally, one that has been produced by a team of scholars, not a single translator. Once you've decided on a translation, my first recommendation is this: your *something-old* Bible should not be a digital one. Go old school and grab yourself a paper edition. Together with the benefit of engaging your senses (touch, sound, and smell!), generally speaking the printed page displays more text in a single glance than does a screen, assisting your ability to appreciate the broader context of what you are reading and follow the flow of the author's thoughts and themes. I will speak to the value of electronic Bibles in a moment, but, for now, trust me: when it comes to familiarising yourself with a Bible of choice—paper trumps screen. Finally, consider a study Bible edition in which editorial notes, maps, graphs, articles and concordances can enhance your reading experience.[18]

For me, my *something-old* Bible is the 1984 edition of the NIV.

Something New

Your *something-new* Bible is a translation that is more fresh than familiar. Its language serves to highlight truths and reveal nuance that may have gone unnoticed in your regular reading version. This is a lesson I learnt from my father.

I have a clear childhood memory from the 1980s of my dad carrying his light brown New American Standard Bible (NASB) to church services and home-group studies. This translation served him well all through his young adult, 'Jesus-people' and Bible college years in the 1970s and today, half a century later, remains his *something-old* Bible, kept in his caravan while my folks spend the best part of their retirement years travelling Australia.

However, more distinct is my memory of his paperback edition of Eugene Peterson's The Message paraphrase, acquired sometime in the mid-1990s. Sat on the dining table each morning alongside his cereal bowl, this so-called contemporary language Bible brought a fresh perspective to the Scriptures my dad had become so accustomed to over previous decades. This was his *something-new* Bible—I'd encourage you to get something new, too.

Reading from a new (or at least *new-to-you*) translation, which is notably different in expression from your *something-old* Bible, will help prevent you becoming overfamiliar with the Scriptures in which you are inclined to never see anything fresh. My current Bible of choice for this purpose is The Passion Translation (TPT) by Brian Simmons.

On the one hand, I sense a unique and very personal affinity with this work. Brian and I share many friends in ministry, so I've had opportunity to see him preach and teach, enjoyed time with him over coffee and have corresponded on numerous occasions via email in which I was invited to provide editorial input for portions of his TPT manuscript during its development.

That aside, I find that both the Scripture content and editorial notes of TPT minister well to my head and heart, while the rhythm and flow of the text encourage me to read it with less speed and greater reflection than I am inclined to give when reading my *something-old* NIV.[19]

If you haven't done so recently, it's time to buy yourself a *something-new* Bible to include in your regular reading routine.

Something Borrowed

Your *something-borrowed* Bible is exactly that. It's a translation you use for a specific purpose, at a specific time and thereafter return to its place.

These are Bibles to draw on for occasional referencing, rather than regular reading. Depending on your purpose, they may include anything from the heavily paraphrased varieties to the more rigidly literal translations. I personally have close to a dozen Bibles like this.

When I'm preparing to speak to a group of students at a Christian school chapel or at a wedding or funeral service with a mixed crowd in attendance, I will often take my Scripture readings from my New Living Translation (NLT) or Good News Bible (GNB). When the event is over, I'll place them back on my bookshelf until next time.

These translations are well suited to a broad-based audience for two reasons. First, they utilise contemporary and easy-to-read English, specifically designed to reach those from a pre-teen reading level. No *thees, thous* or *thines* here! Just everyday language, for everyday people.

Second, they employ what is known as a 'meaning-based' (or 'dynamic equivalent') approach to translation. Here, the translators are concerned primarily with communicating the thoughts of the biblical author, so select words according to how well they express this original meaning. In a sense, these 'thought-for-thought' translations combine the first two steps in the hermeneutical process. What it *says* and what it *means* are brought together to save the reader the work required to think through the interpretation for themselves. In these dynamic equivalent Bibles, editors apply a high degree of interpretation in their translating work and, in doing so, insert *their understanding of its meaning* into the process.

Herein lies their weakness for the serious Bible student. When reading these translations, you are submitting yourself to the editor's understanding of the text's meaning, rather than seeing what the Scripture simply says for itself as a first port of call. This brings us to the more literal, 'formal equivalency', alternatives.[20]

Occasionally, you may find yourself investigating a theological topic, specific Scripture or controversial issue that requires detailed study. In these cases, it is helpful to have a selection of Bibles designed to bring out the most straightforward, 'word-for-word' renderings of the original languages.[21]

I often turn to my Interlinear Bible or Young's Literal Translation (YLT) for this purpose. While terribly clunky and at times difficult to read, these versions nevertheless remain faithful to many of the finer details of grammar and sentence structure often omitted by more contemporary language versions.

My other *something-borrowed* Bibles for this kind of study include the English Standard Version (ESV), The Word (in which the King James Version [KJV] is paralleled to 25 other translations!) and occasionally the Amplified Bible (AMP), which brings out some of the more detailed and nuanced communication present in the original languages.

It's important to note that there is no such thing as a purely *verbatim* version of the Bible in English. Any foreign-language translation of a complex literary work includes an element of editorial interpretation. This means that Bible translators will invariably, from time to time, be guided by their theological persuasions and prejudices as they decide which comparable words and phrases fit best. Be aware, but not afraid, of this inevitable reality.

 Remember Tammy, your first step in the process of healthy hermeneutics is discovering what the Bible actually, and accurately, *says*.

Drawing from a variety of versions will prove vital in this task, even if they are ones you simply 'borrow' on occasion.

Something Blue

In true Jesus style, we've saved the best for last. While I love the feel and flexibility of a printed book for my personal reading and as a pastor delight in the sound of rustling pages from my congregation as I preach, I have to say I don't know how I'd manage without my *something-blue* Bible.

One of the great privileges of our modern technological age is the access it has granted to a vast selection of electronic Bible study packages and web-based applications. These services offer immediate and unfettered access to dictionary tools, interlinear formats, multiple translations, commentaries and concordances, all at the touch of a finger.

Translating Approaches: Formal vs. Functional

Luke 2:1—the Wording	Luke 2:1—the Meaning?
Ἐγένετο δὲ ἐν ταῖς ἡμέραις ἐκείναις ἐξῆλθεν δόγμα παρὰ Καίσαρος Αὐγούστου ἀπογράφεσθαι πᾶσαν τὴν οἰκουμένην *Textus Receptus*	What the..? It's all Greek to me!
It came to pass then in the days those went out a decree from Caesar Augustus to **register all the world** *Interlinear Bible*	Uh... register for what? Does 'all the world' include all living things, or just people?
Now in those days a decree went out from Caesar Augustus, that **a census be taken of all the inhabited earth.** *New American Standard Bible (NASB)*	Oh, a census. So, humans only. Does 'all the inhabited earth' mean all civilisations, globally?
In those days Caesar Augustus issued a decree that a census should be taken of **the entire Roman world.** *New International Version (NIV)*	OK, the Roman world only. Who is Mr Augustus, anyway? A statistician?
At that time **the Roman emperor, Augustus, decreed** that a census should be taken throughout the **Roman Empire.** *New Living Translation (NLT)*	Aha. The emperor of the Roman Empire, named Augustus. Now it all makes sense!

Perhaps the greatest benefit of these programs is that they are a haven for hyperlinks—hence, the reference to the colour *blue* ... in case you missed it.

Most helpful in my personal study are the hyperlinks to Greek and Hebrew lexicons, the cross-references to comparable texts and the search capabilities that allow the user to instantly find every recurrence of the same word or phrase throughout the entire Bible.

A *something-blue* Bible is an essential tool for every savvy and serious student of the Scriptures and I encourage you to find one that suits you. There are many available, on all kinds of platforms, but my current go-to programs are stepbible.org, biblehub.com and (the aptly named) blueletterbible.org.

Tammy, Timothy—get busy growing your personal Bible library. At the very least, ensure you have ready access to something old, something new, something borrowed and something blue.

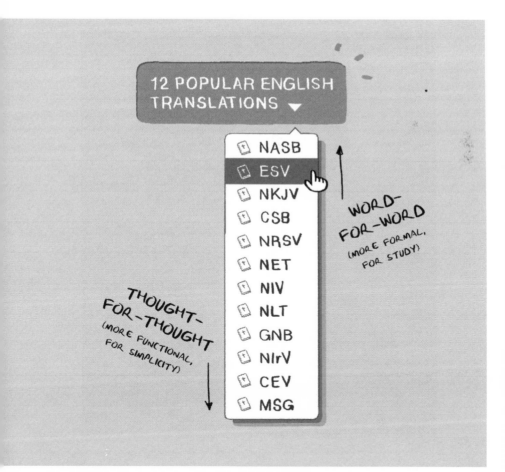

How to Read the Bible

Now that we've established *which* Bible(s) we should read, let's consider *how* we should approach our reading and study. This, from Jesus' summary of His 'parable-of-all-parables':[22]

> **Therefore consider carefully how you listen**. Whoever has will be given more; whoever does not have, even what they think they have will be taken from them. (Luke 8:18)

Despite vowels representing less than 20% of our alphabet, all English speakers know it is near impossible to create a coherent statement of any real value without them. These five little letters (A, E, I, O and U) are absolutely essential to our communication. Just ask any crossword or SCRABBLE® player.

In this section we explore five key points in *how to listen* to the Scriptures. As you read your Bible, always remember to pronounce your vowels:

> A—Appreciation
>
> E—Expectation
>
> I—Intention
>
> O—Openness
>
> U—Understanding

Without these, your ability to comprehend, communicate and benefit from biblical truth will be perilously limited.

CHAPTER 8

Appreciation

When I discovered your words, I devoured them. **They are my joy and my heart's delight**, for I bear your name, O LORD God of Heaven's Armies. (Jer. 15:16 NLT)

The Bible is truly an incredible book. Its importance can hardly be stressed enough. The far-reaching impact and influence of this globally recognised icon and its contribution to human history throughout the ages are second to none. It is, without doubt, the most extensively circulated, cited and scrutinised literary work of all time. There really is nothing like it.

To 'appreciate something' has two meanings, both of which can be true at once, and both of which are vital as we approach our reading of Holy Scripture. First, it infers that we recognise and acknowledge the nature of the Book—we *appreciate* what it is. Second, and just as importantly, we are *grateful* for it—God's Word is a gift we should treasure and delight in. The first concerns the way we *think* about the Book. The second addresses the attitude of our *heart* towards it. Let's start up top. There is much to be said about appreciating the true nature of the Bible, but here's a brief summary of my *big three*.

A Work of Unity and Diversity

In Ancient Greek, '*biblia*' refers to a collection of scrolls,[23] and what a collection it is! Consisting of 66 books written over 1,500 years in three different languages, on three different continents, by over 40 different authors employing a multitude of distinct literary genres—'diverse' seems much too weak a word. Yet weaving through the vast variety is a glorious unity, holding it all together in holy harmony. Such unity cannot be explained by mere coincidence or clever collusion. It is a sure and certain sign of the intelligent and intentional orchestration of a sole Master Artist.

As you open your Bible, appreciate that you are indeed reading one book that tells one unified story. Diverse it may be, with many subplots, characters, purposes and themes, but, believe me when I say the Good Book is both coherent and cohesive, complex but not complicated. Beautifully diverse yet uncompromisingly unified, the Bible is the 'Diverse Anthology' of Holy Spirit's greatest hits.[24]

A Work of Divinity and Humanity

As we accept Christ being at once human and divine, so we must the Scriptures. The 'Word made Flesh' and the 'Word made text' share this common trait, albeit in their own unique way. Just as Jesus experienced some 'co-parenting' in His development, so the Bible was developed by co-*authorship*. God's Eternal Word has been conveyed to us through, in and by the written words of men. Put simply, God spoke by His Spirit, through the mouth of men, who took paper to pen (Acts 4:24–26).[25] This is a mysterious reality and is ultimately what distinguishes the Bible from all other books and so-called sacred texts, granting it an authority not held by others. As with the famous Dead Sea Scrolls,[26] God in His wisdom chose 'jars of clay' to present and preserve this heavenly treasure for us (2 Cor. 4:7).

> And we also thank God continually because, when you received the word of God, which you heard from us, you accepted it not as a human word, but as it actually is, the word of God, which is indeed at work in you who believe. (1 Thess. 2:13)

A Work of Mystery and History

The Bible is a history book. It contains real-life stories of people and places, cultures and conditions, politics and empires, famines and wars, many of which are corroborated by archeology and other historical accounts. I'll say more about the scope of the Bible's historicity in *Big-Picture Background*.

Together with this, the Bible is a book of mystery. It is a human record of heaven's revelations, articulating realities and truths we would otherwise not be privy to had God not gone 'out of His way' to inform us. Said the biblical authors:

> There is a God in Heaven who **reveals mysteries ... who reveals his thoughts to mankind** ... This, then, is how you ought to regard us: as servants of Christ and as those entrusted with **the mysteries God has revealed**. (Dan. 2:28; Amos 4:13; 1 Cor. 4:1)

A Heart-Felt Appreciation

Appreciating what the Bible is (and subsequently what it is *not*) will put us in the right headspace as we approach our reading and study. Healthy hermeneutics, you'll remember, is about handling the Word intelligently. However, it goes much deeper than that. When it comes to correctly handling the Word of Truth, the heart of the issue, is *an issue of the heart*. Coming to the Scriptures with appreciation means also having our *heart* in the right place. Jesus brings this point home for us in what is arguably His most poignant of parables—the parable of the sower.

Each Synoptic Gospel (Matthew, Mark and Luke) records this story.[27] It features a sower scattering seed over four different soils, resulting in four very different degrees of success. It's also one of very few parables in which we have record of Jesus' own explanation of its meaning. His general point is that the level of fruitfulness of God's Word in people's lives is largely dependent upon the condition of their hearts when receiving it.

While every preacher has their own way of articulating the core components and characteristics of a good and fertile heart, most of us would agree that a commitment to thankfulness is key. An *attitude of gratitude* prepares our hearts to successfully receive God's Word, even when our heads cannot fully comprehend it: 'But Mary treasured all these things in her heart and often pondered what they meant' (Luke 2:19 TPT).

 Timothy, God's truth is to be treasured. Develop a deep appreciation for the Word of God. Approach it with awe and respect, gratitude and delight.

Next time you open your Bible, stop. Think. And thank Him. For what you are about to receive, be truly grateful.

> Your word I have treasured in my heart, That I may not sin against You … I shall delight in Your statutes; I shall not forget Your word. (Ps. 119:11, 16 NASB)

CHAPTER 9

Expectation

(But) the message they heard did not benefit them, because it was not **united with faith** [in God] by those who heard. (Heb. 4:2 AMP)

While they hold noteworthy differences in some respects, the esteemed Christian virtues of faith and hope share this: *confident expectation*. You may not have thought about it this way before, but every healthy relationship involves operating in accordance with a set of expectations, either articulated or assumed. Your relationship with God and your approach to His Word, is no different. Each time you open your Bible, you do so expectantly, whether you are conscious of it or not! The question is: what should your expectations be when coming to the Scriptures?

> Then Jesus put his hands over their eyes and said, '**You will have what your faith expects!**' And instantly their eyes opened—they could see! (Matt. 9:29–30 TPT)

There are three areas you should personally expect God to minister to, as you apply yourself to read and study His Word: your *head*, *heart* and *hands*.

Your Head—Expect to Learn

You don't need be a psychologist or neuroscientist to realise that what and how we *think* plays a huge role in determining the course of our lives. God Himself is a thinker, who claims that: 'As the heavens are higher than the earth, so are my ways higher than your ways and my thoughts than your thoughts' (Isa. 55:9). Thankfully, He has chosen to reveal such thoughts to us by His Spirit, through His saints, as recorded in Holy Scripture (1 Cor. 2:10–13).

Expect God's Word to engage your brain. The Bible contains deep and diverse insight into His knowledge, wisdom, will and ways, so set your mind on what the Spirit presents on its pages (Rom. 8:5; Col. 3:2). Expect Him to stir, stimulate and satisfy your questions and curiosities, affect the way you think, and 'open the eyes' of your mind:

> Stop imitating the ideals and opinions of the culture around you, but be inwardly **transformed by the Holy Spirit through a total reformation of how you think**. (Rom. 12:2 TPT)

Your Heart—Expect to Feel

On the day of Pentecost, the message proclaimed through Peter 'pierced the hearts' of his hearers (Acts 2:37). The word for 'pierced' (Greek: *katanussó*) is found nowhere else in the New Testament and is a composite of 'pierced' and 'down, from a higher to lower place'. The content of Peter's message was not essentially new information to his listeners. But on that day, with the atmosphere supercharged with God's manifest presence and power, the spoken Word came to their ears, dropped from their heads and pierced the deep recesses of their hearts, souls and emotions.

This was a mass demonstration of Holy Spirit heartburn, in which God's living and active Word came like a fire to frozen hearts, melting icy barriers and penetrating deep to effect lasting change. Comprehension became conviction and compelled the crowd to respond. The 'eyes of their *heart*' had been opened (Eph. 1:18):

> [Our] gospel came to you not simply with words but also with power, with the Holy Spirit and **deep conviction** … [Now may] the Lord **direct your hearts** into God's love and Christ's perseverance. (1 Thess. 1:5; 2 Thess. 3:5)

CHAD M. MANSBRIDGE

While the Christian is given a new 'heart of flesh' at conversion, it is still possible for us to become hardened 'by the deceitfulness of sin' (Ezek. 36:26; Heb. 3:13). This is one of the reasons Paul so often prayed for the heart condition of his churches, and encouraged them to avoid strange teachings— 'it is good for our hearts to be strengthened by grace' (Heb. 13:9).

Our heart serves as a storehouse from which the issues of life flow (Prov. 4:23; Luke 6:45). Our daily disciplines and soul-diet will witness either good or bad investments placed into this internal depository. Since words act as food for the soul, it is vital for our health that we monitor our intake wisely and feed our hearts on a solid diet of God's life-giving truth (Prov. 18:20; Ezek. 3:1–3; Matt. 4:4).

Listen to me. The state of your internal world holds great import in the heart of God. Expect Him to minister to you deeply, heart-to-heart, each time you incline your ear to His Word:

> For **the word of God is living and active**, sharper than any two-edged sword, piercing to the division of soul and of spirit, of joints and of marrow, and **discerning the thoughts and intentions of the heart**. (Heb. 4:12 ESV)

Your Hands—Expect to Act

Last, we should expect God's Word to engage, equip and empower our hands with practical actions and applications. The Scripture does not exist to simply titillate our intellect or speak sweet nothings to our emotional ear— the Bible contains clear instructions for everyday effective living. We will do well to have 'our hands at the ready' every time His Word is heard:

> Therefore everyone who hears these words of mine **and puts them into practice** is like a wise man who built his house on the rock. The rain came down, the streams rose, and the winds blew and beat against that house; yet it did not fall, because it had its foundation on the rock. (Matt. 7:24–25)

It is both the hearing and *heeding* of God's Word that matters here. Permit me to draw a contrast. When we receive a wise person, we take their words under advisement—we may, or may not, apply their insight. Our options are open. But for us, Christ is not simply a good teacher—He is our Lord.[28] Jesus is no mere adviser; He is our sovereign Master and He *expects us* to apply obedient application to His instructions. We should expect ourselves to do the same:

> Do not merely listen to the word, and so deceive yourselves. **Do what it says.** (James 1:22)

As we will discuss later, not all of God's written Word is ours to apply. It is not right nor reasonable to expect hands-on application from every Bible passage. However, it is incumbent upon us as followers of Christ to approach our readings with *a posture of willing obedience,* in which we stand decidedly prepared to do what He tells us to do, say what He tells us to say and go where He tells us to go.

The Gospel of peace—the knowledge that the One who *knows* what is best for us also *wants* what is best for us—has fitted our feet with the 'readiness' to act the moment our Commander in Chief speaks (Eph. 6:15). All Scripture, you'll remember, is God-breathed—empowering us in ways that are right, and ensuring our hands are 'thoroughly equipped' for good deeds and practical works (2 Tim. 3:16–17):

> Jesus replied, 'But even more blessed are all who **hear the word of God and put it into practice'.** (Luke 11:28 NLT)

 Tammy, next time you open your Bible to meet with God, take stock of the expectations you are bringing to the table.

What are you hoping to achieve? What do you have faith to receive? At the very least, expect His Word to minister to your head, heart and hands. Expect to *learn* something, expect to *feel* something and expect to *do something* about it!

CHAPTER 10

Intention

Experience has taught me that many Christians shy away from reading their Bibles on a regular basis because they find it complicated and confusing. On the rare occasion they reach for the Good Book, these believers do so haphazardly and with a 'lucky-dip' mindset, skimming through masses of seemingly irrelevant verses in the hope of finding at least one nugget of truth to apply to their present crisis or pressing need.

The fact you're reading this book (or at least have reached this far!) demonstrates a desire to develop your Bible-handling skills. You want to grow. You want to improve. This is highly commendable and is a certain sign of *intentionality*. Believe me, if something's worth doing, it's worth doing purposefully. It's time to make a plan:

> **Good planning and hard work lead to prosperity**, but hasty shortcuts lead to poverty. (Prov. 21:5 NLT)

There are three tried-and-tested methods for intentional Bible study: *devotional*, *topical* and *chronological*. Consider each as forming part of your balanced Bible-reading regime.

Devotional Reading

The least technical of the three methods, we begin with the one intentionally designed to serve the health of your heart. The devotional approach is focused primarily on finding inspiration, intimacy and personal implications in the text. Attending a quiet, distraction-free space to meet with God and muse on His Word is a common feature of having a 'devotional time':

> [His] delight is in the law of the LORD, and **on his law he meditates day and night** ... **I will meditate on your precepts** and fix my eyes on your ways. (Ps. 1:2; 119:15 ESV)

This meditative method typically includes reading short sections of Scripture, slowly and (at times) repetitively. It emphasises reflection, contemplation and even memorisation—committing to memory those portions that particularly 'speak to our soul'. It may also include responsive journalling, prayer and song or the accompanying aid of devotional books from Christian authors specifically tailored for this purpose.[29]

'Devotion' is an expression of love and loyalty and, when directed at God, an act of worship. When taking this approach to your Bible reading, you are doing so with the explicit intention of drawing near to and adoring the Author.

Topical Reading

This second approach focuses more on you searching the Scriptures than having the Scriptures search you. You've likely realised by now that the Bible is not organised according to topic or theme. The books are not categorised by subject matter or even (strictly speaking) key characters. It is full of doctrinal terminology and teaching, but is neither a dictionary nor a book of systematic theology.

To discover 'what the Bible says' about a given issue of interest, you'll have to be deliberate in searching for it. It's time to apply some intentional investigation:

> They found that the Jews of Berea were of more noble character and much more open minded than those of Thessalonica. They were hungry to learn and eagerly received the word. **Every day they opened the scrolls of Scripture to search and examine them**, to

verify that what Paul taught them was true. (Acts 17:11 TPT)

This second method involves researching, accumulating and arranging a variety of verses, passages and stories on a given subject. This could be a specific life-topic (such as *conflict resolution, financial stewardship* or *parenting*), a religious activity (*worship in song, water baptism,* or *prayer and fasting*), a character profile (of *Joshua, Elisha* or *Mary Magdalene*), a Christian doctrine (*Christology, Eschatology* or *Gifts of the Spirit*), a particular phrase or word-study (*day of the Lord, propitiation* or *love)* or an examination of the Bible's larger and recurring motifs and themes (*God's unfaithful wife, perfection through suffering* or *exile and return*). Plenty of ideas to get you going, Timothy?

Bible encyclopedias, theological papers and especially your *something-blue* Bible can all be of assistance when performing a productive topical study.

Chronological Reading

Without doubt, this method is my personal favourite. I am, by natural temperament, a 'big-picture guy' and I will spend considerable time discussing the importance of developing a big-picture perspective in Step 2. Stay tuned for that.

The chronological style of study is systematic, methodical and orderly. The reader approaches and follows the text in a straight, linear format, from start to finish. Placing one step ahead of the other, neatly progressing through the information from beginning, to middle and end. For many books of the Bible, this is certainly how the author(s) intended their work to be read.[30]

> I charge you before the Lord to **have this letter read to all the brothers and sisters** … After this letter has been read to you, see that it is also read in the church of the Laodiceans and that you in turn read the letter from Laodicea. (1 Thess. 5:27; Col. 4:16)

What do you think Paul had in mind when he asked this? Did he hope someone would stand before the assembly, open his letter somewhere near the middle, read a few random sentences, then skip ahead to the final greetings? I highly doubt it, yet this is precisely how too many believers treat these epistles. As a result, they completely miss the context and flow of thought that a sequential reading offers.

When we attest that 'all Scripture is God-breathed' (2 Tim. 3:16), we are first referring to its content—the information presented to us is revelation from God. However, does this not also imply that Holy Spirit—the Great Author behind the author(s)—also had His hand in shaping the flow and form each book would take? That the human authors were 'carried along' by Him (2 Peter 1:21), both in regards the substance *and structure* of their work?

Reading each book of the Bible *as it has been presented to us*, from start to finish (and for smaller books, in one sitting!) is an essential strategy for every serious Bible student seeking to discover its message and meaning.[31]

While each individual word may be divinely inspired, we must appreciate that every one of those words is in a sentence; each sentence in a paragraph; each paragraph in a body of thought; and each thought sequenced together to become a composite whole. For us to understand the Bible well, we must first read it well. A consistent, chronological approach to the Bible's contents will serve us well in this endeavour.[32]

This is probably a good time to address the issue of *non-inspired* formatting. Bear with me here as we venture down a little rabbit trail. The books of our Bible were not originally written with 'chapter-and-verse' divisions or distinctions. These were added by scholars, beginning in the thirteenth century, for ease of referencing.[33] For most of its history, the Scriptures contained no such numbering system. Precisely *where* these breaks appear is not entirely arbitrary, but nor are they 'God-breathed'. This formatting is not to be considered sacred. In many cases, such chapter-and-verse partitions can (and perhaps even *should*) be ignored, particularly when they disrupt the flow of the author's thought.

The same holds true for the way in which the 66 books are *ordered* in our Bible. The Old Testament with which you and I are familiar orders its books

THE 24 BOOKS OF THE HEBREW BIBLE (TANAKH)

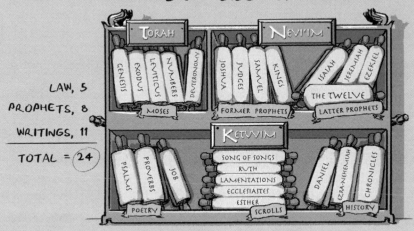

LAW, 5
PROPHETS, 8
WRITINGS, 11
TOTAL = 24

THE 66 BOOKS OF THE PROTESTANT BIBLE

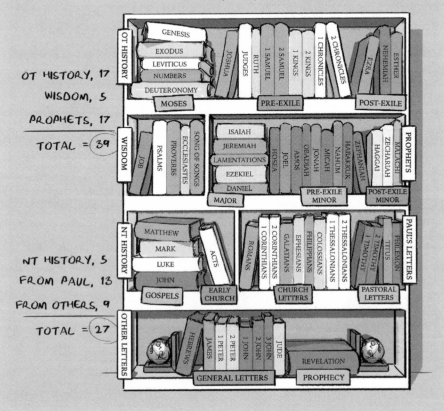

OT HISTORY, 17
WISDOM, 5
PROPHETS, 17
TOTAL = 39

NT HISTORY, 5
FROM PAUL, 13
FROM OTHERS, 9
TOTAL = 27

YOU CAN HANDLE THE TRUTH

according to the Greek translation of the Hebrew Bible, formed sometime around 250–150 BC. This is known as the *Septuagint*, or *LXX*, and its structure differs to the traditional Hebrew. Both formats open with the Books of Moses, Joshua and Judges but where our Old Testament ends with Malachi, the last book in the Hebrew Bible is Chronicles. In the Septuagint, some of the larger books (Samuel, Kings, Chronicles and Nehemiah) were split into two—in fact, one book (The Minor Prophets), was split into 12! This means that while they contain the same content, our Old Testament presents 15 books more than the traditional Jewish version. No material has been added, simply *rearranged*. This variation in book number, order, naming and grouping does not dilute the Bible's accuracy or authority in any way. After all, it is the Septuagint that was read and quoted by New Testament authors. Same substance, different structure.

Ordering the Bible: Same-Same, but Different

Since medieval times it has become commonplace for Jews to refer to their Bible as the *Tanakh,* an acronym derived from its three primary divisions: *Torah* (Law), *Nevi'im* (Prophets) and *Ketuvim* (Writings).

It seems even the old Jewish rabbis appreciated the power of a good acronym!

The Hebrew Bible traditionally contains 24 books although there is some evidence, including from the first-century historian Josephus, that it may have also been presented as 22—combining Judges with Ruth, and Jeremiah with Lamentations. This editorial variation may have some relation to the number of letters found in the Hebrew and Greek alphabets (22 and 24 respectively).

The Greek Old Testament (circa 250–150 BC) divided and reordered the books. This work is also known as the *Septuagint or LXX,* meaning 'seventy', signifying the number of translators who were said to have developed it. This new arrangement was embraced by Jerome when he produced a Latin translation known as the Vulgate (circa. 390–405 AD). It is these works which form the basis to the book order of the Old Testament we read today.

The New Testament comprises 27 books. Their canonisation was firmly established by the end of the fourth century, thanks largely to the Councils of Hippo (393 AD) and Carthage (397 AD). Despite minor variations, the traditional ordering of the New Testament follows that of the Latin Vulgate.

The *Great Bible* of 1539 was the first English edition to order the New Testament according to the sequence we have today. Prior to this, most Protestant Bibles followed Luther's lead by placing Hebrews and James in the back alongside the likes of Jude and Revelation. Apparently, Luther was no fan of these four books!

In the same way, the organisation of the 27 books comprising our New Testament has changed over time and varied between certain ecclesiastical (church) traditions. As with the Old Testament, these first-century Scriptures are not presented to us chronologically, but are grouped primarily according to genre and author. Which brings us back to considering *chronology*.

I have already explained the value in taking an *individual book* of the Bible and reading it from start to finish as it has been presented. But what about reading the whole thing? Is there any benefit to reading the books from Genesis to Revelation as they have been laid out for us by church tradition centuries after the fact? Or rather, should we walk through the Bible employing a chronological methodology to (in a sense) experience the unfolding story 'as it happened'?[34]

Some time ago, I challenged my church community to read through the Bible in a year by following a weekly schedule designed to highlight the narrative unity of the Scripture and the progressive flow of its *one big story*. This method involves reading prophecies, psalms and epistles in the context of their historical narratives, allowing you to see where the details fit with the overall picture and appreciate how all the books beautifully dovetail together. The feedback and testimonies of those who completed the challenge (helped by my weekly video tutorials) echoed my own. It really is a worthwhile experience. I personally and strongly recommend it to you.[35]

My point is this: 'If something's worth doing, it's worth doing purposefully'. If you don't currently employ some sort of Bible-reading plan, now is the time to start one. Whichever method you choose—devotional, topical or chronological—approach the Scriptures with *intention*.

CHAPTER 11

Openness

The first step in the process of healthy hermeneutics requires us to examine what the Bible *says*—to which I have encouraged you to read it with appreciation, expectation and intentionality. In this chapter we consider a fourth quality: openness.

When we come into relationship with Christ, we are bestowed with a bevy of new identities. We are called saints, servants, sons, soldiers, citizens and more: each designation communicating something of who we are and Whose we are, each holding true at once, complete in itself and yet complemented powerfully by the others in forming the whole 'new creation' we are in Christ (2 Cor. 5:17).

In this point, however, we are primarily concerned with our status as *students*. So long as Christ is a 'good teacher' (Luke 18:18), we're to commit ourselves to Him as good students.

I Don't Know it All—and I May Be Wrong

Coming to His Word with *openness* means being willing to learn, unlearn and relearn; to challenge and change your opinions, and to see something you've not seen before or, at the very least, to be willing to look upon a familiar truth from an unfamiliar standpoint. Being open means you are prepared to be surprised and confronted, and (if required) to persevere through offence and discomfort in the pursuit of truth. Openness is about being humble enough to admit: 'I don't know it all—and I may be wrong'.

As a pastor, I often remind people that God (or perhaps just life itself) is committed to presenting us with human exemplars from which we can learn. We are provided both positive and negative role models, and can take lessons from either. When it comes to being open to change, God's old-covenant community consistently demonstrates the kind of attitude we are *not* to embrace when confronted with His truth:

> For I know how stubborn and obstinate you are. **Your necks are as unbending as iron**. **Your heads are as hard as bronze** … Yes, I realize that you are descendants of Abraham. And yet some of you are trying to kill me because **there's no room in your hearts for my message** … You stubborn people! You are heathen at heart and **deaf to the truth**. Must you forever resist the Holy Spirit? That's what your ancestors did, and so do you! (Isa. 48:4; John 8:37; Acts 7:51 NLT)

Quite a list, isn't it? Stubborn, obstinate and resistant to the Spirit of Truth, Israel was time and again rebuked and called to repent from their stiff necks and hard heads, deaf ears and closed hearts. The call to repent means literally to *change the way you think*. To obey such a call, we must first be open to hearing anything and everything our Teacher has to say. Said Cornelius to Peter, 'Now we are all here in the presence of God to **listen to everything** the Lord has commanded you to tell us' (Acts 10:33). Such is the attitude of the good Bible student.

There are three potential impediments to growth that almost every student of the Scripture will face as they approach their Bible reading, each of which can be remedied by a little dose of openness—*presuppositions, preferences* and *pride*.

Presuppositions

Presuppositions are pre-existing beliefs. Including anything from lightly held assumptions to firmly established convictions, these beliefs may be concerned with a specific topic or, at times, a much broader paradigm of thought through which we filter all information presented to us. Theological presuppositions are things we 'pre-suppose' to be true of God and His Word.

Approaching the Scripture with openness means we are willing for our taken-for-granted notions to be exposed and (when necessary) expelled. The Gospels are full of examples in which Jesus encountered and confronted the pre-supposed beliefs of His contemporaries:

> **Do not suppose** that I have come to bring peace to the earth. I did not come to bring peace, but a sword. (Matt. 10:34)

When I first opened my 1984 NIV as a teenager, I held multiple presuppositions regarding what the Bible said. I believed God was real and personal, that He was Creator of all things and that Genesis 1 offered a scientific description of how He formed the universe, planet Earth and every living thing over six 24-hour days. I believed God would be angry at me each time I sinned, yet was willing to show mercy if I was sorry enough and asked His forgiveness. After all, Christ paid the price for my sins on the cross. I believed Jesus was both God and man, born to a virgin mother in a farmer's stable in the early hours of 25 December, 0 AD, who would later work as a carpenter alongside His father, Joseph Christ. I believed speaking in tongues was proof that somebody was full of the Spirit, that God's miraculous power was active today as it was in biblical times, and that I was growing up in the 'last days' and the 'end of the age'. I believed that, in my lifetime, Jesus would physically and literally *come down* on a cloud, *lift away* Christians, *burn up* the planet and *cast aside* unbelievers to be tortured with unceasing agony for all eternity. I believed that because of my faith in Christ, I was 'saved', despite still being a sinner with a heart that was deceitful and desperately wicked.

These are just a few of the preconceptions I brought into my Bible reading. Be assured, there were many, many more. Over the course of my life and learning, each one of these beliefs has been challenged. Some I still cherish. Others I have changed.

Today, I still hold many presuppositions, some of which I am not (yet) even conscious. And that's okay. We cannot help but bring implicit background beliefs to our Bible reading. This is unavoidable. However, we can commit to being humble enough to admit we have them, and open enough to having the

Good Teacher address and adjust them as He deems appropriate. Remember, openness is about being prepared to admit: 'I don't know it all—and *I may be wrong*'.

Preferences

As with presuppositions, there is nothing inherently wrong with having preferences towards certain aspects of biblical revelation. After all, our personal preferences play a huge part in defining and distinguishing who we are as individuals. It does become problematic, however, when we refuse to adjust when our partialities are proven unhelpful.

Let's face it; we all have biblical truths, teaching and topics of which we are particularly fond. We all hold passion for certain aspects or portions of Scripture to which we grant more time and attention than those we favour less. Any passion for the things of God should be celebrated, but this comes with a caution. If kept unchecked, personal bents and biases towards things *we like*, can easily form blind spots to things we *don't like*:

> (P)reach the word; be ready in season and out of season; reprove, rebuke, and exhort, with complete patience and teaching. For the time is coming when people will not endure **sound teaching**, but having itching ears they will accumulate for themselves teachers **to suit their own passions**. (2 Tim. 4:2–3 ESV)

The word Paul uses here for 'sound' teaching (Greek: *hugiainó*) literally means *healthy and whole*, to be in good working order. His challenge to Timothy is clear. A considered combination of encouragement, correction and rebuke would be required of this young leader to bring people into health with a wholesome, well-balanced doctrinal diet. The Scriptures reveal so many nourishing truths on which we are invited to feast. At times, we just need to step out of our comfort zones and let our ears taste something we've never tried before!

I say this, of course, from much personal experience. I too have preferences (and prejudices) when it comes to the Scriptures. Here is one of them. I was more than 14 years into my pastoral career when I preached my first ever message on the second coming. I had committed to a teaching series on Thessalonians, and in doing so, had backed myself into a corner. There was no escape. I had to finally address issues like the return of Christ, the resurrection of the dead and the rapture of the church. Yep, you heard me right. I *had* to. I didn't *want* to.

I had avoided tackling eschatology (the study of 'last things') for years, and I had my reasons. I found the whole thing unclear, unnecessary and unpleasant. There, I said it. I was happy to sing along to the triumphant closing lyrics of hymns and songs that spoke of Jesus 'coming back soon', but I knew enough to know that it wasn't all beer and skittles. Oh, and I had also seen too many Christians become downright weird (and divisive) when it came to their end-time positions—something I did not wish to encourage in my local church community.

That said, the main reason I avoided this subject as a teacher in public was because I had so often avoided it as a reader in private. I habitually ignored the many 'coming of the Lord' passages (particularly their judgment and wrath elements) so I could read the bits I had a better grasp of and that provided me with greater comfort.

I'm not saying my evasion strategy was right … but it was a reality. My preference for easy-to-understand, familiar and feel-good truths led me to practise prejudice against those I considered difficult, foreign and uncomfortable. Left unchecked, preferences produce prejudices. A good student acknowledges such tendencies and is willing to adjust their perspective when an unhelpful bias is revealed.

Pride

I'm no gamer, but I've played enough video games in my lifetime to know that the enemy at the end of the battle is the biggest and baddest of them all. So, it's fitting that we've kept the worst until last. When it comes to the obstacles we face in our journey into biblical truth, the big boss of them all is pride.

But mark this: There will be terrible times in the last days. People will be lovers of themselves, lovers of money, **boastful, proud … rash, conceited … always learning but never able to come to a knowledge of the truth**. (2 Tim. 3:1–7)

Pride says, 'I know it all—and what I know is right' and in so doing, denies, discards and demeans the truths that expose our erroneous presuppositions and unhealthy prejudices. Pride arrogantly and intentionally employs confirmation bias, in which we apply a filter to the truths we hear, receiving those that prove us right and rejecting those that prove us wrong. Openness is both the antithesis and remedy to conquering this destructive force, and conquer it we can!

While it is impossible (and unnecessary) to rid ourselves of presuppositions and preferences, the archenemy known as pride can be defeated and stripped of his evil influence in our lives: '**So get rid of all the filth and evil in your lives, and humbly accept the word God has planted in your hearts**, for it has the power to save your souls' (James 1:21).

Retaining humility in your study of Scripture is a challenge that will remain with you for the rest of your life. It takes considerable courage to confess 'I was wrong' (even if it is just to ourselves) but the rewards of doing so far outweigh the costs.

Sometimes, you may face the (perhaps even greater) challenge of witnessing the ideas of your pastor, parents or church tradition proved incorrect or incomplete. Openness also says '[my favourite Bible teacher] doesn't know it all—and may be wrong'. No human preacher or author, system or seminary, denomination or movement, college or creed is infallible or inerrant. As much as we respect the teaching and perspectives of other saints, it is vital that we remain committed to embracing an openness to adjust our belief systems, as God Himself guides us.

Tammy, please understand that none of us approach the Bible from a truly objective standpoint. Each of us wears 'lenses' through which we observe life and literature, and you are no exception.

As the old adage asserts, 'We don't see the world as it is, we see the world as we are'. Your lenses colour how you read the Bible and, at times, obstruct your pursuit of biblical truth before (presuppositions), during (preferences) and after (pride) revelation comes to you. But again, be assured—you *can* handle it!

As I said earlier, my hope in this book is to bolster your confidence in handling the Word of God, so that your faith for being led into truth is greater than any fear you may have of being led into error. With this, I also hope to stir your curiosity, to inspire you to ask questions and seek answers and insights for yourself. So, please, be a good student. In both your heart and mind, remain open.

CHAPTER 12

Understanding

Finally, we must bring to our Bible reading an understanding of the practice, principles and process of hermeneutics. Before running out onto the field to play, we need to be aware of the rules and guidelines that govern our game. Back to Timothy:

> We know that the law is good if one **uses it properly** … Similarly, anyone who competes as an athlete does not receive the victor's crown except by competing **according to the rules**. (1 Tim. 1:8; 2 Tim. 2:5)

I bring together the two statements above for this reason: they contain the New Testament's only uses of the word *nomimōs*.[36] In doing so, Paul draws a parallel between the sportsperson and the Bible student—both vocations are governed by rules. To have any hope of success, players must adhere to the proper prescriptions of their particular profession.

Here in Australia, we have our own unique brand of football: Aussie Rules— the greatest game on the face of the earth, as any true-blue Australian will tell you. But for international sports fans, the game is often deemed nonsensical, confusing and messy. Believe me, I get it. Upon first viewing, there seems no rhyme or reason to it. Compared with other football codes, it appears disorganised, disorderly and disorientating, leaving the unschooled observer despondent and dissatisfied with the experience.

However, with just a little bit of explanation, most sports-lovers can eventually be won over and become diehard footy fans. The more they understand the rules, the more they are inclined to watch. The more they watch, the more they understand the rules—and so, we witness the upwards spiral of familiarity and fandom.

The same applies to the Bible student. The more we engage with the Word, the more we understand how it works. The more we understand how it works, the more we are inclined to engage. Think back to where we began, at Jesus' parable of the sower: 'Therefore consider carefully how you listen. **Whoever has will be given more**; whoever does not have, even what they think they have will be taken from them' (Luke 8:18). It would seem that when it comes to being faithful with the seed of God's Word, the reward for *good* understanding is even *greater understanding.*

It's never too late to start reading the Scriptures, and it's never too late to learn the rules by which they operate. The goal of this book is to help develop your understanding of hermeneutics, and thereby position you to become a better *observer*, *practitioner* and *teacher* of God's Word.

Observer

Like spectators at a football match, there will be times in life when you find yourself in the position of an observer, watching and listening as others handle the Word of Truth before you. A good observer of preaching ministry is like the Bereans who were considered 'noble-minded' because they engaged in the apostles' teaching with educated enthusiasm (Acts 17:11). They were open, but not naïve, combining zeal with knowledge, eager to learn from Paul and Silas, but unwilling to take their Gospel 'as gospel' until they had investigated the issues for themselves.

Understanding the principles of biblical interpretation will help you apply healthy discernment as you feed on the ministry of others, enhancing your ability to 'eat the meat and spit out the bones' as necessary.[37]

That said, the best and most discerning observers are those who know through personal experience what it's like to be in the game. Sports stadiums are often full of loudmouthed critics who consider themselves experts, but have never stepped on the field. God forbid we (as Christians) allow ourselves to become professional sermon-connoisseurs but never progress to hands-on participation.

Practitioner

When it comes to understanding how something works, there's no better teacher than the rubber-hits-the-road reality of personal experience. In an age in which information is fed to us fast and free, it is tempting to think that because we've *heard* something, we *know* something. According to Jesus, it is the truth you hear, heed and 'hold to' that will bring freedom and form a firm foundation for your life (Matt. 7:24–25; John 8:31–32).

Over the years, I have read and listened to hundreds (if not thousands) of hours of teaching from some of the world's best Bible preachers. But the truths that have had the greatest impact on me, the ones I hold nearest and dearest, are those that came as a result of my personal curiosity, investigation and discovery. The biblical convictions I truly 'own as my own' are revelation that have come through research, reflection and my one-on-one relationship with God.

Think back to Eden for a moment. As I see it, Eve was the one most susceptible to the serpent's cunning because, unlike Adam, she had only *second-hand revelation* of God's Word. Eve was not on the scene when God gave His instruction regarding the forbidden fruit, and so relied on the information passed on to her from her hubby. When the serpent (who, it seems, *was* an eyewitness to this instruction) presented a different story to that of Adam, Eve was confronted with a classic 'he-said-he-said' situation. Who was correct: her spouse or the snake?

That fateful day, faced with a discrepancy between the two accounts, Adam and Eve made the same mistake—neither sought clarity direct from God Himself, but instead trusted and acted upon the testimony of another (Gen. 2:15–3:6).

By all means, observe those who play the game well. Watch and listen to them. Be encouraged, enthused and equipped by preachers you enjoy and trust. But understand this: it's not enough for you to simply feed and depend on the teachings of others. Grow up. Get out of the stands and onto the field. Understand how the Bible works, read it for yourself, follow the rules, learn by trial-and-error and put some points on the board.

Just as football players develop their ball-handling skills through routine training and gameplay, it is only by regular practice and hands-on participation that we will improve our Bible-handling abilities. Watching others play is not enough. It's time to step into the game for yourself. The more you personally participate in handling the Word of Truth, the better an observer you will be and the more qualified you'll become to instruct others.

Teacher

If spectators and players require a healthy understanding of the rules of the game, then how much more the coach! The influence coaches wield over the course, condition and culture of the team is greater than that of the most ardent fan or star recruit. When it comes to instructing others in the Scripture, says James, those who assume such a role should anticipate a greater degree of scrutiny (James 3:1). Yet, according to Paul and John, there is nothing more fulfilling than being coach to a winning team:

> For what is our hope, our joy, or the crown in which we will glory in the presence of our Lord Jesus when he comes? Is it not you? **Indeed,**

you are our glory and joy … For now we really live, since you are standing firm in the Lord … **I have no greater joy than to hear that my children are walking in the truth**. (1 Thess. 2:19–20; 3:8; 3 John 1:4)

For a good coach, the success of their players is its own reward. For these apostles, the crown in which they rejoiced was the fact that their students had successfully continued in the truth they had been taught.

Having been in pastoral preaching and teaching ministry for most of my adult life, I can absolutely attest to this. As exciting as it is when Holy Spirit personally illuminates something to me from His Word, it's nothing compared with the delight I encounter when that same Spirit works *through me* to 'switch others on' to His glorious truth!

 Timothy, I encourage you to take the content of this book seriously and commit yourself to understanding the rules and principles of biblical hermeneutics.

I do this not so that you would simply become a better spectator or player and benefit only yourself, but that you will take on the role of coach to the many Timothys that come after you:

> You then, my son, be strong in the grace that is in Christ Jesus. **And the things you have heard me say** in the presence of many witnesses **entrust to reliable people who will also be qualified to teach others**. (2 Tim. 2:1–2)

SUMMARY REMARKS—STEP 1

Time to sum up Step 1. Your first and foundational task in the process of healthy hermeneutics is to answer the all-important question: what does the Scripture *say*?

For those of us not trained in its original languages, this means choosing a variety of versions from which to read. Since no single translation (on its own) is capable of fully conveying the complexity of the message communicated in the ancient text, I suggest that every serious student of Scripture should have ready access to at least four different Bibles: something old, something new, something borrowed and something blue.

Yet it's not enough to know *what* to read—one must also know *how* to read.

Each time you approach your Bible reading and study, remember to pronounce your vowels. Come to God's Word with appreciation, expectation, intention and openness, and finally, with a commitment to understanding (and undertaking) the art and science of healthy hermeneutics.

Step 2

What Does it Mean?

Having established what the Bible *says*, we now turn our attention to our second task, discovering what the text *means*. As anyone in a serious relationship will tell you, listening to your partner is one thing, *understanding them* is another thing entirely! Yet as royal members of God's family, seeking understanding of His Word is both our privilege and priority: 'It is God's privilege to conceal things and **the king's privilege to discover them**' (Prov. 25:2).

My son, if you accept my words and store up my commands within you, turning your ear to wisdom and applying your heart to understanding—indeed, if you **call out for insight and cry aloud for understanding**, and if you look for it as for silver and search for it as for hidden treasure, then you will understand the fear of the Lord and find the knowledge of God. For the Lord gives wisdom; from his mouth come knowledge and understanding. (Prov. 2:1–6)

Since this is where the bulk of our work lies, I have dedicated significantly more space to this section of our study (Step 2) than I have to the others. When considering the workload that is required of us as good students of the Scriptures, especially when dealing with complex issues, I'd suggest that more than two-thirds of our labours (some 70% or more) belong in this critical second step.

Pay attention, Tammy. It is here that most battles for sound doctrine are won or lost.

CHAPTER 13

The ABCS of Exegesis

Work hard so God can say to you, 'Well done.' Be a good workman, one who does not need to be ashamed when God examines your work. **Know what his Word says and means**. (2 Tim. 2:15 TLB)

Healthy hermeneutics, you'll recall, is a discipline that seeks to answer three questions of the Scripture: *What does it say? What does it mean? What does it matter?* The second step in this process is so important, so indispensably imperative to the interpretive method, that it warrants its own technical term: *exegesis*.

Again, the origins of this word are Greek: *exegeisthai* is a composite word meaning 'to guide out'. When applied to the field of literary interpretation, exegesis essentially means 'to draw out the original intended meaning' of the text.[38] Exegesis is fundamentally a historical task to determine the original meaning of the original words to the original audience in the original context into which they were originally delivered.

Essentially, this means (funnily enough) that *there's nothing original about exegesis*!

This critical second step in healthy hermeneutics is not about discovering a new or novel meaning in the text, but rather about establishing what the text has *always meant*. When we exegete a portion of Scripture, we are setting our minds to hear and embrace the text on *its own terms*. To achieve this, it is helpful to imagine ourselves in the minds of the ancient authors, considering their intent as they spoke and wrote.[39]

Authorial Intent

Think back to our web-based traffic app analogy. When the program declares, 'the road is red', what does that *mean*? Has the road been painted? Is it hot, angry or in love? Is the road socialist, flowing with blood, a Manchester United fan or in financial deficit? Are only red vehicles permitted to drive it? No, no and no.

There is only one meaning to the statement 'the road is red': slow-moving traffic. That meaning is determined by the author of the program. It matters not what 'red' means to you. That is not the question here. The question is, 'what does the *author* mean'?

True, there is an *art* to biblical interpretation. There is space in hermeneutics to bring one's unique perspective, creativity and personal expression to the process. But not here, not now, not yet. With exegesis, we are dealing wholly and solely with the cold, hard *science* of hermeneutics.

Once we clarify the text's original then-and-there meaning (i.e., the intended meaning of the author), we can seek to apply the truths the text reveals to comparable situations in our here-and-now. It is there (in Step 3) that some creativity is required.

Until then, exegesis is about asking, 'What did the author intend to communicate when he spoke/wrote, and how were those words to be understood by the target audience?':[40]

> Jesus looked directly at them and asked, '**Then what is the meaning** of that which is written: "The stone the builders rejected has become the cornerstone"'? (Luke 20:17)

The Aim of Exegesis

Healthy hermeneutics insists the original intended meaning of the text is fixed; the text *means what it has always meant*, and that cannot be changed.

It is not your task to *decide* what the text means, but to *discover* the meaning that has always been there. While the communication method may be nuanced or layered with multiple implications, the meaning of the text is fixed in history.

That is not to say that the biblical authors always understood the full meaning of their message.[41] Remember, when dealing with the Scriptures, there are *multiple authors* involved—the human and the Divine. This is particularly relevant in prophetic texts. Even Daniel, having received a long and detailed revelation concerning the future of his people, openly confessed: 'I heard, but I did not understand' (Dan. 12:8). Such men were indeed 'carried along by the Holy Spirit' as they spoke, but then reviewed their own utterances 'intently and with the greatest care' in an attempt to develop a clearer picture of what God had just communicated through them (2 Peter 1:21; 1 Peter 1:10–12).

If, at times, you find yourself at a loss to know precisely what God meant when He communicated a particular message, take heart. You are in good company, indeed. Exegesis can be difficult. Discerning the intended meaning of the biblical text is not always as straightforward as we might hope. Even the first-century apostles acknowledge this! Says Peter of the apostle Paul:

> He writes the same way in all his letters, speaking in them of these matters. **His letters contain some things that are hard to understand**, which ignorant and unstable people distort, as they do the other Scriptures, to their own destruction. (2 Peter 3:16)

Answering the all-important question, *What does it mean?*, can be a challenging task, but our target remains clear. To correctly handle the Word of Truth, we must set our sights on the *aim* of exegesis: the *author's intended meaning*.[42]

Learning Your ABCS

Since the aim of exegesis is to discover the author's intended meaning, the *practice* of exegesis is largely concerned with *clarifying the context* into which the text was written. When it comes to discovering 'what the Bible means', context is king. After all, when you take a text out of context, all you are left with is a con.

There are four major considerations in establishing the context of Scripture. I call them the ABCS of exegesis, in which we consider the:

A—Author and Audience

B—Big-Picture Background

C—Corroborating Content

S—Style of Speech

The remainder of Step 2 will focus our attention on these crucial exegetical concerns. As we work our way through, I will draw on a variety of biblical case studies for illustrative purposes. Many of these will be simple. Some more challenging. Others will even have you laughing. But please know, this is serious business.

Exegesis is absolutely indispensable to the proper process of hermeneutics. I cannot stress this enough. Like laying the foundation of a brick wall or constructing a timber frame for a house, how well we exegete the text has serious ramifications for the overall alignment, strength and success of our final result. If we are to rightly divide the Word of Truth, perhaps an old carpentry motto would be helpful here: 'measure twice, cut once!'.

 Proceed with caution, Timothy.

Author and Audience

When it comes to correctly exegeting a text, authorial intent is crucial. Therefore, the first step in establishing context is to *ascertain the author and audience* of the text in question. As we read the Bible, we need to be conscious of who is speaking and to whom their words are directed. When it comes to the who, what, when, why and how of contextual considerations, remember, 'who's on first!'.[43]

> 'You also must be ready, because the Son of Man will come at an hour when you do not expect him.' Peter asked, '**Lord, are you telling this parable to us, or to everyone?**' (Luke 12:40–41)

Largely, determining the author and audience of a given text is relatively simple. Approximately two-thirds of the Bible's books have been attributed names that instantly identify either the author or audience in question.[44] Further, publishers of modern study Bibles commonly include a preface to each book, outlining each work's likely author, intended audience, approximate

dates and historical setting. For the most part, such commentaries from biblical scholars are both accurate and helpful.

But, ultimately, it will be your personal growing familiarity with the Bible that will serve you best in the long term. Your competence and confidence in discerning author and audience will increase with regular practice and a consistent, systematic approach to Bible reading.

Before we move on to practical examples, allow me to stress that while all Scripture is written *for* you, not all Scripture is written *to* you. In fact, while all Scripture is written for you, none of it (in purely historical terms) was written directly to you.

Exegesis, you'll remember, is about establishing the author's original intended meaning as addressed to the original intended audience. While you and I today, here in the twenty-first century, may very well be a *subsequent* audience, none of us can accurately claim that we are the actual audience the authors considered as they wrote and spoke.

While we believe (correctly) that the Eternal God had us in mind as the human authors were empowered to write—and should take to heart Jesus' exhortation to be one who 'has an ear [to] hear what the Spirit says to the churches' of antiquity (Rev. 2:7 ESV)—we must accept that from a literary perspective, every time we pick up our Bibles, we are effectively reading somebody else's mail.[45]

I'll say it again: while all Scripture is written *for* you, not all Scripture is written *to* you.

To address *What does it mean?*, it is useful to imagine ourselves in the 'pews and shoes' of the original recipients, and more importantly, in the minds of the human writers. This is no small task, especially considering the significant linguistic, historical and cultural disparities between the original author and audience, and us today!

Tammy, let me assure you, this is a discipline that becomes easier with time, practice and familiarity. For now, the best way to observe how this works is by walking together through some practical examples:

> The Advice in Job
>
> The Laws in Leviticus
>
> The Wisdom in Proverbs 31
>
> The Woes of the Prophets
>
> The Citations in the New Testament
>
> The Books by John

Let's go.

CHAPTER 14

The Advice in Job

Ever been at a place in your life in which you have been so desperate for God's counsel that you have simply opened your Bible and stuck your finger in some random page, hoping you would receive the Word of the Lord for your situation? Believe it or not, I'm not about to entirely negate this practice (in fact, God has actually spoken to me in that way before!), but I must say, if your Bible opens up close to the middle, and your finger ends up pointing at a passage in Job, it is highly likely that what you are about to read is some very *bad advice* indeed!

While the book of Job may very well be a Spirit-inspired account, a good portion of what you'll read in that book is not Spirit-inspired advice! Most of what is recorded in Job are words spoken by men whose perception of God, and therefore, perspective on life, were seriously flawed. Their faulty claims and the discussion that ensues span no fewer than 25 chapters of the book, as three of Job's friends spout their misinformed beliefs and misleading rants:

> You say to God, 'My beliefs are flawless and I am pure in your sight.' Oh, how I wish that God would speak, that he would open his lips against you … What are mortals, that they could be pure, or those born of woman, that they could be righteous? If God places no trust in his holy ones, if even the heavens are not pure in his eyes, how much less mortals, who are vile and corrupt, who drink up evil like water … How then can a mortal be righteous before God? How can one born of woman be pure? If even the moon is not bright and the stars are not pure in his eyes, how much less a mortal, who is but a

maggot—a human being, who is only a worm! (Job 11:4–5; 15:14–16; 25:4–6)

Later, over just two brief verses in the closing chapter, God finally calls these men out, describing their words as 'folly' and rebuking them: '**You have not spoken the truth about me**' (Job 42:7–8). In other words, much of what you will read in the book of Job concerning the nature of our Lord is not accurate. According to God Himself, 'the truth' was not spoken by these men.

The same can be said regarding statements made by Job. As the story of his suffering proceeds and his situation intensifies, the grieving protagonist levels scathing accusations against God's good and righteous character:

> The LORD gave, and now he has taken away ... Almighty God has shot me with arrows, and their poison spreads through my body. God has lined up his terrors against me ... God's anger is constant ... He sends storms to batter and bruise me without any reason at all. He won't let me catch my breath; he has filled my life with bitterness ... When an innocent person suddenly dies, God laughs. (Job 1:21; 6:4; 9:13, 17–18, 23 GNB)

Do not assume that Job's assertions here are correct—nowhere does God Himself endorse or support these claims. While considered 'blameless and upright' in regards his character (Job 1:1), like his three deluded friends Job's knowledge of God was seriously deficient. Sincere he may have been, but, in many cases, Job was sincerely wrong: 'Then out of the storm the LORD spoke to Job. Who are you to question my wisdom with your ignorant, empty words?' (Job 38:1–2 GNB).

The point is, be aware of *whose words you are reading* when you approach a passage of Scripture. While, collectively, the Bible is the Word of God, not everything uttered in the Book are the words of God. At some points, our Bible even contains out-and-out lies:

> '**You will not certainly die**,' the serpent said to the woman. 'For God knows that when you eat from it your eyes will be opened, and you will be like God, knowing good and evil.' (Gen. 3:4–5)

YOU CAN HANDLE THE TRUTH

You may be reading something that has been recorded correctly, but, in essence, is all wrong. It all depends on who is speaking.

That said, were your finger to fall somewhere in the last 10 chapters of the book of Job, in which the main contributors are God and Job's wise friend Elihu, it is likely you will find some great nuggets of truth. But like Elihu, allow me to be a good friend and counsel you with these words: while it may succeed occasionally (*very* occasionally), I suggest you limit your random, finger-falling, lucky-dip approach to the Scripture to begin with!

As discussed in Step 1, most of your Bible reading should be done systematically—choose a book and read it through from start to finish as was originally intended. For the most part, this approach will help you to clearly identify the author of the words, determine how these words fit into the broader context of the statements, situation and story surrounding it, and hopefully avoid the problematic pitfalls of an out-of-context interpretation.

Thanks for Your Message: May I Ask Who's Speaking?

Legend has it, a classified advertisement was once placed in the Personals pages of the Atlanta Journal. It read something like this:

SINGLE BLACK FEMALE seeks male companionship, ethnicity unimportant. I'm a very good-looking girl who loves to play. I love long walks in the woods, riding in your pickup truck, hunting, camping and fishing trips, cozy winter nights lying with you by the fire. Candlelight dinners will have me eating out of your hand. Rub me the right way and watch me respond. I'll be at the front door when you get home from work, wearing only what nature gave me. Kiss me and I'm yours. Call (404) 875-6420 and ask for Daisy.

As the story goes, over 15,000 men responded to the advertisement that week, only to find themselves talking to the Atlanta Humane Society about an eight-week-old black Labrador retriever.

Since the aim of exegesis is to discover the author's intended meaning, it stands to reason that, every time we approach a biblical text, we first establish the identity of the one speaking.

CHAPTER 15

The Laws in Leviticus

The first five books of our Bible are known collectively as the law of Moses, the books of Moses, or simply the Law (*Torah* in Hebrew, and *Pentateuch* in Greek).[46] Leviticus is third in this collection and literally means 'relating to the Levites'. Identifying the author and original audience here is pretty straightforward—you need look no further than the first and final verses:

> The Lord called to Moses and spoke to him from the tent of meeting. He said, 'Speak to the Israelites and say to them: "When anyone among you brings an offering to the Lord, bring as your offering an animal from either the herd or the flock"' … **These are the commands the LORD gave Moses at Mount Sinai for the Israelites**. (Lev. 1:1–2; 27:34)

From these top-and-tail passages, we observe that Leviticus is primarily a book of instructions issued by God, through Moses, while camped at Mount Sinai. The target audience of these instructions are the Israelites, the ancient nation of Israel, a collective body of 13 identifiable tribes who traced their natural ancestry to the patriarchs Abraham, Isaac and Jacob.[47]

The commands and regulations contained within Leviticus concern such things as: the correct animals to offer to the priests to atone for sin and guilt, how to hold a lamb's head while it is slaughtered and where to sprinkle its blood, dietary restrictions (including shellfish, pig, rabbit and snake), mandatory male circumcision, burning clothing affected by mildew and avoiding clothing of mixed-materials, bathing after sex, the purchase of

YOU CAN HANDLE THE TRUTH

foreign slaves, how not to clip one's beard and so on.

 Be assured, Timothy, as you read the ancient instructions contained in Leviticus, you are most certainly reading somebody else's mail!

The regulations, routines, rites and rituals prescribed in Leviticus are not written to you, or for that matter, to anybody you know. God's commands they may be, but to *whom* He is issuing them is of fundamental importance. Says Paul to the Christians in Rome: 'Now we know that whatever the law says, it says to those who are under the law … [however] you are not under the law, but under grace' (Rom. 3:19; 6:14).

Again, I am not saying that Leviticus is irrelevant to us. On the contrary, the modern-day reader can learn plenty from this book. Remember, '**All Scripture** is God-breathed and is useful' to the Christian community (2 Tim. 3:16) and 'all Scripture' includes the Levitical Law:

> **The old system under the law of Moses was only a shadow**, a dim preview of the good things to come, not the good things themselves. The sacrifices under that system were repeated again and again, year after year, but they were never able to provide perfect cleansing for those who came to worship. (Heb. 10:1 NLT)

The first-century Scriptures (i.e., the New Testament) explain that many of the processes and prescriptions pertaining to Moses' tabernacle, the Levitical priesthood and the related offerings, sacrifices, seasons and festivals, served as temporary 'shadows' to which Jesus Christ provided a permanent substance. In other words, the physical rites and rituals performed by the Israelites and their priesthood would become spiritual realities through the ministry of Christ centuries later. In turn, the work of Christ would render these practices redundant, as the old was set aside by a new and superior system of worship.[48]

Consequently, if you are unfamiliar with the concepts of Leviticus in relation to the major national festivals of Israel (for example), you will fail to recognise much of the nuanced language in the first-century Scriptures that indicates the fulfilment of those festivals in Christ. In doing so, you will be left with an incomplete understanding of the implications of His work for you as a new-covenant believer. Familiarity with the ancient worship practices of Israel outlined at Sinai will provide you with a helpful framework (or scaffolding) with which to build a working knowledge of the many benefits and blessings available and accessible to you through the Gospel of Christ today.[49]

By all means, read the law of Leviticus and learn from it. There's plenty of good stuff in there that can bless and benefit you, so long as you handle it properly. Despite not being addressed to you, it should most definitely *matter to you*. Just keep in mind that you are far removed (in many respects) from the audience both God and Moses had in mind.

CHAPTER 16

The Wisdom in Proverbs 31

Now for something a little more lighthearted and perhaps not so obvious. A few years back, I preached one of my all-time favourite Mother's Day messages using the famous *Wife of Noble Character* poem from the closing chapter of Proverbs. I began by thanking the mums present and encouraging them to put their feet up, sit back and relax. This Mother's Day Sunday, I was not going to preach to them. Instead, my message was to be directed at the men in the room. My first objective was to draw attention to both the author and intended audience of this great collection of wisdom. From the opening prologue:

> The proverbs of Solomon son of David, king of Israel … **Listen, my son, to your father's instruction and do not forsake your mother's teaching**. They are a garland to grace your head and a chain to adorn your neck. **My son**, if sinful men entice you, do not give in to them … **my son**, do not go along with them, do not set foot on their paths. (Prov. 1:1, 8–10, 15)

King Solomon is clearly identified as the principal author of this body of work, one of many he was credited for during his life and reign as king (1 Kings 4:29–34). Saying after saying, discourse after discourse, the book of Proverbs reads as a collection of advice from a father to his son. That is, until the final chapter. You see, Proverbs 31 was authored by a woman—the Queen mother.[50]

Two things are worth noting here. First, when deciding how to finish this epic work of wisdom, even Solomon knew well enough to leave the final word to the woman in his life! A valuable lesson indeed. Second—and more seriously—while the author of this chapter may shift from the words of Solomon to those of his mother, the intended audience does not change. The royal son is still the target.

This means the famous *Wife of Noble Character* poem is not directed to a woman. It never was. It was written to a prince.

Proverbs 31 was not written to tell women what they should be like. It was not given as a list of instructions to which a daughter should aspire to attain in life. This beautiful poem was never intended to be some type of checklist for women the world over, trying desperately to break through glass ceilings and striving to make their mark in a 'man's world'. After all, Proverbs 31 was not directed to a woman at all. While I am fully aware that this poem has been the subject of many a sermon at Christian women's events and countless articles, books and blogs all directed at female audiences, I believe this passage should primarily be preached to men.

Now please, Tammy—don't misunderstand me. If you are inspired by the woman described in this poem and choose to view her as some type of exemplary figure on whom you wish to model your life, by all means, do so! Be open to whatever lessons Holy Spirit wants to highlight to you through her example. My point is simply that we need to accept that the intended audience of this poem was male, Solomon and then his son. By doing this, we can accomplish our exegetical goal: to discover the *author's intent*. Don't believe me? Let's take a closer look.

The poem opens with a question: 'A wife of noble character, who can find?' (Prov. 31:10). The question is not: 'A wife of noble character, who can *be her*', but rather, 'who can *find her*'. In other words—'what kind of man gets a woman like that?'.

As we now search for the answer to that question, our focus needs to be directed primarily towards the male character it describes. Without doubt, the poem paints a glorious picture of an industrious, favoured, wise, hardworking, respected, entrepreneurial, asset-rich, creative, multiskilled, strong, joyful and God-respecting woman. But the intent of the poem is to draw the readers' attention to the *qualities of the man who is worthy of wedding her*. It is the male's character and conduct under scrutiny here. This is an intent that we will miss, with the likely result of a faulty interpretation and misguided applications, if we do not exegete the text well by paying attention to the original target audience.

 Have I sparked your curiosity, Timothy?

Great. Now go read Proverbs 31 with these things in mind.

CHAPTER 17

The Woes of the Prophets

Now for something far more serious that I feel warrants a word of warning. What I am about to say may come as a shock, so please take a deep breath and brace yourself. Are you ready? Here goes.

None of the great warnings and woes uttered by the Bible's prophets were written to your nation. They are not directed at you, the city in which you live or to the church in which you participate. The doom-and-gloom predictions of divine judgment pronounced by Nahum, Obadiah, Isaiah, Jeremiah and others are not addressed to the United Nations, capitalist America, communist China, secular societies of Modern Europe, Islamic societies in the Middle East or to any twenty-first century nation-state or religious body corporate.

Every Bible prophet spoke by the Spirit of God to a particular constituency, at a particular time in history. That audience is fixed in time and antiquity.

I stress this point with a touch of drama because perhaps more than any other part of our Bibles, the prophetic writings are the most often mishandled by modern-day readers and preachers. Let's be clear—you will never handle the Prophets properly unless you first establish the author and audience in question.

Identifying the prophetic authors is quite straightforward given that many have their books named after them, at least those post-Solomon.

Other significant prophetic ministers include Moses, King David and the psalmists, John of Revelation and, of course, Jesus and John the Baptiser, who themselves did not write but, nevertheless, had many of their prophetic discourses recorded by others.

That said, identifying the *audience* of the Prophets is not so simple. Some prophetic discourses clearly identify their target (typically a nation or significant leader), whereas other oracles are less specific, leaving the Bible student to dig a little deeper to ascertain the most likely intended recipient(s).

While there is a great deal to be said regarding understanding prophetic literature, allow me to highlight three simple facts to consider when approaching these unique ministers of God: prophets are *messengers*, prophets are *messy* and prophets are *mindful*. Remember, Step 2 in healthy hermeneutics (i.e., exegesis) is all about discovering the *author's intent*. This is something you will likely miss, should you not appreciate these simple realities.

Prophets are Messengers

In the Hebrew Bible, the two most commonly used terms to denote God's prophetic messengers are *seers* and *prophets*.[51] Prophets are very much engaged with 'seeing' the spiritual. Theirs is a ministry of heaven's courtroom.[52] Prophets take what they see and hear in the spirit realm and speak that reality to their earthly audience as instructed. At times, this means their words are predictive in nature, a preparative warning for their listeners; but often, their words are not foretelling but simply forth-telling, and carry a more here-and-now observation or directive.

Prophets also concern themselves with the Scriptures. Theirs is a ministry of the covenant. Prophets take what God has recorded in the Scripture and, like a prosecuting attorney, pronounce both the positive and negative consequences of the covenant conditions to its adherents. This is one of the reasons the language of biblical prophets so often reflects that of Moses. God used Moses to *pen* the law and later used prophets to *prosecute* that law.[53]

While some were addressed to individuals, the bulk of the Bible's prophecies had a collective or national audience. For the most part, this would include Israel (God's covenant community), whereby the prophets would plead God's legal case against them upon their violation of the Torah. Occasionally, the prophets turned their attention to Israel's neighbouring nations, issuing rebukes for general misconduct, or more commonly for their specific mistreatment of His covenant people. After all, despite Israel's frequent failure to keep God's law, the Israelites were still the children of Abraham to whom He had promised 'whoever curses you I will curse' (Gen. 12:3). We will further discuss the importance of covenant in *Big-Picture Background*.

Prophets are Messy

We all know prophets are a little peculiar. Whether it's wedding a well-known harlot, dining on honey-dipped locusts, baking cakes over cow dung or walking around naked for extended periods, prophetic people are often a little more 'creative' than the rest of us. And when it comes to reading the Prophets, things often become messy.

For starters, while often including a narrative element to their work, prophets don't necessarily set out their story in a linear fashion, but are known for jumping back-and-forth through various periods as their purpose dictates. Some prophetic oracles are time-stamped (by referencing the current king's reign, for instance), but others are not, making it difficult to pinpoint when in the chronology certain prophecies were given.

In their writing, prophets can switch from speaking God's words to people to speaking people's words to God. One moment they'll be directing their woes to a community, and the next, they'll begin to bare their own hearts to heaven. At times, their books seem biographical in nature (i.e., penned by others) and then, suddenly, they appear autobiographical, with the prophet speaking of, and even to, themselves![54]

Further, the Prophets are famous for their great variety of literary genre, mixing metaphors and combining historical narrative with heavenly nuance. At times, their oracles are recorded as psalms, or other forms of poetry, using emotive and exaggerated language to highlight their point. Therefore, what prophets *say* and what prophets *mean* are often two very different things. Once more, something we will discuss in further detail in *Style of Speech*.

Prophets are Mindful

When the prophets spoke, they were always aware of their audience.

While they may not have completely understood the full implications of their prophetic visions and oracles, prophets did not speak mindlessly. In terms of their communication, they were 'carried **along** by the Holy Spirit', not carried *away* by Him (2 Peter 1:21). The prophets' words were both performed and recorded while in a cognisant state, being fully aware of the intended audience for whom they shaped and structured their speech.

Therefore, it is imperative that when considering the prophetic warnings and woes, we are also aware of the audience being addressed and, particularly, their historical, political and covenantal contexts.

When Moses foretold the day that God would say of His people, 'I will heap calamities on them and spend my arrows against them. I will send wasting famine against them, consuming pestilence and deadly plague' (Deut. 32:23–24), he was speaking of the nation-state of Israel, bound to the old-covenant system of Law, some 1,400 years before Christ. By no means assume these words are addressed to you.

When Isaiah described the coming day of the Lord as, 'Cruel, with fury and burning anger, to make the land a desolation', when God would 'exterminate its sinners' (Isa. 13:9 NASB), he was specifically addressing the inhabitants of Babylon in the sixth century BC. The armies of the Medes and Persians are not coming for you, your city or any modern-day nation-state! The day of the Lord cited in this passage had a very particular audience in mind, and the fulfilment of that prophecy has well and truly been and gone.

When John the Baptiser warned that 'The ax is already at the root of the trees, and every tree that does not produce good fruit will be cut down and thrown into the fire' (Matt. 3:10), please understand that he was not a

Christian preacher speaking to a Christian crowd. The fact is, 'Christians' did not exist during John's ministry, or his entire lifetime for that matter! As did the prophets before him, John used well-established old-covenant language to address an old-covenant audience, at a time when the old-covenant agreement was still in effect.[55]

Similarly, when Jesus delivered His famous *Seven Woes Sermon* and *Signs of the End of the Age* prophecy, we must be aware of His audience. The warnings, worries and woes of the Olivet Discourse (including wars, famines, earthquakes, persecution and great distress) and the survival advice given (fleeing to the Judean mountains, not returning to fields, praying that it would not occur in winter or on a Saturday) were not directed to twenty-first century Christians! These pronouncements and predictions of wrath were specifically issued to a first-century Jewish audience, particularly, as with John the Baptiser, to those living in and around Jerusalem at the time.[56]

The Prophets—Closing Comments

As established earlier, healthy hermeneutics requires you to 'keep your head' and approach the Bible intelligently (2 Tim. 4:5). Especially when reading the Prophets, remember to always consider the author and intended audience.

All Scripture is written *for* you, but not all Scripture is written *to* you.

CHAPTER 18

The Citations in the New Testament

Moving on to some New Testament examples, we will begin with a little game I like to call 'Whose line is it anyway?'. Question: which prominent first-century figure claimed the following?

> For God so loved the world that he gave his one and only Son, that whoever believes in him shall not perish but have eternal life. (John 3:16)

Were you to present me with this touch of Bible trivia a decade ago, my answer would have come without the slightest hesitation: 'For God so loved the world' is a quotation from none other than the one and only Son of God Himself, the Lord Jesus Christ. Anybody could tell you that. After all, it's right there in red and white. Or at least it was in my *something-old* Bible.

Some years ago, I acquired a copy of the 'slightly revised' 2011 NIV. Having been assured that it contained only minor edits to the 1984 edition, somewhere in the vicinity of a 5% variance, you can imagine my shock when I turned to John 3:16 and found it written in black! Not red ... black! No longer was it the Beloved Son claiming, 'For God so loved the world'. This quotation was now being credited instead to the beloved disciple.

My world was rocked. How dare they alter God's Holy Word! Did this new breed of translators not realise that those who did such a thing would have their share of the Tree of Life taken from them (Rev. 22:19)? I was grieved; then my sorrow turned to anger. Righteous indignation bubbled in my belly, as I began to experience my own 'cleansing the temple' moment. It was one thing to use the gender-inclusive phrase 'brothers and sisters', but this change was pure sacrilege. What were these translators thinking? How dare they remove these glorious words from the lips of my Lord and attribute them to a mere mortal? Surely this was the nearest to the unpardonable sin that one could get!

It should please you to know that I didn't make a whip that day, nor did I storm into NIV publishing headquarters and start kicking over tables. Instead, I did a little research. Turns out, when our New Testament was first written, it contained virtually no annotation or punctuation: no commas, periods, colons or question and quotation marks. In fact, until the ninth century, Koine Greek was written entirely in upper-case (uncial) letters and barely included spaces between words![57] It was as though the first-century apostles had typed out a document without a functioning spacebar and with the caps lock key permanently depressed. Needless to say, the result doesn't make for easy reading.

The absence of such markers in the earliest biblical documents has meant that, over time, and to accurately convey intended meaning, translators have had to employ a considerable degree of discretion and deliberation when punctuating our Bibles.[58] This brings us back to John 3:16, and the matter of how the translator's placement of quotation marks, or lack thereof, affects our understanding of who spoke a particular line of text.

Where New Testament authors directly cite an Old Testament passage, the placement of quotation marks is simple enough to determine—one only needs to reference the original. Likewise, when quoting verifiable sources from outside the biblical canon (including secular proverbs, philosophers, poets and pseudepigraphal works), and for what appear to be early Christian creeds and hymns, translators generally agree as to where these citations begin and end, even if they remain uncertain of the original sources.[59]

Conversely, as with John 3:16, there are instances in which citations are more ambiguous and, thus, the placement of quotations marks more speculative. In some cases, this can have significant implications for our exegesis.

Women: Forbidden to Speak in Church?

Since we're considering New Testament examples, what are we to make of this?

> Women should remain silent in the churches. They are not allowed to speak, but must be in submission, as the law says. If they want to inquire about something, they should ask their own husbands at home; for it is disgraceful for a woman to speak in the church. (1 Cor. 14:34–35)

When Punctuation Matters: He Said What?!

That Ancient Greeks would write their letters in upper-case with no spacing between words reminds me of a fun social experiment I conducted some years back when I logged into my social media platform and posted the following:

Almost immediately an old classmate of mine, an outspoken religious sceptic, applauded my confession: 'Exactly what I've been telling you for years, Chad!' he replied with glee, believing I had finally been won over to his atheistic worldview. Yet, following his comment, my GODISNOWHERE post was liked, shared and commented on by close family, Christian friends, members of my church and even fellow pastors. 'He sure is here right now', said one, 'God IS now here! Yes!' declared another.

At the time, the point of my post was largely to illustrate the power of perception but for current purposes it demonstrates something else: the power of punctuation. 'God is nowhere' and 'God is now here' present two entirely conflicting ideas, yet all it takes is a variance in the spacing.

The fact is, punctuation matters. After all, there's a big difference between saying: 'I like cooking my family and my pets', and saying 'I like cooking, my family, and my pets'. If you're somehow not convinced punctuation is vital to communication, try leaving out the semicolon when you tell someone 'I'm sorry; I love you'.

Paul's Corinthian epistles are commonly referred to as 'occasional letters' in that they came about in response to a specific set of circumstances. The occasion for this particular epistle began when Paul received a visit from concerned church members and a letter the leadership, presumably, had addressed to him (1 Cor. 1:11; 7:1). Picture that for a moment. When Paul penned 1 Corinthians, sat right by his side was the letter they had written to him.

Because of this, many translators believe that the apostle references their letter with direct citations. In other words, Paul makes a habit of quoting the Corinthians' letter back to them—performing a quick 'copy-and-paste'—before addressing the issues raised:

> Now concerning the matters about which you wrote: '*It is good for a man not to have sexual relations with a woman.*' But because of the temptation to sexual immorality, each man should have his own wife and each woman her own husband. The husband should give to his wife her conjugal rights, and likewise the wife to her husband (1 Cor. 7:1–3 ESV, italics added).

Seems straightforward enough. The Corinthians had suggested that sexual abstinence was a positive move, to which Paul responded with an 'I hear you, but' qualification: '*I hear you* that celibacy is a good thing, *but* sex within marriage is both a delight and a duty for those involved. Don't neglect it!'. Over and again, this 'I hear you, but' pattern is repeated as Paul recalls and rebuts the Corinthians' views:

> '*All things are lawful for me,*' but not all things are helpful. '*All things are lawful for me,*' but I will not be dominated by anything. '*Food is meant for the stomach and the stomach for food*'—and God will destroy both … '*All things are lawful,*' but not all things build up … we know that '*all of us possess knowledge.*' This 'knowledge' puffs up, but love builds up. (1 Cor. 3:4; 6:12; 10:23; 8:1 ESV, italics added)[60]

This brings us back to his 'women should be silent' remarks. Here, is Paul issuing heaven's inspired instruction regarding female voices in the church, or is it possible he is quoting another source—perhaps a false teaching that was circulating among the Corinthians at the time—and then refuting the claim with his 'I hear you, but' retort?

> '[The] women should keep silence in the churches. For they are not permitted to speak, but should be subordinate, as even the law says. If there is anything they desire to know, let them ask their husbands at home. For it is shameful for a woman to speak in church'. What! Did the word of God originate with you, or are you the only ones it has reached? If any one thinks that he is a prophet, or spiritual, he should acknowledge that what I am writing to you is a command of the Lord. If any one does not recognize this, he is not recognized. (1 Cor. 14:34–38 RSV, quotation marks and italics added)

Is it possible that, because of a lack of punctuation, Bible readers for centuries have wrongly attributed the 'women should keep silent' command to Paul, when instead he was correcting an anti-female heresy propagated by a so-called prophet in the Corinthian church? Does this not make more sense in light of the fact that just three chapters earlier, he detailed specific instructions regarding female voices praying and prophesying in church meetings (1 Cor. 11:5, 13), and that nowhere in the Law were women ever forbidden to speak, as it is here claimed?

Was Paul insisting that women be silent in the church, or was this a proposal he was rejecting and refuting? The text clearly states that women 'are not permitted to speak' (1 Cor. 14:34 ESV), but to whom is this claim attributed? Paul may have penned it, but who authored it?[61]

New Testament Citations—Closing Comments

Discerning the original source of certain statements and citations can prove difficult. Placement of quotation marks is by no means a haphazard process, but neither is it a precise science—in many cases, a degree of *informed speculation* is required. What we do know for sure is that annotation and punctuation can make all the difference to our understanding of both the text's author and meaning, and vary according to the discretion and preference of translators, some of whom simply refuse to insert quotation marks in the first place. This is all the more reason to draw on a variety of translations when studying the Scriptures.

CHAPTER 19

The Books by John

For the most part, the author and audience of the New Testament books are easy to identify, at least in broad terms. This is especially the case with the apostle Paul, who habitually names himself and his recipients in the opening verses of almost all of his letters. We'll save the argument about the authorship of Hebrews for another time.

But things aren't always so straightforward. Some authors are not as systematic in their approach to writing as Paul is, so don't follow his principles of address and introduction. Case in point: the five books of John.[62]

John's Intended Audience

Let's first examine the *audiences* of John's three epistles, before shifting our attention to the identity of the author himself. First, 3 John:

> The elder, **to my dear friend Gaius**, whom I love in the truth … I hope to see you soon, and we will talk face to face. Peace to you. (3 John 1:1, 14)

Although we are not told a great deal about him, it seems quite plain that the intended audience of this epistle is a man named Gaius—an individual known and loved by the author. The use of a singular inflection on the pronoun 'you' in the closing verse indicates that this little letter was intended to be received and read by Gaius *personally*.[63]

Well, that was simple enough. Let's move on to the second epistle:

The elder, **to the lady chosen by God and to her children**, whom I love in the truth … I hope to visit you and talk with you face to face, so that our joy may be complete. The children of your sister, who is chosen by God, send their greetings. (2 John 1:1, 12–13)

A number of theories surround the identity of this 'chosen lady'. The Greek word employed here is *kuria*, and so could simply refer to a female who bears that name (i.e., Kyria or Cyria). Alternatively, John may be using *kuria* as a term of respect, as would be appropriate for a woman of prominence and influence (i.e., a 'lady' of distinction).

But, unlike in his letter to Gaius, in this epistle John frequently uses 'you' in its plural form, much like Americans may with the term 'y'all', or we Australians with the colloquial 'youse'. This suggests his target audience is not an individual, but a group of believers. One theory is that the author's terms 'chosen lady', 'sister' and 'children' are being used as code for local church leaders and/or their assemblies, in an attempt to deliberately conceal their identities. Considering the severe persecution Christians were experiencing at the time this epistle was written, could it be that 'the elder' was employing cryptic terms to safeguard himself, his audience and his letter courier against unnecessary attention from their adversaries? Could the 'chosen lady' be a female pastor and her 'children' the church she leads?[64]

Certainly, an interesting thought. The point is, the intended audience of this second epistle is not as clear as it is for 3 John. This brings us to the largest of the three letters, in which the identity of the original audience is even vaguer still:

That which was from the beginning, which we have heard, which we have seen with our eyes, which we have looked at and our hands have touched—this we proclaim … **we proclaim to you the eternal life … we proclaim to you what we have seen and heard, so that you also may have fellowship with us. And our fellowship is with the Father and with his Son, Jesus Christ** … This is the message we have heard from him and declare to you: God is light … if we walk in the light, as he is in the light, we have fellowship with one another … If we confess our sins, he is faithful and just and will forgive us our sins and purify us from all unrighteousness. (1 John 1:1–9)

Nowhere in the opening chapter of 1 John is an audience clearly identified. The author simply employs the pronouns 'you', 'us', 'we' and 'our'. It is clear, however, that 'you' in this poetic prologue[65] speaks of those who do not yet share Christian fellowship with either the author or—more significantly—with 'the Father and his Son' (1 John 1:3). Is it possible, therefore, that this opening discourse is not addressed to fellow believers: that the 'you' to whom is being proclaimed 'the eternal life' are those who are not in fellowship with Christ? It is not until the second chapter that the author begins to employ identity terms denoting family, faith and fellowship. These include 'my dear children', 'friends' and 'brothers'. He refers to his audience from here as those who do 'know the truth', '**know the Father**' and '**have been forgiven** on account of his name' (1 John 2:1–14).

In other words, this epistle seems to be addressing a mixed crowd. Between Chapters 1 and 2, the author's target audience appears to change from those who are not (yet) in the Father's fellowship, to those who are.

Acknowledging this shift helps bring clarity to an apparent contradiction in this epistle, one that has confused many a Bible reader. The author insists that his audience confess their sins so that God may (in response) forgive them, but then later asserts their sins have already (in the past) been forgiven (1 John 1:9; 2:12). Well, which is it? Are the sins of Christians held against us, to be forgiven in the future on condition of our ongoing confession, or is forgiveness a thing of the past, a done deal for those who 'know the Father'?

One possible solution to this doctrinal dilemma is to recognise the shift in intended audience. Targeting non-believers in Chapter 1, the author speaks rhetorically and employs a universal 'we' in Verses 6–10 to address those who must confess their sins to be forgiven (either 'we-the-human-race', or more likely 'we-the-Jewish-people'), whereas from Chapter 2 onwards, he specifically addresses those who have already made this confession at some point in their past and '**have been** forgiven on account of His name' (1 John 2:12).[66]

The point is, some books in our Bible address both a believing and non-believing audience. Just because the authors of the New Testament letters are Christians, we mustn't assume their readers always are: 'But these are written that you **may believe** that Jesus is the Messiah, the Son of God, and that by believing you may have life in his name' (John 20:21).

Is Author John the Apostle John?

We will now turn our attention to the identity of the author—how does the man responsible for these writings identify himself? Let's work our way backwards.

The book of Revelation is written in the first person by a character identifying himself simply as 'John, your brother and companion'. In the two smaller letters, he refers to himself as 'the Elder', whereas in the larger letter, he provides no name or title at all, except to indicate that he was among the direct eyewitnesses of Christ. In his Gospel account, the author uses another designation altogether, describing himself in the third person as 'the disciple whom Jesus loved' and then, when appearing alongside the apostle Peter, as simply 'the other disciple'.[67]

It is widely held that the author John is none other than the apostle John, son of Zebedee and fellow thunder-brother to James, a fisherman from Galilee, cousin to Jesus and one of His chosen Twelve who ministered alongside Peter post-Pentecost. This position is based predominantly on extra-biblical scholarship dating back to Irenaeus (Bishop of Lyons, France) in the latter part of the second century. But let's set aside church tradition for a moment and turn our attention to the text itself—what does the internal evidence teach us about the man responsible for this fourth Gospel? Is there an alternate candidate who fits the description of the 'beloved disciple', who may also (as is the case with many characters in the New Testament) be known by another name?[68]

I believe there is. Ladies and gentlemen, I present to you Lazarus of Bethany, the resurrected brother of Mary and Martha. Consider the following.

First, the apostle John is nowhere identified as being uniquely 'loved' by Jesus, but Lazarus is described this way three times! In fact, Lazarus is singled out as the *only* character in the entire Bible who is personally named with this honour, and the only individual Jesus is known to have wept over: 'So the sisters sent word to Jesus, "Lord, **the one you love** is sick" … Jesus wept. Then the Jews said, "See how **he loved him**!"' (John 11:3–5, 35–36).

Second, this disciple is said to be 'known to the high priest' in Jerusalem, allowing him privileged access into his courtyard during Jesus' trial (John 18:15–16). Compare this with the book of Acts, which indicates that the apostle John was not known to the high priest when he and Peter were called to give account of their ministry (Acts 4:5–13). Such familiarity with Caiaphas and his servants suggests the beloved disciple resided locally, which Lazarus did.

Third, the Synoptics claim that the apostle John, as one of the Eleven, abandoned Jesus at His arrest and did not believe He had risen until Jesus appeared in person on resurrection evening (Matt. 26:56; Mark 16:11–13; Luke 24:33–45). In contrast, this 'other disciple' was beside Mary at the crucifixion and believed in the resurrection that morning, the moment he saw the linen cloths lying abandoned in the empty tomb (John 19:25–27; 20:1–8). Burial cloths similar, perhaps, to the one he himself had worn just weeks prior? Certainly, food for thought.

There are many more indicators supporting the 'Lazarus as the beloved disciple' view, but I shall leave it there. You can do your own research should this interest you.[69] Whether we believe the content of the Fourth Gospel came from the pen of John, brother of James, or from John-Lazarus, brother of Mary and Martha, nothing diminishes the great preciousness and power of this sacred work.

Author and Audience—Closing Comments

The task of establishing the author and intended audience of a biblical text is an important consideration in the process of exegesis. At times, it is simple and straightforward. At other times, it is more complex and challenging.

Either way, we must never forget that, ultimately, the Great Author and Originator of the Scriptures is God Himself. Even if you did not quite catch the identity of the messenger, remember that his job, to begin with, was simply to speak on behalf of his Master.[70]

Whether it was originally delivered by the Lord Jesus, the apostle John or the beloved disciple Lazarus, this fact remains: 'For God so loved the world that He gave His only Son' is a glorious and eternal truth. God Himself is the Source of all Scripture and we should never forget that.

Let me stress again that while not all Scripture is written to you, *all Scripture is written for you.* By asking you to consider the original intended audience of a given text, I am by no means encouraging you to view any part of the biblical corpus as irrelevant for you as a follower of Christ today. The written Word is living and active, ready and waiting to leap from the pages and make a deep and abiding impression on your life (Heb. 4:12)!

Almost 1,500 years after God thundered His commands to the Israelites at Sinai, the evangelist Stephen said that Moses 'received living words to pass on to **us**' (Acts 7:38). Jesus likewise claimed of His first-century audience: 'It was because **your** hearts were hard that Moses wrote **you** this law' (Mark 10:5), despite the obvious fact that none of His audience were physically present that day. Referring to that same exodus generation, Paul said to the Corinthians: 'these things happened to them as examples and **were written down as warnings to us**' (1 Cor. 10:6–11). To persecuted Jewish Christians, the authors of Hebrews claim the ancient wisdom of Solomon was addressed *to them* (Heb. 12:5–6).

The practice of perpetually passing God's eternal words to the next generation of His covenant community is as important for the modern church as it was for Ancient Israel (Deut. 6:7; 11:19). The power inherent in the Word of God when it was first delivered is just as potent today, and with the presence of the Spirit and the perspectives of His saints, your Teacher is committed to meeting and speaking with you through the entire scope of His Holy Scripture.

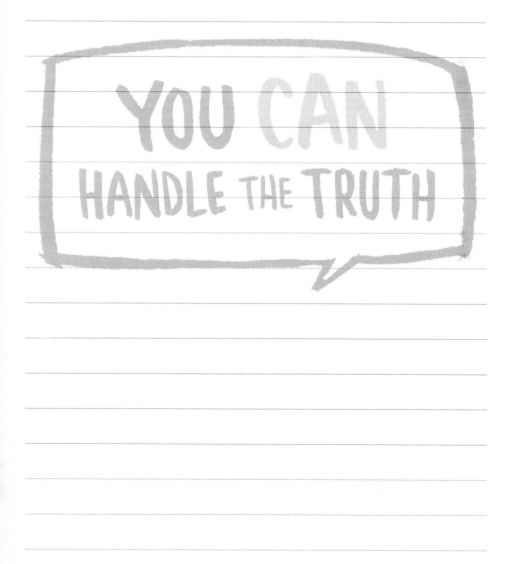

Big-Picture Background

Before we move on, let's pause for a moment and establish our bearings. Healthy hermeneutics (interpreting the Bible well) involves addressing three key questions of the Scripture: *What does it say? What does it mean? What does it matter?* We are currently concerned with the second step in this process, an activity known as exegesis. The aim of exegesis is to ascertain the author's intended meaning; to do this, we need to recognise that context is king.

Just as there are three golden rules to achieving success in real estate (location, location, location!), so too are there three essential components to successful exegesis: context, context, context![71] After all, context determines meaning.

Allow me to illustrate. A fad hit the online world some years ago, in which meme-makers would take photographic images of high-end athletes competing at track and field events and superimpose them onto varied

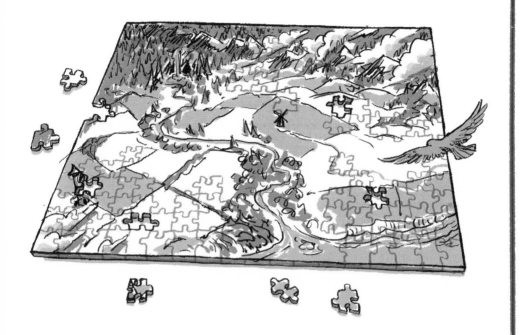

backdrops, typically involving ferocious animals or natural disasters. The results were laugh-out-loud funny, with famous sportspeople depicted running for their lives from wild bears, raging bulls, dinosaurs, molten lava and the like. The motivation behind the runner's stride and the meaning behind their expressions of exhilaration changed depending on the background. But when asking, 'Why is this individual running so?', the correct answer can only be reached when the athlete is observed in their original context. The lesson here is simple: how we understand the foreground information is largely dependent on what lies behind. It is not enough to simply focus on the detail directly in front of us. Context is everything.

Somewhat related to this is the famous maxim, 'They can't see the forest for the trees'. This describes a person so preoccupied with detail that they have lost sight of the bigger picture at hand and, as a result, become lost in a forest of facts, trapped in their pursuit of truth. Students of the Scripture are certainly not immune from this fate, but fortunately, the solution is simple. One only needs to rise above the immediate and embrace a birds-eye view of their surroundings. Such is the power of a big-picture perspective.

In the chapters that follow we will examine three contextual considerations, each of which play a significant role in forming the backdrop upon which much of the Bible's content is presented:

The Context of Covenant

The Context of Chronology

The Context of Culture

But before then, let's begin with a brief word on the Bible's borders and boundaries.

Borders and Boundaries

Reading the Bible without a big-picture perspective is like looking at a pile of jigsaw puzzle pieces scattered on a table. While each individual piece is, in a sense, a work of the artist and valuable in its own right, when *brought together* they reveal a true 'work of art'. A panoramic view of the Bible helps us appreciate its beauty and gain confidence in setting its pieces in place. As we approach the Scripture and tackle the critical *What does it mean?* step in our interpretive process, it's important to consider where the text fits in the broad backdrop of the Bible's big-picture background.

Now, don't misunderstand me. The finer details of Holy Scripture do matter. Every jot and tittle of the inspired text has inherent value and divine purpose.[72] In the next section (*Corroborating Content*), we will examine the importance of reading Scripture closely, zooming in on specific detail to further discover a text's true meaning. But first, I want to encourage you to take a step back.

We begin by noting the *limits* of the Scripture's historical accounting. As with any work of art, the biblical narrative fits within the confines of a set perimeter. As with a jigsaw puzzle, the first step to success is putting the border pieces in place.

The historical backdrop for the Bible's stories has distinct boundaries in relation to both time and place. In terms of time, the span covered is quite vast, with more than 2,500 years between the lives of Abraham's ancestors (in early Genesis) and those of the first-century apostles. In the broadest of terms, historians refer to this entire period as 'ancient history'.[73] Regarding place, however, the borders of the biblical narrative are relatively limited. Its every character, community and civilisation were constrained to the lands of the modern Middle East (i.e., the Near East) and parts of North Africa, Europe and Central Asia, with Israel the geographical focal point.

You see, *the Bible is fundamentally a book of covenant history*—not global history.[74] Our Bible does not concern itself with the great exploits or empires of antiquity the world over. It says nothing of the ancient Harappan civilisation of India or the great dynasties of China, nor does it mention the mighty Mayan conquests in South America or the age-old cultures of Indigenous Australia, Central Africa or South-East Asia. From a geographical and anthropological perspective, the scope of the Bible story does not spread far.

This is because, from beginning to end, the biblical narrative is concerned specifically with God's unique relationship with His *covenant people*, the children of Israel. Other nations and political powers feature as well, of course, but only as they relate, or are relevant to the unfolding tale of God's covenant community.

This is not to say that the historicity of the Bible is somehow irrelevant to the rest of the world's population. Absolutely not! The coming of the Jewish Messiah, and the ministry, mandate and message He brought to the earth was, and still is, a global event that has ramifications for humankind everywhere. As an Australian, I live just about as far as you can possible from the Near-Eastern lands where the Bible's stories are based. And yet, through my relationship with Jesus, biblical history has, in a sense, become my history. Their story is now my story. Through the Gospel, every believer in Christ has been grafted into the unbroken line of God's covenant family (Rom. 11:24).

Still, the Bible is not so much a book of *human* history as it is of *Hebrew* history. From Adam to Absalom, Zedekiah to Zerubbabel, and all the way through to Joseph, Jesus and John the Revelator, the Bible tells of communities in relationship with Yahweh,[75] describing how those ancient societies functioned and found their place in the world.

That established, we will now examine three major components of the Bible's big-picture background: the contexts of *covenant*, *chronology* and *culture*.

 Tammy, it's time to rise on eagles' wings and develop a birds-eye view of the Bible.

CHAPTER 21

The Context of Covenant

When God decided to enter into a special relationship with humankind, He chose covenant. While not mentioned a great deal today, covenant was commonplace in ancient cultures and particularly in the Ancient Near East. It is no surprise that the term is frequently used by the biblical writers who, by virtue of their upbringing, were steeped in covenant thinking. Comprehending covenant is essential to understanding the biblical narrative and achieving the aim of exegesis—to discover the author's intended meaning to his primary intended audience.

So, what is 'covenant'?

A covenant is a binding relational agreement, made between two or more parties and secured by an irrevocable oath. In many respects a covenant is akin to a legal contract. Entering a covenant arrangement typically involves the exchange of promises, the performance of a ceremony and the institution of a sign by which it may be remembered and referenced in the future. Marriage is perhaps the most common form of covenant relationship witnessed today, in which most (if not all) these four elements are practised: *promises*, a *ceremony*, a *sign* and an *oath*.[76]

Whether bilateral or unilateral, written or oral, between individuals, families, nations and kings, or (as observed in Scripture) between the Creator and His created, covenant is serious business. So much so that in ancient times, covenant ceremonies often involved the shedding of blood to assert the solemnity of the oath and strength of the bond. Indeed, the Hebrew word for covenant—*beriyth*—literally means *a compact made by cutting* (Gen. 15:10; Jer. 34:18). To be sure, a covenant agreement is far more serious than a 'handshake deal'. It is a bond in blood, a weighty pact that is not entered into lightly.

While there is some disagreement as to the precise number of divine covenants mentioned in the Bible,[77] the three that feature most prominently in the teachings of the New Testament are those of Abraham, Moses and Jesus. 'Rightly dividing' these covenants is a critical key to exegesis.

Three Covenants—Three Conditions

In my first book, *He Qualifies You!*, I dealt exclusively with the distinctions between these three major agreements and discussed how they each found their place in the Bible's big-picture narrative. My case was simple:

Under the *Abrahamic Covenant* (communicated, cut and confirmed in Genesis 12, 15 and 22 respectively), God's people qualified for His promised blessings purely because of their *pedigree*. God promised to favour His covenant family on the basis of their Abrahamic birthright. Nothing more, nothing less. No matter how abhorrent their attitudes or defiant their disobedience, God never punished, cursed or even corrected Abraham's early descendants for their crooked conduct. Under this covenant, God, in many ways, treated His people like infants. So long as someone identified as one of Abraham's kids, God blessed and favoured them unconditionally.

Under the *Mosaic Covenant*, however, (introduced in Exodus 19), terms radically changed. At Mount Sinai, the nation of Israel entered a law-keeping agreement, which promised both divine favour and divine fury, depending upon the people's *performance*. Under this system, only when the covenant community were faithful in their obedience were God's blessings guaranteed. His special favour was now a reward for good behaviour. Together with this came the promise of covenant curses. Like a stern and ever-present disciplinarian, the Law (Hebrew: *Torah*) would demand severe punishment for those who dared step out of line. In this sense, God was now treating His people like children.

However, under *Christ's Covenant* (inaugurated in Acts 2), God introduces a whole new arrangement. Here, those of us who believe in Jesus qualify for the blessings of God on the basis of our *position* in Christ. Jesus, who possesses both the purest pedigree and most perfect performance, cuts covenant with God on our behalf. Through His completed work of redemption, Gospel believers are brought together (legally and literally) into a new-covenant community of faith in which we are declared righteous, holy and blameless in His sight in love. God's presence and provisions are our rightful inheritance, both now and for all eternity, as we are declared sons and daughters of God regardless of our family pedigree or fluctuating performance. Consequently, those with faith in Christ are no longer mere infants or children, but fully-fledged adults—accepted, affirmed and authorised heirs of our Father's rich and royal estate. Amazing grace, indeed!

You see, when it comes to His nature, character and essence, God does not change (Mal. 3:6; James 1:7), yet a simple read through the Bible shows us that He clearly does change how He relates to His people.

Contrasting the Covenants: Abraham, Moses, Jesus

	Abraham	Moses (Old)	Jesus (New)
Commencement	~2081 BC at Hebron Gen. 15 & 22	~1446 BC at Sinai Exo. 24 & 32	30 AD at Calvary Luke 23 & Acts 2
Sign	Male circumcision Gen. 17:11–12	The Sabbaths Exo. 31:12–17	The Spirit Rom. 8:16; Eph. 1:13
Obligation	Walk before God Gen. 17:1–2, 19	Love God, love others Matt. 22:36–40	Be loved, love others John 13:34; 1 John 3:23
Confidence	Pedigree Phil. 3:4–5	Performance Phil. 3:5–6	Position Phil. 3:7–9
Status	Infant Gal. 3:6–9	Child-heir Gal. 4:1–3	Adult son Gal. 3:26–29; 4:4–7

Different Relationship = Different Response

Take, for example, the exodus account. Before reaching Sinai, the children of Israel worship false gods, break the Sabbath, murmur against both God and Moses and complain consistently about their desert experience. Yet, through it all, God responds time again with blessing, provision, kindness and care. In contrast, just a few months later, no sooner does Moses return from the mountaintop with stone tablets in hand, *the very same behaviour* results in God's anger burning against them! Now, Israel becomes the object of God's cursing, punishment, wrath and vengeance, resulting in sickness, suffering, pain and death![78]

Neither God nor His people changed in or of themselves—the only change was the covenant relationship to which they were party. Prior to Sinai, God was relating to Israel solely upon the Abrahamic covenant and was blessing them accordingly. Post-Sinai, the very same people were now being judged by their performance under Moses' Law, and were being cursed accordingly.

Same people. Same behaviour. Different covenant. Different response.

Bible readers who fail to distinguish between the divine covenants often struggle in trusting God, because they see Him as being inconsistent: 'How can I rely on the God who rescues His children from Egypt one moment, and then punishes them with plague and pestilence the next? Which God am I going to see today? The peaceful and loving God of the New Testament or the stern and angry God of the Old?'.

My point is, comprehending covenant helps us understand that any variation in God's conduct is not a variation in His character. Rather, it has everything to do with the covenantal agreement in effect at the time.[79] The Bible is, indeed, a book of covenant history, and the arrival of these three major covenants ushered in their own eras and audience of adherents.

This brings us back to the issue at hand—considering the significant role covenantal context plays in the backdrop of the Bible's big-picture.

Most of us are taught right from the outset that the Bible comprises two major parts: the Old and New Testaments. Or, since the words can be used interchangeably, the old and new *covenants*.[80] However, this editorial division can prove problematic. Here's how.

The Assumption of Covenant Audience

This point takes us back to our first consideration in exegesis: ascertaining the intended audience. Many Bible readers assume that a directive issued by Jesus in the Gospels (for example) is immediately a 'Christian teaching', since it is part of the New Testament canon. However, this may not be the case.

You see, prior to Pentecost, Christians did not even exist! Jesus certainly had disciples during the Gospel years, but it wasn't until the combined work of Calvary and Pentecost that His followers could become born again, Spirit-filled, believers and beneficiaries of the new covenant. During His three-and-a-half-year earthly ministry, Jesus never addressed a Christian community.

Instead, most of His audience were members of old-covenant Israel, living under the requirements of the Mosaic law.[81] While He occasionally reached out to non-Jewish people, the primary audience of Jesus' teaching and preaching ministry was the old-covenant community: 'Jesus said, "I've only been sent to the lost sheep of Israel"' (Matt. 15:24 TPT).

An example may help illustrate this. During His Sermon on the Mount, Jesus claimed: 'For if you forgive other people when they sin against you, your heavenly Father will also forgive you. But if you do not forgive others their sins, your Father will not forgive your sins' (Matt. 6:14–15). Simple, right? Forgiveness from God is contingent on one's first forgiving others—you do your bit, God will do His. Therefore, the Father's forgiveness is conditional on one's behaviour. Jesus said so. It's right there in the New Testament.

But hold on a sec. To *whom* was Jesus speaking? To which audience does He target this teaching? At this point in history, both Jesus' disciples and the crowd at large were (predominantly) members of the Jewish community. These words were spoken to an old-covenant audience, not to Christians.

Therefore, Jesus' teaching here is consistent with old-covenant conditions, under which God's blessings are based on performance. If people did their bit, God would do His.

Let me be clear: I affirm that these words, uttered by Christ Himself, are true. However, I equally affirm that these words are *not directed to the Christian*. Forgiveness under the new covenant is not determined by our behaviour, but by our belief in Christ. It was Jesus' performance at Calvary that earned our forgiveness, not our own. So, to the new-covenant community positioned 'in Christ', Paul declares forgiveness an already done deal, a once-for-all irrevocable gift of God's grace:

> God made you alive in Christ. **He forgave us all our sins, having cancelled the charge of our legal indebtedness**, which stood against us and condemned us; he has taken it away, nailing it to the cross … **In Him we have redemption through his blood, the forgiveness of sins** in accordance with the riches of God's grace. (Col. 2:13–14; Eph. 1:7)

At the Sermon on the Mount, they were told, 'you forgive others then God will forgive you'. In the Epistles, the sequence is reversed: 'Instead, be kind to each other, tender-hearted, forgiving one another, just as God through Christ **has forgiven you**' (Eph. 4:32 NLT). Once more, divine forgiveness is described here as a past-tense reality.

Jesus and Paul do not contradict one another on this issue. They are simply speaking to different audiences at different times. Jesus' words were spoken to the old-covenant community, prior to His death, before the new covenant was made available. Conversely, Paul was teaching post-Calvary, to those in Christ, members of the new-covenant community of faith. Jesus purchased and proclaimed our forgiveness at the cross—'Father, forgive them, for they know not what they do' (Luke 23:34 ESV)—as He ushered in an entirely new arrangement for those who would believe in Him and receive His atoning work.

Please understand, I am not claiming that Jesus' pre-Calvary teachings hold no application whatsoever to Christian audiences. I simply stress that considering the *covenantal context* of a biblical teaching is essential when *discerning the audience* to which a particular truth is addressed. To which covenant community does the target audience belong? What relational agreement (if any) do they have with God at the time?

This brings us to my next concern with the traditional Old/New Testament divide.

The Timing of Covenant Commencement

It is misleading to describe the New Testament as beginning at Jesus' birth. The fact is, the new covenant could not begin until sometime after His death. Remember, no divine covenant comes into effect without the shedding of blood—this 'seals the deal' for the parties concerned.

It was at the time of His crucifixion, not His incarnation, when Jesus announced to His disciples: 'This cup is the new testament in my blood' (Luke 22:20 KJV). What is most relevant here is not the blood Mary shed at Christmas, but the blood Christ shed at Calvary.[82]

> **For where a covenant is, there must of necessity be the death of the one who made it**. For a covenant is valid *only* when men are dead, for it is never in force while the one who made it lives. Therefore even the first *covenant* was not inaugurated without blood (Heb. 9:16–18 NASB).

Think back to Sinai for a moment.

Soon after the exodus, the Israelites heard the commands of God thunder audibly from the mountain, and personally witnessed His manifest glory. They then had the book of the covenant read aloud to them and thrice agreed to adhere to its conditions, confidently claiming: 'Everything the Lord has said we will do' (Exo. 19:8; 24:3–7). Despite their verbal exchange, it was not until the shedding of blood that this covenant would be 'put into effect' (Heb. 9:18). Words would not suffice.

Once promises are exchanged, Moses performs a covenant ceremony, sprinkling the blood of bulls over the people. He then ascends the mountain with Israel's elders, who eat and drink in the presence of God. Soon after the group returns, he leaves camp again, this time with Joshua, spending seven days on the mountainside and forty more in God's presence (Exo. 24:8–18).

 Do the maths, Timothy.

Moses' descent from Sinai with the stone tablets took place some 50 days after the covenant was cut. In other words, it wasn't until seven weeks had passed that the covenant was eventually inaugurated and God began to apply the conditions specified in their new agreement. On that fateful day, with no first-chance warning or grace-period given, the fire of God's wrath broke out against His idolatrous community, just as He promised it would. The result? Three thousand Israelites were slaughtered by the swords of their Levite brothers, and names were blotted from His heavenly book, as the Lord 'struck the people with a plague because of what they did with the calf Aaron had made' (Exo 32:25–35).[83] Some 15 centuries later, this same process is repeated with Christ's covenant, but with vastly different outcomes!

On the day of Pentecost, seven weeks after Jesus' blood was shed, three thousand sinners were saved when the sword of Peter's preaching pierced their hardened hearts. As the fire of God's love, grace and empowerment was poured out upon His people, many names were added to the Lamb's book of life and a whole new covenant-era began (Acts 2:1–41). The covenant Jesus communicated at the Last Supper and cut with God at the cross had now commenced. The pattern established by Moses had been repeated by Christ—seven weeks after covenant blood was shed, inauguration day had come.

> For the law was given through Moses; grace and truth came through Jesus Christ. (John 1:17)

The contrast between these two covenants could not be clearer! It is no wonder Paul described one as 'the ministry of death' and the other that which 'gives life'; the old was a 'ministry of condemnation', the new a 'ministry of righteousness' (2 Cor. 3:6–11). At Pentecost, this long-awaited agreement was finally put into effect, and the promise of Israel's prophets was fulfilled:

> 'The days are coming,' declares the Lord, '**when I will make a new covenant** with the people of Israel and with the people of Judah. It will not be like the covenant I made with their ancestors when I took them by the hand to lead them out of Egypt ... For **I will forgive their wickedness and will remember their sins no more**.' (Jer. 31:31–34)

I appreciate that your Bible likely contains an 'Old Testament' title page before Genesis 1, and a 'New Testament' title page separating Malachi from Matthew. I know mine does. Please understand that these editorial pages were inserted by the publishers, not by Holy Spirit.

The old covenant did not commence until the second half of Exodus. Similarly, the new covenant began in Acts 2, not at Matthew 1.

The Timing of Covenant Completion

It is likewise inaccurate to suggest that the Mosaic covenant suddenly reached its end come that first Christmas morn. The truth is, the entire New Testament period was one of *covenantal transition*, in which the old covenant continued to operate despite the onset of the new.

Although Jesus announced the Law's fulfilment and set it aside by introducing the new, the old-covenant community continued to operate their Mosaic economy at full steam, adhering to Torah and observing its worship rituals, sacrificial system and religious requirements. Despite the offer of a vastly superior, eternal, never-fading, unshakeable, better-in-every-way arrangement, the first-century Jewish world, as a whole, remained stiff-necked in their rejection of Christ and were determined to retain that which their promised Messiah had died to replace.[84]

Consider the apostle Paul. On a personal level, Paul frequently describes his relationship to the Law as a past-tense experience, an aspect of his previous life before coming to know Christ: 'I myself am not under the law ... for through the law **I died to the law**, so that I might live to God ... **whatever were gains** to me I now consider loss for the sake of Christ' (1 Cor. 9:20; Gal. 2:19; Phil. 3:4–7).

Yet, when referencing the Law in a more general sense, Paul speaks of the old covenant as a present-tense reality. For as long as the temple system was functioning, it continued to serve its primary prophetic purpose, providing shadows and signs pointing people to Christ (Col. 2:17–18).[85] While it may have been removed from his personal life, the old covenant had not yet been removed from the world in which he lived: 'for to this day the same veil remains when the old covenant is read. It has not been removed' (2 Cor. 3:14).[86]

This is why Paul often warns his fellow Christians not to put themselves under the Law's influence! This from Galatians, written in the mid-50s AD, more than 20 years after the new covenant was put in effect:

> Oh, foolish Galatians! Who has cast an evil spell on you? For the meaning of Jesus Christ's death was made as clear to you as if you had seen a picture of his death on the cross. Let me ask you this one question. Did you receive the Holy Spirit by obeying the law of Moses? Of course not! You received the Spirit because you believed the message you heard about Christ. How foolish can you be? After starting your new lives in the Spirit, why are you now trying to become perfect by your own human effort? ... [For] those who depend on the law to make them right with God are under his curse ... [Tell me], you who want to live under the law, do you know what the law actually says? (Gal. 3:1–3, 10; 4:21 NLT)

These Galatian believers faced the same challenge as Adam in the garden— would they continue to feed from the Tree of Life (i.e., Jesus) or be beguiled into believing that the knowledge of good and evil (i.e., the Law) would somehow complete them? At this time in history, the old covenant was still very much in play and remained accessible and available to anyone who would submit their faith to it and feed on its fruit. Redundant? Yes. Replaced?

Yes. Removed? Not yet.

Just as Sarah and Hagar cohabited in Abraham's house for a time, so too did the old and new covenants exist side-by-side until the older was eventually expelled:

> The women represent two covenants. One covenant is from Mount Sinai and bears children who are to be slaves: This is Hagar ... [who] corresponds to **the present city of Jerusalem**, because **she is** in slavery with her children. But the Jerusalem that is above is free, and she is our mother. (Gal. 4:21–31)

While obsolete, ageing, faulty and fading, the old-covenant system was kept alive and active until the Roman Empire's three-and-a-half-year war on the Jews brought it to a dramatic and definitive end. Only then, almost 40 years after Jesus' crucifixion, did the Levitical sacrifices forever cease, and their furnishings and items of worship melt down with fire. The entire temple complex was destroyed and dismantled stone-by-stone, just as Christ had foretold (Luke 21:5–22).

The old created order, made by human hands and destined to perish with use, was shaken 'once more'—first by the Babylonians in 586 BC and again by the Romans in the first century AD. Only this time, with a heavenly replacement made ready, the Sinaitic system of worship was completely removed, never to return.[87]

Throughout the Gospels and even beyond the final chapter of Acts, the old covenant was still very much present and practised. It did not end in Malachi 4.

The Tendency to Bifurcate the Bible

My final concern with the traditional Old/New Testament editorial divide is that it develops a tendency in Bible readers to split the Scriptures into two entirely different books, with the implication that one is immediately less important, less valuable or less necessary than the other.[88]

This can lead to Christians making simplistic and sweeping judgements on the relevance and implications of certain passages based solely on which side they fall on the Malachi/Matthew divide. 'We're a new-covenant grace church, the Old Testament is not relevant for us! That Scripture is 'old covenant'; you can't preach the Law to me! I'm a New Testament Christian and I don't need to read the Old!'

 Tammy, do not fall into this trap.

The Bible is best viewed as one book, with one consistent and progressive narrative. The Scriptures tell the tale of God's developing relationship with His covenant people, spanning multiple epochs of Hebrew history. While the nature of these covenants may change over time, together with the names and faces of recipients, the fact remains that the Bible does not tell two stories—it tells one.

The Good News of Christ does not first come to us in Matthew, Mark, Luke and John. It is proclaimed, prophesied and promised through the entire scope of the biblical narrative. From the promise in Genesis 3 that the seed of the woman would crush the serpent's skull, to that of Malachi 3, where the 'messenger of the covenant' would come like a refiner's fire to His holy temple (Gen. 3:15; Mal. 3:1–2); the Hebrew Scriptures set the stage for the glorious revealing of Jesus Christ. Consider these top-and-tail verses from the book of Romans, arguably Paul's greatest dissertation of the new-covenant Gospel:

> Paul, a servant of Christ Jesus, called to be an apostle and set apart for the gospel of God—**the gospel he promised beforehand through his prophets in the Holy Scriptures** … my gospel, the message I proclaim about Jesus Christ, in keeping with the revelation of the mystery hidden for long ages past, but now revealed and made known **through the prophetic writings** by the command of the eternal God. (Rom. 1:1–2; 16:25–26)

Covenantal Context—Closing Comments

The Bible is a book of covenant history, detailing the developing relationship between God and His covenant community over more than two millennia.

While it contains record of multiple covenant agreements, the three that feature most prominently are those associated with Abraham, Moses and Jesus. These three divine arrangements are each distinguished by their own set of obligations and requirements and are put into effect at different points in the biblical narrative. Rightly dividing them is essential to understanding the context in which much of the Bible's content is given.

The covenant in which Christians participate is the new covenant, brought through the life, death and post-ascension ministry of Jesus. While the Old Testament books, in particular, contain detailed record of Ancient Israel's covenant requirements, rites and rituals, it is important to note that this covenant was later made redundant by Christ, and is not binding on those who believe in Him today. In what may be described as a *1,500-year parenthesis* in biblical history, the law covenant given at Sinai served as a temporary tutor for God's people until such a time as Messiah would come and offer a far superior form of relationship at Calvary (Gal. 3:23–25).

That said, while not necessarily applicable to the new-covenant community, the entire Old Testament canon is to be treasured by Christians today. From beginning to end, the Bible is His-story and while it is not all directed to us, all Scripture is written *for* us. Each and every verse, regardless of covenantal context, is to be upheld as significant and sacred: 'For everything that was written in the past was written to teach us, so that through the endurance taught in the Scriptures and the encouragement they provide we might have hope' (Rom. 15:4).

CHAPTER 22

The Context of Chronology

As discussed in Step 1, it's important to appreciate that the Bible is a work of incredible diversity. The Word of God is a collection of 66 books written by over 40 human authors, living in a variety of ages and places, speaking diverse languages, belonging to different cultures, possessing unique personalities and backgrounds, and writing with varying purpose and choice of literary genre. The multifaceted Scriptures truly reveal a multifaceted God!

At the same time, the Bible is a work of breathtaking unity. Ultimately, it is one book. A collaborative, complete and cohesive work with a single developing narrative, the Bible reveals the unfolding story of God's interactions with His covenant people. Unfortunately, however, the structure of our Bible makes it difficult to see this unity.

When approaching literature with a strong narrative element, we typically anticipate a linear presentation. We expect to walk through the story from beginning, to middle, to end. But unlike most history books, the Bible is clearly not presented to us in this way. Instead, most of the Bible's books are grouped according to their author or genre, leaving us with a disjointed chronology and, for many readers, a fragmented feel.[89]

It's like grouping together puzzle pieces according to their primary colour. Sure, some of them may fit together, but ultimately what proves most helpful is returning to a big-picture perspective. What big story, or 'metanarrative', has the artist put before us? And where does my particular piece of the puzzle (a biblical character, event or teaching for example) fit in the broader scheme of things?

We now turn our attention to the chronology of the biblical narrative. What follows in this chapter is my attempt to summarise the sequential flow of the Bible's big story by identifying a series of seven significant periods in the development of God's people. Seven 'governmental ages' of God's covenant community, from creation to Christ.[90]

Age of the Ancients: Pre-2100 BC[91]
from Adam to Abram | Genesis 1–11

> These are **the generations of the heavens and the earth** when they were created, in the day that the LORD God made the earth and the heavens … This is the book of the generations of Adam … These are the generations of Noah … Now these are the generations of Terah. Terah fathered Abram. (Gen. 2:4; 5:1; 6:9; 11:27 ESV)

The opening chapters of Genesis, the book of origins, begin with a creation story, followed by a collection of genealogies. From a narrative perspective, the primary purpose of these first 11 chapters is to list the ancestral generations of Israel, tracing the ancient path from Adam to Abram.[92]

Here, we are introduced to some of the Bible's classic characters. This begins with Adam and Eve and their cohabitation with the cunning serpent, who successfully deceives them into disobedience resulting in their eastward expulsion from Eden, the garden of God's pleasure and presence. Following this is the rivalry of Cain and Abel, with the favoured younger son being persecuted by the jealous older brother. Next comes Noah, who heeds prophetic warnings of a destroying flood, provides a means of salvation through the ark and then returns as part of a righteous remnant once God's judgment is complete. Finally, we witness the rise and fall of Babylon (aka Babel), a civilisation built in defiance to God for the glory of man.[93]

While there is much debate over the precise nature of these primeval sagas,

A Seven-Age Summary of the Biblical Chronology

7. Age of Fulfilment

from Incarnation to Re-creation

Beginning with the births of John and Jesus (circa 5 BC), the New Testament details the life and ministry of Christ; His death, resurrection, and ascension; and the outpouring of Holy Spirit (30 AD). Thus begins the new covenant era, as foretold by the Prophets. Despite hostile opposition from Jewish authorities, the Gospel spreads beyond Judea and saturates the Roman Empire. The Acts narrative concludes with Paul preaching in Rome (60–62 AD), and persecution of the church intensifies. The New Testament canon is completed (circa 65/95 AD).

| Matthew – Revelation |

Narrative Gap: Intertestamental Period (432–5 BC)

6. Age of Second Temple Judaism

from Babylon to the Baptiser

The kings of Persia allow groups of Jewish exiles to return to Judah (538–444 BC). Led by Zerubbabel, Ezra and Nehemiah this remnant construct a new temple for worship and rebuild Jerusalem's walls.

Ezra, Nehemiah, Esther
Haggai, Zechariah, Malachi

5. Age of the Divided Kingdoms

from Division to Destruction and Deportation

The 10 northern tribes secede and claim the title 'kingdom of Israel'; appoint their first king from the tribe of Ephraim; and eventually establish Samaria as their capital. Wicked kings rule one after the other as tribes vie for power. Meanwhile, the two southern tribes are renamed 'kingdom of Judah' with Solomon's sons retaining the throne in Jerusalem. The Lord's prophets rebuke both kingdoms for their sinfulness before Israel is destroyed by Assyria (722 BC), and Judah defeated by Babylon (586 BC). Many Judahites/Jews are carried away into exile. Ezekiel and Daniel, captured prior to Jerusalem's fall, prophesy in Babylon, while Jeremiah serves as an eyewitness to the destruction. After 70 years of dominance (609–539 BC), Babylon is conquered by the Persian Empire.

1–2 Kings, 2 Chronicles
Isaiah, Jeremiah, Lamentations, Ezekiel, Daniel
Hosea–Zephaniah (9 Minor Prophets)

4. Age of the Unified Kingdom

from Saul to King Solomon

Saul becomes Israel's first king, uniting the 12 tribes behind him; David claims Jerusalem as the capital; and Solomon builds the Holy Temple. He dies in the knowledge that the kingdom will split (circa 930 BC).

1–2 Samuel, 1 Chronicles
Psalms, Proverbs, Ecclesiastes, S-Songs

3. Age of the Judges

from Moses to Samuel

Beginning with the birth of Moses the rest of the Torah narrates the exodus from Egypt; the cutting of the law covenant at Sinai; and the establishment of Israel as an independent nation (circa 1446 BC). After 40 years in the wilderness Joshua leads the people into Canaan where they settle in their new tribal homelands. Following Joshua's death, other judges arise and lead as required (circa 1375–1050 BC) up until the time of Samuel.

| Exodus, Leviticus Numbers Deuteronomy Joshua, Judges, Ruth |

Narrative Gap: Israelites in Egypt (1805–1525 BC)

1. Age of the Ancients

from Adam to Abram

Following the creation narrative come the accounts of Adam, Eve, and their sons through to Noah; the Table of 70 Nations; and the birth of Abram (circa 2166 BC). The story of Job is also set in this period.

| Gen. 1–11 Job |

2. Age of the Patriarchs

from Abraham to Joseph

The bulk of Genesis concerns God's call and covenant with Abraham; the lives of Isaac, Jacob and his 12 sons; and the migration of Israel's family to Egypt. Genesis closes with the death of Joseph (circa 1805 BC).

| Gen. 12–50 |

START HERE!

one thing is clear: they are each intended to serve as archetypes—prophetic precursors to future fulfilment. This is why they are revisited many times throughout the biblical narrative, by prophets and apostles, who reimagine and recapitulate their moral lessons for future generations of God's people. In other words, these origin stories also serve as *prophetic* stories. This should not surprise us. After all, our God is He who makes known 'the end from the beginning, from ancient times, what is still to come' (Isa. 46:10). But I digress.

What's important to note here is that during this era, which Peter terms the 'ancient world' (2 Peter 2:5), God's people had essentially no collective identity. There was no body of believers for example. God did not yet have a people who together identified as being His. Rather, this part of our Bible tells of ancient individuals who simply 'walked with God' with little evidence of such faith being communal or shared by others.[94]

At this time in history, the covenant community lacked both structure and substance. God's covenant world was, to coin a phrase, formless and void, effectively indistinguishable among the cultures and communities of the Ancient Near East.[95]

To establish a perpetual and lasting legacy, God first had to find a faithful mum and dad.

Age of the Patriarchs: Circa 2100–1805 BC
from Abraham to Joseph | Genesis 12–50

> And I will establish my covenant between me and you **and your offspring after you throughout their generations** for an everlasting covenant, to be God to you and to your offspring after you. (Gen. 17:7 ESV)

In Genesis 12, we are introduced to the notion of a covenant family, with God offering Abraham, Isaac, Jacob and their descendants a shared promise of both divine blessing and a place for them to call home. Thus, the age of the patriarchs begins, taking us through to the end of Genesis.

Throughout this era, God's people were simply a family led by fathers—a group of successful semi-nomadic farmers in the Near-Eastern lands of Mesopotamia, with a growing knowledge of God and a developing sense of collective identity, custom and culture.

While the family of Abraham primarily included those born or married into it, 'foreigners' were also included by essentially being adopted.[96] Make no mistake—from its very beginning, there has always been provision for outsiders to be welcomed into God's covenant community. After all, there are numerous ways one can join a family. Again, I digress.

From the calling of Abraham to the death of Joseph in Egypt some three centuries later, the bulk of Genesis is concerned with the lives of the patriarchs, their wives, children and important others.

From a chronological perspective, the stories of the patriarchs provide the background to Israel's unique relationship with Yahweh, their claim to the land of Canaan, their historical association with neighbouring peoples and their centuries-long sojourn in Egypt. As the Genesis account concludes a 300-year narrative gap commences, in which, under Pharoah's suspicious eye, the family of Jacob 'multiplied greatly, increased in numbers and became so numerous that the land was filled with them' (Exo. 1:7).

Age of the Judges: Circa 1525–1050 BC
from Moses to Samuel | Exodus–Ruth

This third phase begins with Moses and the exodus, placed sometime around 1446 BC. Upon leaving Egypt, Jacob's descendants, now known as Hebrews and Israelites, were baptised into the collective body of Moses (1 Cor. 10:1–2) and entered into a new covenant with God at Sinai. From a civil perspective, this is also where God's people are united and identified as a distinct populace, complete with their own law, land, calendar, rituals, festivals and newfound traditions. The *family* of Israel had now become the *nation* of Israel and required a new governing structure by which to operate.

This leadership was largely provided by the judges—military leaders and prophetic seers whom God empowered at certain times and places for particular tasks. Moses' and Joshua's influences were unique among the other judges in that their leadership was universally acknowledged by all 13 tribes. In contrast, once Israel had dispersed, expanded and settled in the promised land (thanks largely to Joshua), the ministry scope of subsequent leaders like Deborah, Gideon and Samson was mainly localised, according to the need at the time.[97]

The age of the judges spans some 400 years and ends with the widely recognised ministry of the prophet Samuel. For some untold reason, and as the first and only judge to do so, Samuel appointed his sons as successors to his leadership.[98] While these sons proved deeply unpopular and were rejected by the people, the idea of paternal succession caught on. In response, God's people sought to institute a formalised system of national governance by demanding a king be installed over them.

In this way, the Israelites no longer had to call on God to give them the right leader at the right time. A monarchy would mean that the current leader's son would automatically be appointed as the nation's next ruler. Rather than relying on the Spirit to supply their needs, a man-made system would take care of them instead.

Thus, Samuel's final task as Israel's final judge was to appoint a king and ensure a smooth transition to this new form of national governance.

Age of the Unified Kingdom: Circa 1050–930 BC
from Saul to King Solomon | Samuel & 1 Chronicles[99]

While displeasing, but certainly not surprising to God, the people of Israel ask for a king to lead them and a monarchy to govern them (1 Sam. 8:1–22).[100] The *family* of Israel, which had become the *nation* of Israel, was now the *kingdom* of Israel.

Despite some occasional intertribal tension, God's people expanded, prospered and flourished as a unified kingdom for some 120 years under the rule of Saul, David and Solomon. Jerusalem was dubbed *Zion: City of*

David and became Israel's spiritual, political and cultural capital, housing a substantial palace precinct and, most significantly, the magnificent Holy Temple.

These were the glory days—the golden years, if you like—of Israel's history.

Most of the Psalms were written during this period, as were Solomon's books of wisdom. Although prominent prophets and priests, such as Samuel, Nathan, Gad and Zadok, performed powerfully in their ministries at this time, these men do not have dedicated books in our Bibles.[101]

This privilege is reserved for those who would prophesy during the next chapter of Israel's story.

Age of the Divided Kingdoms: Circa 930–538 BC
from Division to Destruction and Deportation | Kings & 2 Chronicles

Here's where things become really mixed up.

After Solomon's death (circa 930 BC), the kingdom is split into two. David's tribe of Judah remains in Jerusalem and surrounds, accompanied by the Levites and baby brother Benjamin. Having seceded, the 10 northern tribes select their own king and assemble their own military force. These majority tribes retain the name 'Israel' as their collective identity, establish Samaria as their capital city and appoint their own priesthood and places of worship with no regard for the books of Moses or the dynasty of David (1 Kings 12–14; 2 Chron. 10–11).[102]

The *nation* of Israel, which became the *kingdom* of Israel, has now divided into *two separate kingdoms*; Israel in the north and Judah in the south.

This is a tumultuous time for God's people—the two kingdoms engage in constant conflict with one another, break covenant with God by their widespread idolatry and, ultimately, suffer defeat and destruction by powerful foreign forces.

In 722 BC, some two centuries after their split (and 19 kings later!), the

Kingdom of Israel falls to the mighty Assyrian Empire. Its people are driven from the promised land and scattered among foreign nations. Make no mistake, however, what happened here was far more than a military defeat or collapse of a nation-state. According to the prophets (Amos, Micah, Hosea and Isaiah), and in keeping with Moses' Law, God Himself had orchestrated Israel's demise. Behind the scenes, from a covenantal perspective, these northern tribes were now divorced from, and ultimately 'dead' to, God.[103]

In the same way that Adam's ejection from Eden was a consequence of his sin and a physical sign of his relational death to God, so it was with the northern kingdom. Their eastward expulsion from the promised land was described in covenantal terms as being 'removed [from] his presence' (2 Kings 17:18–23). The people of Israel had broken their covenant and God had punished them accordingly. The dreaded day of the Lord had come upon them.[104]

Meanwhile, in the southern kingdom, despite the occasional good king in charge, things weren't looking good. In 586 BC, a similar fate befalls Judah. After a number of targeted military campaigns, Jerusalem and her temple are destroyed by King Nebuchadnezzar, and deployments of Judean captives find themselves deported as political exiles in Babylonia.[105]

Here, in the age of the divided kingdoms (and Babylonian exile), the ministry of the prophets really comes to the fore. There are 16 distinctly prophetic books in the Old Testament, the so-called Major and Minor Prophets, and all but three find their place in this period of the historical narrative.

Making sense of the Prophets, Kings and Chronicles is nearly impossible if you do not appreciate the dynamic of the divided kingdoms. At the very least, one must grasp the basic concept that during this period, the people of Israel (also known as Ephraim)[106] and the people of Judah were two distinct kingdoms, with capital cities Samaria in the north and Jerusalem in the south.

While the Prophets have an overwhelmingly doom-and-gloom feel, they are nevertheless smattered with hints of hope—designed to inspire repentance and positive expectation in the people of God. Time and again, the Prophets predict the rise of a righteous remnant and an age when all things would be restored. This future restoration would include a *return* to the land, a *rebuilt* sanctuary, *resurrection* to covenant life, *remarriage* to God and a *reunification* of Judah and Israel as one glorious Davidic kingdom.[107]

A new King and new covenant were coming.

Age of Second Temple Judaism: Circa 538–5 BC
from Babylon to the Baptiser | Ezra–Esther

From a chronological perspective, the Old Testament narrative concludes with the books of Ezra and Nehemiah, presented as a single work in the Hebrew Bible, covering some 100 years, from approximately 538 BC to 432 BC. It is here that a restoration (of sorts) ensues.[108]

Having spent 70 years under Babylonian servitude, a remnant of Judean captives, now known as 'Jews', returns to Jerusalem by the decree of King Cyrus, just as the prophets had foretold.[109] With political support from the Persians and prophetic encouragement from Haggai, Zechariah and Malachi, the temple is rebuilt, the Levitical priesthood, offerings and festivals are reinstated and the law of Moses is returned to its rightful place. What is sorely missed, however, is the manifest glory of God (Hebrew: *Kabowd*).

In Israel's past, at the consecration of both Moses' tabernacle and Solomon's temple, Yahweh's supernatural presence and power was displayed in dramatic fashion. Supernatural fire fell from heaven, consuming temple sacrifices and resting visibly on the tent of meeting. Such was the weightiness of God's manifest glory that neither prophets nor priests could draw close to perform their sacred duties (Exo. 40:34–38; 2 Chron. 7:1–3). But this time was different. Here, at the dedication of the second temple, no such divine endorsement was conferred.

During the age of second temple Judaism, both the holy place and the royal throne stood empty.

Put simply, this generation of Judeans were restored to their covenant land, but not to their covenant Lord. Though they practised His principles, they

Ezekiel's Sticks: No Longer Two, but One

The northern kingdom of Israel was destroyed by Assyria in 722 BC. A century later, Babylon took out Assyria and became the ruling empire of the Ancient Near East for the next 70 years (609–539 BC). Having claimed dominance, Nebuchadnezzar launched a series of military campaigns against the kingdom of Judah and in doing so executed three major waves of deportation to Babylon. The prophet Daniel was captured in the first (605 BC), Ezekiel in the second (597 BC), while Jeremiah was left in Jerusalem and witnessed its destruction firsthand (586 BC). This final conquest and captivity began what is known as the Babylonian exile (586–538 BC).

It was during this time Ezekiel had his vision of the *Valley of Dry Bones*. The bones belonged to a once mighty army, the 'whole house of Israel', and Ezekiel was tasked with prophesying them back to life. The message was clear. A time was coming when God would raise His people from their state of death and hopelessness, put His Spirit within them, and return them to their promised land (Ezek. 37:1–14).

Immediately following this is the story of the *Two Sticks* (Ezek. 37:15–28). Ezekiel wrote the names of Judah and Joseph on two pieces of wood, a visual representation of the divided kingdoms. He then joined the sticks together and held them up in the sight of the exiles. This prophetic illustration was to demonstrate how God would one day reunite the nation under a Davidic ruler, and, at the same time, into an everlasting covenant with Himself.

> I will make them one nation in the land, on the mountains of Israel. There will be one king over all of them and they will never again be two nations or be divided into two kingdoms ... I will save them from all their sinful backsliding, and I will cleanse them. They will be my people, and I will be their God. My servant David will be king over them, and they will all have one shepherd ... David my servant will be their prince forever. I will make a covenant of peace with them; it will be an everlasting covenant. I will establish them and increase their numbers, and I will put my sanctuary among them forever. (Ezek. 37:22–26)

The apostle Paul brings these powerful Ezekiel 37 prophecies together in Ephesians Chapter 2. He begins by claiming that Jewish and Gentile believers alike were 'dead in the trespasses and sins', before then being made 'alive together with Christ'. Dead bones made alive—to be saved is to be resurrected (Eph. 2:1–5 ESV).

He then makes the point that in Christ, Jew and Gentile are no longer divided communities: 'For he himself is our peace, who has made the two groups one'. No longer two, but one new covenant-body, where once opposing tribes are reconciled to one-another, and to God, 'through the cross' (Eph. 2:14–18).

The marvellous mystery of the cross of Christ: where the two are brought together as one.

lacked His presence. Ezekiel's vision from some 77 years earlier was still in full effect—the glory had departed (Ezek. 10:18–19; 11:22–23). Zerubbabel may have rebuilt the temple, but God had well and truly left the building. His glory had not returned.

While glad to be back from exile at home in the promised land again, God's covenant community were living far short of His purposes and promises. The Judean returnees were given a new *start*, but not a new *heart* and before long, the errors of their ancestors were repeated as the people failed to submit to God's ways. As expected, prophetic rebukes come thick-and-fast, accompanied yet again by predictions of another day of the Lord against the Holy City and her temple (Zech. 14; Mal. 3–4).

As the pages of the Old Testament come to an end, and the centuries rolled on, in this environment of form-without-substance, the religion of second temple Judaism developed, complete with its political power play, doctrinal divisions, extra-biblical traditions and innumerable religious requirements. With no Kabowd in the temple and no king on the throne, national Israel remained a shadow of its former self. But still, hope remained.

Their promised King would most certainly come in due time and the Glorious One would return to His temple. The question is: would those who longed for Him recognise His coming and His Kingdom? And how would they respond to His arrival?

Age of Fulfilment: Circa 5 BC–65/95 AD[110]
from Incarnation to Re-creation | Matthew–Revelation

While our Bibles are essentially silent in the 400 years between Malachi and Matthew (or Nehemiah and the nativity), these were anything but silent years in Hebrew history! By the first century CE, the cultural landscape of Israel had witnessed monumental change, due largely to the philosophical and political influences of the Greek and Roman empires. However, these cultural shifts were nothing compared with the great spiritual storm about to break upon them! These first-century Scriptures introduce us to the life and teachings of Jesus Christ, the implications of His work and the coming of His messianic age as the birth of Christ ushered in the age of fulfilment:

> All this took place **to fulfill what the Lord had said through the prophet**: 'The virgin will conceive and give birth to a son, and they will call him Immanuel' ['God with us'] … Do not think that I have come to abolish the Law or the Prophets; I have not come to abolish them **but to fulfill them** … He began by saying to them, '**Today this scripture is fulfilled** in your hearing' … Jerusalem and their rulers did not recognize Jesus, yet in condemning him **they fulfilled the words of the prophets** … We tell you the good news: **What God promised our ancestors he has fulfilled for us**, their children, by raising up Jesus. (Matt. 1:22; 5:17; Luke 4:21; Acts 13:27–33)

Matthew to Revelation details the great and final act of the unfolding story of God's covenant people. Here, the 'end of the ages' and the 'fullness of times' had come. The culmination of all that Israel's prophets had pointed towards was being realised—their longings were being fulfilled, bringing healing to sick and hardened hearts and opening access to the Tree of Life from which they had been estranged for so long. At last, the mystery as to *how* exactly God would fulfill Israel's prophetic promises was being revealed from heaven and made known to the earth by a new breed of prophets and preachers.[111]

Whereas Zerubbabel and Nehemiah had overseen a *physical restoration* of God's people, the ministry of Christ brought a *spiritual transformation* of epic proportions. Israel's Messiah, the Word made Flesh, would here perform a complete *re-creation* of God's covenant community whereby His holy nation was now identified not as an earthly 'flesh-and-blood' kingdom, but as a heavenly one. Signs, wonders and healings would be included in the many visible evidences of this kingdom's influence (Luke 7:22; 11:20), but the kingdom itself would not be seen by the natural eye: 'You won't be able to say, "Here it is!" or "It's over there!" For the Kingdom of God is already among you' (Luke 17:20–21 NLT).

From a covenantal perspective, the work and ministry of Christ would render the many visible and physical hallmarks of Israel's identity (established under Abraham and Moses) null and void. That which was seen would be rendered obsolete by that which is not seen, the temporal by the eternal. As physical shadows found their fulfilment in heavenly substance, external rites gave way to internal realities and the natural body was superseded by the spiritual.[112]

In terms of her ancestry, identity, essential essence and very being, 'the Israel of God' was now a community fundamentally spiritual in nature, where 'what counts is the new creation' (Gal. 6:15–16). The age of the Spirit had come and would require a childlike innocence and imagination to embrace it (Luke 18:17).

As Paul illustrates so clearly, the new covenant (Sarah) had given birth to a new-covenant community (Isaac), and though not all were willing to accept it, this newborn community would inherit all the blessings of the Father (Gal. 4:21–31). Hence, the entire New Testament describes a time of turbulent transition, a period of *out with the old, and in with the new*. The authors of the Gospels, Acts, Epistles and Apocalypse constantly reinforce this idea.[113]

As Jesus predicted so accurately, the emergence of the church was met with fierce opposition from the previous administration, as the old community struggled to come to terms with the new covenant-kid on the block. The baton was being passed from the older to the younger, a high-stakes shift characterised by much contention, conflict and consternation. Just as Cain hated Abel, Ishmael harassed Isaac, the house of Saul opposed David and the older brother rejected the prodigal, so here, in the age of fulfilment, the old-covenant brotherhood would persecute the favoured younger son: the newly formed body of Christ.[114]

Sadly, yet predictably, their refusal to acknowledge Jesus as Prophet, Priest and King would lead to a tragic end. The old-covenant community had entered their *last days*, just as Moses, their national founder, had foretold over 14 centuries prior:

> They abandoned the God who made them and rejected the Rock their Savior [Hebrew: *Yeshuah*] ... 'I will hide my face from them,'

he said, '**and see what their end will be; for they are a perverse generation**, children who are unfaithful … If only they were wise and would understand this and discern what **their end will be!**' (Deut. 32:15–29)[115]

Thus, the biblical narrative comes full circle as the origin stories from early Genesis find their prophetic fulfilment in the Revelation of John. Babylon, that proud and wicked city with its monumental tower of idolatry and self-righteousness, is brought to her ruin, suffering a swift and decisive judgment, while a remnant wisely heeds warnings to escape, and finds salvation from the impending flood of her destruction (Rev. 17–19).

With the adulterous wife out of the picture, a pure and holy bride, the wife of the Lamb, is presented. This wife, as with Eve in Eden, was birthed from the side of 'the Last Adam' as He shed blood and water at the cross.[116] Having waited patiently for Him, she is now wed to Christ in a glorious garden ceremony:

> Then I saw '**a new heaven and a new earth**,' for the first heaven and the first earth had passed away, and there was no longer any sea. I saw the Holy City, **the new Jerusalem**, coming down out of heaven from God, prepared as a bride beautifully dressed for her husband. And I heard a loud voice from the throne saying, 'Look! God's dwelling place is now among the people, and he will dwell with them. They will be his people, and God himself will be with them and be their God. He will wipe every tear from their eyes. There will be no more death or mourning or crying or pain, for the old order of things has passed away.' He who was seated on the throne said, '**I am making everything new!**' Then he said, 'Write this down, for these words are trustworthy and true.' (Rev. 21:1–5)

In a breathtaking demonstration of the Bible's symmetry, Jesus Christ, the Living Word through Whom the entire first creation came into being in Genesis 1, draws the Scripture's story to a close as He declares the transition from old to new complete: 'It is done. I am the Alpha and the Omega, the Beginning and the End' (Rev. 21:6).

From beginning to end, biblical history is His story—the unitary tale of a covenant-keeping God and His faithful dealings with His covenant creation. Wow. What a tale! What an intricate, complete and breathtaking work of art, and what a privilege it is to be included at this point in the story, in this covenant community, on this side of Christ's completed work:

> Oh, the depth of the riches both of the wisdom and knowledge of God! How unsearchable are His judgments and unfathomable His ways! For who has known the mind of the LORD, or who became his counselor? Or who has first given to him that it might be paid back to him again? For from Him and through Him and to Him are all things. To Him be the glory forever. Amen. (Rom. 11:33–36 NASB)

Chronological Context—Closing Comments

Timothy, I trust that seven-age summary was helpful. My intent in this section is to encourage you to step back and embrace a big-picture perspective by considering three key contexts into which the Bible's passages, thoughts and truths find their place.

So far, we have examined the context of covenant and the context of chronology. Despite not being presented to us in chronological order, there is a logical and sequential progression to the Bible's narrative.

Next time you open your Bible, pause for a moment, take a step back and gain clarity as to where in the chronology your reading is situated. Your puzzle piece will make a great deal more sense when you understand where it fits in the context of the Bible's big picture.

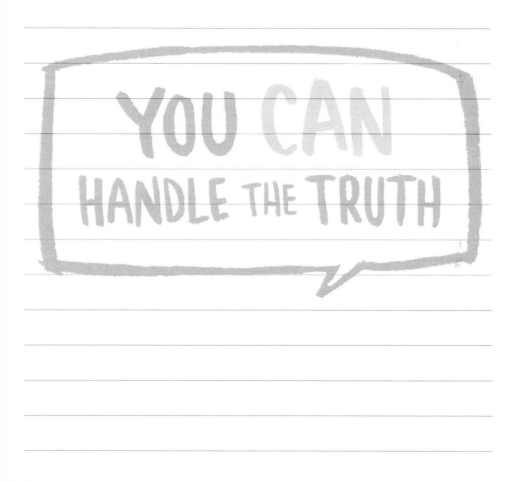

CHAPTER 23

The Context of Culture

We complete our discussion on the Bible's big-picture background by considering the all-important context of culture. How did the worldview and way of life of biblical authors and audiences influence their communication? And what should we, as modern readers, understand about ancient cultures (particularly Hebrew culture) that we may better come to terms with the authors' intended meaning?

Shortly, I will highlight *four critical aspects* of ancient Hebrew culture that have the potential to make or break our exegesis, especially for Western readers. But first, time for another story: the one about Bert and Ali.

A Clash of Cultures

In my childhood years, Bert Newton was one of the most recognised and revered personalities in Australian media. His television appearances began in the mid-1950s and he soon became a household name, a national icon and one of the longest serving television performers in the world. However, Bert's broadcasting career was almost cut short in 1979 thanks to a cross-cultural controversy with boxer Mohammad Ali.

Bert was doing what he did best, compering a television awards show, broadcast live across the nation, when heavyweight champ Ali joined him at the podium. For a couple of minutes, the two men played to the crowd with amusing and lighthearted banter, until Bert recognised the time had come to move on with the presentation. Once Ali had finished his final comments, the smiling host looked out to the audience and uttered the now infamous words, 'I like the boy!'.

Laughter erupted from the crowd, but the response from Ali was one of dismay. His change in demeanour was immediately obvious. Silencing the audience with a hand gesture, the world champion turned to the host and sought clarity on what he had just heard. 'Did you say Roy or boy?' he asked while gently placing his hand on the Australian's forearm. 'I like the boy', repeated Bert, before turning to Ali's handlers and asking, 'Is there something wrong with saying that?'. The tension in the room was almost tangible. Sat at a front table close to the podium was an American actress. 'He said Roy!' she shouted to Ali, in an attempt to dispel the obvious offence taken by the athlete and civil-rights activist. 'No, I didn't' replied Bert, somewhat bemused. 'What's wrong with saying that? I like the boy!' he asserted once more.

Fortunately, this story ends well for all involved. Bert was quickly set straight on the implications of his faux pas, followed by his sincerest apologies, with Ali accepting that his colleague acted in ignorance and with the most innocent of intentions.

That day, our country learnt a significant lesson in the complexities of cross-cultural communication. In the late-1970s, most Aussies were unaware of the history of race relations in the United States (US), and with it the disparaging connotations of the term 'boy' when associated with African American males. Bert's comment exemplified this cultural illiteracy, leaving the Americans in the room aghast at his words.

Conversely, the bulk of the crowd and those of us watching from home recognised Bert's well-meaning and witty intent. After all, his comments had a contextual background. In the months leading up to this incident, Bert had played the role of Colonel Sanders on a series of television commercials for Kentucky Fried Chicken. 'I like the boy' was the catchphrase his character recited in each of these advertisements and Bert was famous for it. When he repeated this phrase on stage with Ali, his fellow Australians understood it as a clear reference to those commercials. They recognised the comedic nuance in his comment and responded accordingly. Bert's intent was to deliver quick, clean and clever humour, despite the fact his words could have had him knocked out cold, were it not for the incredible grace demonstrated by the late, great Ali.

I tell this story for good reason. Cultural ignorance and insensitivities are the cause of many a misunderstanding and the further apart two cultures are, the more likely it is that miscommunication will result.

In the simplest of cases, such cultural misunderstandings stem from differences in the meaning of particular words. Here in Australia, it is not uncommon during the summer to see Christians, and sometimes even preachers, wearing *thongs* to church, a thought that would horrify North Americans! After all, in the US, a thong is a scanty piece of underwear. For us, it describes a casual type of footwear known in other cultures as *flip-flops*. The same word holds a different meaning, depending on the cultural context.

However, cultural variance extends well beyond vocabulary. Most cross-cultural misunderstandings occur when we fail to appreciate what is left *unspoken*—that is, ideas, thoughts and norms that exist in the world behind the words. When Bert said, 'I like the boy', he took for granted that his audience would catch his meaning. The fact that he was quoting a humorous advertising catchphrase was intentionally left unsaid on the assumption that his audience would make the connection. He never imagined it would be interpreted any other way.

A Cross-Cultural Experience

This has powerful implications for our understanding of the Bible. Walking through the pages of Scripture is like stepping into another world, in which cultural values, customs and worldviews are, in many respects, different from yours and often seem nothing short of bizarre!

Consider Abraham, who offered his wife to the sexual whims of another man as part of a political treaty, sliced animals in two for a blood-soaked ceremony, impregnated his female servant at the insistence of his spouse and was willing to sacrifice his son as an act of worship (Gen. 12–22). Think about King Saul, who demanded a bag full of foreskins from David as a dowry for his daughter (1 Sam. 18:25), while Ruth proposed to her would-be husband by uncovering his feet as he slept (Ruth 3). Jesus' expectation of a complimentary foot-washing upon entrance to somebody's home, or Paul's insistence that women in Corinth wear a head covering when they prophesied in church seem tame in comparison (Luke 7:44–46; 1 Cor. 11:1–16). Each of these 'bizarre behaviours' have this in common: they reflect the life and culture of the communities in Bible times. When viewed against the backdrop of their original cultural contexts, these practices appear far less peculiar.

Think of it this way: every time you open the Bible you are engaging in a cross-cultural experience. As a guest in those environments, it is incumbent upon you to be sensitive to both the cultural norms of the world you are entering, and the unspoken communication that accompanies such norms and mores. If we are to grasp the intended meaning of the ancient text, we must extend a listening ear to the ancient world from which it has emerged.

After all, the Scriptures were not written in a historical vacuum. The Bible did not simply drop out of heaven independent of human involvement. Its every thought, truth and tale was recorded by men anchored in a distinct time and place in antiquity. Each author was a product of their culture, and every story and instruction they narrated has a particular cultural setting.

At one end of the Book, we have the works of Moses, born during Egypt's new kingdom era to a family of Semitic slaves, raised in a royal household and later married into the priestly family of a Midianite, where he spent 40 years working as a Bedouin shepherd. At the other end, some 1,500 years later, we have Saul of Tarsus, born to a Benjamite family as a citizen of Ancient Rome and raised in a Jewish community immersed in Hellenistic culture, a radical devotee of second temple Judaism, where he was schooled as a Pharisee under the tutelage of Jerusalem's Rabbi Gamaliel. Be assured, when Paul and Moses put pen to paper, they did so under inspiration of the one-and-the-same Holy Spirit. However, each was also deeply influenced by their distinct cultural environments and experiences in the Ancient Near East (Moses) and the Greco-Roman Empire (Paul).

 Timothy, don't allow these realities to overwhelm you. When it comes to appreciating the specific cultural influences of the biblical authors, you simply need to draw on the expertise of others.

Over the years, extensive research and scholarship has been committed to this area, resulting in books, courses and even study Bibles dedicated to highlighting and explaining cultural nuance in the Scripture.[117]

For our purposes, however, here are four key characteristics of ancient Hebrew culture that shaped the worldview of the biblical authors and lie discreetly, but most definitely, behind much of the text they wrote: *collectivism, ethno-nationalism, parochialism* and *supernaturalism*.

To see how these cultural features may enhance our understanding of the authors' intended meaning, let's refer to one of my all-time favourite Bible passages from Ephesians, Chapter 1:

> Paul, an apostle of Christ Jesus by the will of God, To the saints who are in Ephesus, and are faithful in Christ Jesus: Grace to you and peace from God our Father and the Lord Jesus Christ. Blessed be the God and Father of our Lord Jesus Christ, who has blessed us in Christ with every spiritual blessing in the heavenly places, even as he chose us in him before the foundation of the world, that we should be holy and blameless before him. In love he predestined us for adoption to himself as sons through Jesus Christ, according to the purpose of his will, to the praise of his glorious grace, with which he has blessed us in the Beloved. In him we have redemption through his blood, the forgiveness of our trespasses, according to the riches of his grace, which he lavished upon us, in all wisdom and insight making known to us the mystery of his will, according to his purpose, which he set forth in Christ as a plan for the fullness of time, to unite all things in him, things in heaven and things on earth. In him we have obtained

an inheritance, having been predestined according to the purpose of him who works all things according to the counsel of his will, so that we who were the first to hope in Christ might be to the praise of his glory. In him you also, when you heard the word of truth, the gospel of your salvation, and believed in him, were sealed with the promised Holy Spirit, who is the guarantee of our inheritance until we acquire possession of it, to the praise of his glory. (Eph. 1:1–13 ESV)

Collectivism: How Ancient Hebrews Viewed Themselves

Notice Paul's repeated use of the pronouns 'we', 'us' and 'our' in this passage. Next time you read the Scriptures, watch for plural pronouns like these—they are everywhere. This is partly because, as discussed previously, the Bible is a community book designed to be read, and lived out, with others. But more than that, the Scriptures were written by men from *collectivist societies*, and this cultural influence is writ large on the backdrop of the Bible's big picture.

All societies in the ancient world, Israel included, functioned from a collectivist paradigm. Collectivist communities place the values, goals and interests of the team above the individual. Group identity, commitment to collective aims and working together towards the peace and prosperity of the tribe are paramount in collectivist communities. Conversely, individualistic societies (a relatively recent phenomenon)[118] emphasise the rights and distinctiveness of the individual, and encourage the pursuit of personal autonomy, aspirations and achievement.

In short, people within collectivist cultures tend to think, speak and act in terms of 'we' rather than 'me'. It is not the individual, but the group—family, tribe and nation—that is the most important entity. This worldview stands in stark contrast to how many Westerners, me included, are inclined to view things.[119]

For starters, those of us from Western individualistic cultures are prone to consider the Bible as 'God's Word to *me*'. After all, He chose me before the creation of the world, came knocking on the door of my heart, offered to wash my sins away and, in response, I repented, I believed and I submitted my life to Him. 'I have decided to follow Jesus', and though none go with me, still I will follow. Now God is my heavenly Father, Jesus my personal Lord and Saviour, and my body a temple of Holy Spirit who lives in me. Hence, when I open my Bible, I expect to find God's direction for *my* life.

While each of these statements contain a measure of truth, they demonstrate the individualist's proclivity to hear the Scriptures 'in the key of me'. After all, for many Westerners, religious belief and one's relationship with God are viewed as a deeply personal issue. This is not the case with collectivist societies in which religious identity is inextricably linked to family. In these communities, it is not uncommon for entire households to come to faith together, a phenomenon we witness again and again through the book of Acts.[120]

When Words Fail Us: Ye and Thee, You and Y'all

The limitations of English present several challenges for our Bible translators. One in particular plays well into the collectivist vs. individualist conversation—and I think *you* should be made aware of it.

When employing the second-person pronoun 'you', modern literary English uses the identical word for both individual and collective audiences. It is not immediately obvious whether the question, 'how are you?' is addressing an individual or a group. In the old days, Elizabethan English—used by the likes of Shakespeare and the King James Bible—offered 'thou, thine and thee' as singular, while 'you, your and ye' indicated a plural audience. Sadly, these conventions have been lost to us in modern times, certainly in a formal sense. The creation of the contraction 'y'all' or the colloquial 'youse', indicate a desire for a plural-form option, regardless of whether they are formally sanctioned.

In contrast, the bulk of written languages, and especially Greek and Hebrew, draw clear distinctions between you-singular and you-plural. This is primarily done using inflections (word endings). Herein lies a significant challenge for the English Bible reader. More often than not, the differences between you-singular and you-plural are lost in translation, opening up yet another opportunity for a misunderstood meaning.

The New Testament contains over three thousand uses of the pronoun 'you' and more than two-thirds of these are in plural form. When Jesus declared: 'You are the salt of the earth ... You are the light of the world' (Matt. 5:13–14), in both cases the 'you' here is plural. In other words, *y'all* are salt and light. In his letter to the Corinthians, Paul makes the repeated claim that

Consider this. When the New Testament introduces us to Jesus, it begins by describing His placement in a lengthy genealogy. The Messiah was not born in isolation. He was a member of a family, clan, tribe and nation. Indeed, the prophetic words Jesus came to fulfil were all collective in nature, framed as national, not personal, promises. Christ was the one who 'will save **his people** from their sins', be called 'Immanuel ("God with **us**")', be born 'king of the **Jews**' who would 'shepherd my **people** Israel' (Matt. 1:21–23; 2:1–6). To the collectivist, Messiah is viewed more as the people's Saviour than as a personal Saviour. His message is for 'we', not simply for 'me'.

I am not here to advocate or argue for either the collectivist or individualist perspective, but simply to make this point: the tendency of the biblical authors was to communicate with the collective in mind. For these men, God's revelation was primarily heard 'in the key of we'. This reality must be

'you are God's temple' (1 Cor. 3:9, 16–17; 6:19; 2 Cor. 6:16). In each case, again the pronoun is plural.

While there are certainly individual implications for these metaphors, the grammar makes clear that the *primary* intent was to communicate a collective reality.

Combine the absence of a plural-form 'you' with the western tendency to read 'in the key of me', and we witness the perfect conditions for creating cross-cultural miscommunication. The solution? Develop the habit of thinking more in terms of 'we' than 'me' as you read. When in doubt, youse should all just use your *something-blue* Bible.

considered as we exegete their texts.

This brings us back to Ephesians 1 and its insights into the hotly contested topic of *predestination*. Both mentions of predestination in this passage are given in a collective context: 'In love **he predestined us** for adoption to himself as sons ... In him **we have ... been predestined** according to the purpose of him' (Eph. 1:5, 11). Let me propose to you that Paul is not saying that particular individuals are preselected to sonship, but rather that God's preselection was of a certain group. In other words, God predestined us-as-a-collectively-identified-group, not us-each-as-individuals.[121]

While Westerners may read the words 'he chose us in him before the foundation of the world' to mean that He chose each of us (and most especially *me*!), the collectivist-minded apostle was saying that God chose *our group*. That is, He predestined us-Jews 'who were the first to hope in Christ' before 'you also' were included. He chose our group, and then He chose your group.

The notion of God foreordaining people for salvation has been a strongly contested one for the past 2,000 years, but the nature of the debate varies according to culture. In the individualistic West, we concern ourselves largely with personal predestination. Which individuals has God chosen for salvation, which has He destined to perish, and what part does one's own free will play in the process? For the early church, this was not the issue. When the leaders in Jerusalem gathered with Paul and Barnabas to discuss who could or could not be saved, they were thinking in terms of group identity, not individual choice. As collectivists, the debate was whether or not God had predestined just one people-group or multiple people-groups (Acts 15:1–11).

 Tammy, my goal here is not to unpack the doctrine of predestination, but simply to demonstrate that the cultural context of the ancient Hebrews was significantly coloured by collectivism.

My practical advice on this point is to be prepared to think more in terms of 'we' than 'me' as you read the Scriptures. This is not a call to negate or neglect the personal nature of biblical application, or dismiss occasions in which an individual reading is clearly indicated by context. I am simply encouraging you to recognise that collective thinking was a significant behind-the-scenes influence on the biblical writers and readers.[122]

Appreciating this background will help us discover the author's intended meaning and hopefully avoid cross-cultural misunderstandings. This brings us to a related characteristic of ancient cultures: ethno-nationalism.

Ethno-Nationalism: How Ancient Hebrews Viewed Others

To which nation do you belong? How is that nation defined? How is your nation differentiated from others?

I am Australian. My birth certificate, passport, tax and medical registrations all say so. Both legally and literally, I identify as a citizen of the Australian nation, yet the sense of belonging I have here is not based on my particular ethnicity. I am Australian primarily by virtue of my relationship with Australian law, her language, lifestyle and land. I am part of a modern, Western, multicultural nation-state, and my membership here is entirely unrelated to my racial background. In other words, my belonging is based on my civic status, not my ethnic status.

Such was not the case in the ancient world, in which nationhood and ethnicity were inseparable. One's nation was essentially one's extended family. Ethnic identity was paramount.[123]

Biblical characters like Joseph, Moses, Daniel and Esther each enjoyed a significant measure of status and authority during their time in Egypt and Babylon/Persia respectively, yet through all the years of their residency in those nations, they were Hebrews first and foremost. In many respects, they remained outsiders in these communities by virtue of their ethnicity. Likewise, the apostle Paul, a citizen of Rome and beneficiary of the privileges that status bestowed upon him, never identified as a Roman. He was a Jew, a proud member of the Hebrew people. His civic identity was trumped by his ethnic identity.[124]

What's important here, from a cultural perspective, is that ethno-nationalism tends to develop an us-versus-them mentality in relation to race. Like it or not, this thinking was prevalent within the cultures of biblical times, particularly within Hebrew/Jewish society and, understandably so. After all, God had chosen the children of Israel from among the nations for a divine and distinguished purpose. In the exodus, Yahweh distinguished between the Israelites and the peoples of Egypt, in keeping with the covenant He had made with their forefathers. At Mount Sinai, He 'set them apart' from all surrounding nations when He cut a new covenant with Israel, and with Israel only. The ancient Hebrews were supposed to view themselves as different from other nations by virtue of the fact that they were God's covenant people! Indeed, perhaps we could speak of Israel's nationalism as more motivated by their covenantal distinctiveness than by their ethnicity. Food for thought.[125] The point is, the cultural attitude of 'us versus them', along ethnic lines, is witnessed throughout much of the biblical narrative and comes to the fore strongly in the New Testament era, when it manifests as 'Jew versus Gentile'.

Time and again, this cultural divide is spelt out clearly in the text. The woman at the well was startled when Jesus asked her for water because it

was culturally understood that 'Jews have no dealings with Samaritans'. This point was echoed by Peter, who said to the crowd at Cornelius' home: 'You are well aware that it is against our law for a Jew to associate with or visit a Gentile' (John 4:9; Acts 10:28). Years later, a city-wide riot rocked the streets of Jerusalem when certain men declared of Paul, 'Fellow Israelites, help us! This is the man who teaches everyone everywhere against our people and our law and this place. And besides, he has brought Greeks into the temple and defiled this holy place' (Acts 21:28). It turns out these agitators had observed the apostle fraternising with an Ephesian. Simply unacceptable behaviour.

This brings us back to his letter to the Ephesian church—note the 'we-versus-you' distinction as Paul closes this opening passage: 'So that **we who were the first to hope in Christ** might be to the praise of his glory. In him **you also**, when you heard the word of truth, the gospel of your salvation, and believed in him, were sealed with the promised Holy Spirit' (Eph. 1:12–13).

As we learn from his life testimony, Paul was hardly one of the first to follow Christ. His encounter on the Damascus road occurred a good four years or more after Jesus' ascension, in which time many thousands had come to faith before him. So, how can he claim to be included in the 'we' who first believed? What did Paul mean by the term 'we'?

As suggested previously, it is likely that Paul's meaning here is that 'we Jews' were the first to hope in Christ, after which 'you Gentiles' also came to believe.[126] Although he could mean 'we apostles' and 'you Ephesians', it seems more likely that the we-and-you distinction here is ethnic. After all, Paul uses the 'we Jews' and 'you Gentiles' phrasing throughout the following chapter, when explaining how both groups are now joined together in the one body, of Christ:

> Therefore, remember that formerly **you who are Gentiles by birth** ... were separate from Christ, excluded from citizenship in Israel and foreigners to the covenants of the promise ... [But] He came and preached peace to **you who were far away and peace to those who**

were near. For through him **we both** have access to the Father by one Spirit. (Eph. 2:11–18)

As most of Paul's epistles were addressed to multiethnic congregations, this 'we-Jews and you-Gentiles' distinction is littered throughout his work.[127] Take note of this because it will help you see when Paul shifts his attention from one group to the other. In 1 Corinthians, he makes a point of addressing Jews and Gentiles separately, while simultaneously recognising both as his 'brothers' (1 Cor. 10:1; 12:1–2). Romans Chapter 7 is clearly directed to Jewish believers ('those who know the law'), while Chapters 9–11 seem to be primarily aimed at Gentile Christians (Rom 7:1; 11:13). When Paul asserts in Galatians that 'Christ redeemed **us** from the curse of the law [and] the law was **our** guardian until Christ came', he was speaking to his fellow Jewish brethren who, like him, had lived under the law of Moses.[128] Soon after, his attention shifts to the non-Jewish believers, whom he describes as '**you** [who] did not know God [and] were slaves to those who by nature are not gods' (Gal. 3:13, 23–25; 4:1–12).

Let's be clear on this: Paul made much of the fact that the coming together of Jews and Gentiles in the body of Christ was a magnificent 'mystery' stemming from God's eternal and unsurpassable wisdom. He also argued vehemently that a believer's ethnicity contributed nothing to their status or standing in the new-covenant community.[129] Indeed, while grateful for his own Hebrew heritage, Paul also recognised that from a Gospel perspective, his Jewish roots were as worthless as 'garbage' (Rom. 3:1–2; Phil. 3:1–9).

That said, while one's ethnic identity may have no theological significance in light of the new covenant, the fact remains that the ancient world into which the new-covenant Scriptures were written was deeply entrenched in a Jewish/Gentile divide, thanks largely to a strong ethno-national mindset.

As you read through the pages of your Bible, be conscious of this powerful cultural influence.

Parochialism: How Ancient Hebrews Viewed the World of Men

Now for something a little more subtle: the influence of parochialism.

> The Sovereign LORD said, '**Look at Jerusalem. I put her at the center of the world**, with other countries all around her'. (Ezek. 5:5 GNB)

To be parochial means to have a small view of the world. The word stems from the Greek *pároikos*, meaning 'alongside the house', and the Latin *paroecialis*, indicating that which falls within the bounds 'of a church parish'. Over time, it has essentially come to describe a person who cannot see beyond the borders of their own neighbourhood. Simply put, a parochial person is concerned with matters local, with no reference or regard for matters global.

Those in ancient cultures had a much smaller view of the world than have we modern folk. After all, there was no world atlas on classroom shelves or spinning globes on teachers' desks. There were no cable news channels, no Google Earth and no sophisticated transcontinental communication system of any kind. The ancient world had no satellite imagery, no jumbo jets and no international trade agreements with governments on the opposite side of the planet. The so-called age of exploration, when Europeans would 'discover' the new-world civilisations of the Americas, Asia, Australia, greater Africa and eventually circumnavigate the globe, would not begin until well into the fifteenth century after Christ.

Until then, the ancients lived in a much smaller world than you and I do today; this difference in perspective needs to be considered when exegeting the texts they wrote. After all, what may sound like a worldwide event to the modern reader may in reality be the ancient author's way of describing a situation far more limited in geographical scope.

Consider how Daniel addresses King Nebuchadnezzar when called upon to interpret his dream: 'Your Majesty, you are the king of kings. The God of heaven has given you dominion and power and might and glory; **in your hands he has placed all mankind** and the beasts of the field and the birds in the sky. **Wherever they live**, he has made you ruler over them all' (Dan. 2:37–38).

Sounds impressive, doesn't it? But are we to believe that Nebuchadnezzar's reign extended to the ancient civilisations of South-East Asia or Central America? When Daniel speaks of 'all mankind, wherever they live', what precisely does he mean by that? Is he thinking globally, or locally?

Either way, this prophecy appears to go to Nebuchadnezzar's head! Soon after, he erects a large golden image, and decrees that 'nations and peoples of every language' were to worship it. With the exception of some Jews, notably Shadrach, Meshach and Abednego, we are told that 'as soon as they heard the sound of the horn, flute, zither, lyre, harp and all kinds of music, **all the nations and peoples of every language** fell down and worshipped the image' (Dan. 3:1–12). Similar phrasing is used in the following chapter, in which the same king addresses a letter to 'the nations and peoples of **every language**, who live in **all the earth**' (Dan. 4:1).[130]

Without doubt, both Nebuchadnezzar's letter and legal decree were issued to a local audience. The Babylonian ruler was not addressing all the peoples on earth—only those within the limited jurisdiction of his kingdom. To the modern reader, the language of 'all nations, peoples and tongues' conjures thoughts on a global scale, but this ancient king was addressing *his* world, not *the* world.

It was this same king who destroyed Jerusalem in 586 BC. The Judean king at the time was Zedekiah, whom God promised would be made 'an offense to **all the kingdoms** of the earth' and his city 'a curse among **all the nations** of the earth' (Jer. 15:4; 24:9; 26:6). Are we to believe this included the kingdom of Zhou in China, or the Nok civilisation in sub-Saharan Africa? Did the ancient Austronesian nations of Borneo and New Guinea catch wind of Judah's fall to Babylon? Of course not. Although God was fully aware of these distant communities, Jeremiah was not. While today, the destruction of cities and collapse of nation-states receives instant global attention courtesy of modern technologies, this was not the case in the ancient world. Once more, 'all kingdoms and nations of the earth' refers not to a global audience, but a local one.

Fast forward to the first century and parochialism continues to make its mark. In his account of Jesus' birth, Luke tells of Caesar Augustus, who decreed that '**all the world** should be registered' and later claims that the crowd at Pentecost consisted of devout Jews 'from **every nation under heaven**' (Luke 2:1; Acts 2:5 ESV). While the language here may sound global in scale to you or me, again, the context demands a localised interpretation of both statements—'all the world' and 'every nation under heaven' both describe the world of Rome. After all, there were no Aboriginal Australians, native Americans or Alaskan Inuits in Jerusalem at that time. Those gathered at Pentecost were all residents of the Roman Empire. The text itself tells us so just a few verses later: 'Parthians, Medes and Elamites; residents of Mesopotamia, Judea and Cappadocia, Pontus and Asia, Phrygia and Pamphylia, Egypt and the parts of Libya near Cyrene' (Acts 2:5–11). In fact, many English translations go as far as to add the word 'Roman' to the nativity passage to ensure their twenty-first-century audience catches the author's meaning.[131] The emperor's census was limited to the population of the Roman world, not the entire global world. As with Nebuchadnezzar, the biblical writer is describing a political, not a planetary world.

At other times, Luke's attention turns to the world of Judaism. Contrast his account of the Olivet Discourse with those of the other Synoptics. Matthew and Mark describe 'great days of distress, unequalled from the beginning [or the creation] of **the world**'. However, Luke is very deliberate in specifying the world of which Jesus was speaking, leaving no doubt that the 'great distress and wrath' was to be limited to the land and people of Judea and Jerusalem (Matt. 24:21; Mark 13:19; Luke 21:23). Later in Acts, he recounts the prediction from Agabus that 'there would be a great famine over **all the world**' (Acts 11:28 ESV). These words were fulfilled soon after when food shortages struck the regions of Palestine and Judea. In these cases, the subject matter of these prophecies is the *Jewish world*—a local community, not a global one.[132]

One could even argue that the apostle Paul was somewhat parochial in his outlook, at least from a modern-world perspective. How else could he so confidently affirm that the faith of the Roman Christians sometime in the late-50s AD was already 'being reported **all over the world**' or that the voice of the evangelists 'has gone out into **all the earth**, their words to the **ends of the world**' (Rom. 1:8; 10:18)? How else could he say to the Colossians that 'the gospel that you heard and that **has been proclaimed to every creature under heaven** ... is bearing fruit and growing throughout the **whole world**' (Col. 1:23, 6)? Was Paul under the impression that the Gospel had already reached the entirety of human civilisation, a mere 30 years after the giving of the Great Commission? What precisely did the apostle mean when he spoke of the *whole world* in these contexts?

This brings us back to the opening discourse of Ephesians and Paul's claim that God 'chose us in him before the foundation of the world'. Just which 'world' is he speaking of here? Does Paul mean that God chose believers to be united with Christ before the galaxy existed? Or that God had destined Jews to be in Christ prior to the founding of the *Jewish world*? Is Paul referencing the planet, or a particular people in this context?

Further, since we're considering the issue of world origins, what are we to make of the stories in early Genesis? Was God speaking of a local or global event when He said to Noah 'I am going to bring floodwaters on the earth to destroy **all life under the heavens**' (Gen. 6:17)? Was this a universal extinction of all humans on planet Earth, or does it describe a localised judgment of the land and people familiar to Noah? Later at Babel, we are told, 'the Lord confused the language of **the whole world**' and scattered the people 'over the face of **the whole earth**' (Gen 11:9). Did this migration result in the birthing of all human civilisations globally, or did it simply have regional implications, limited to the known lands of the Ancient Near East? Now think forward to the similar catastrophes described in the final book in our Bible, Revelation, in which the sounding of trumpets results in a third of the earth being burnt, a third of the sea turning to blood and a third of humankind killed by plagues of fire, smoke and brimstone (Rev. 8:7–8; 9:13–18). Are these plagues universal or merely regional? Following this, it is said that those from '**every people, tribe, language and nation**' will gaze upon the corpses of the two witnesses laid in streets of the great city Babylon, who had made '**all the nations**' drink the wine of her adulteries (Rev. 11:9; 14:8; 16:19). Are the angels here declaring Babylon to be a city of global influence, or does the reference to 'every people, tribe, language and nation' have a far more localised meaning, as it had in the book of Daniel? Which interpretation are we supposed to believe? What do Moses and John mean when they use terms and phrases that sound, to the modern reader at least, universal in scope?

 Timothy, my point is this: every character in the pages of our Bible was a product of their ancient culture and their parochial worldview at times shaped their communication.

As modern readers tasked to discover the intended meaning of their text, this cultural consideration can prove critical. While we may be worlds apart from the biblical authors culturally, we do not want to be worlds apart from them in the conclusions we reach. As always, context is key.

Supernaturalism: How Ancient Hebrews Viewed the World of the Divine

My final point regarding cultural considerations is to appreciate that all biblical societies held to an unquestioning belief in what we moderns would term the 'supernatural'. In contrast to Western civilisation, which emerged out of the technological innovations of the Renaissance, the biblical authors came from a world whose citizens were more inclined to think and speak in terms of spiritual realities than in scientific ones.[133] That the world of the divine directly exerted influence upon the world of humans was an everyday assumption. It simply went without saying that much of what took place in the seen realm was a result of unseen activity in the realm of the spirit.

Belief in angels, demons and otherworldly creatures, an afterlife, underworld and glorious heavenly places were all part of the ancient Hebrew perspective. Stories of human interaction with the supernatural not only receive frequent airplay throughout the Scriptures, but actually direct the entire form and flow of the narrative itself. Were one to remove paranormal phenomena from the pages of our Bible, we would be left with almost no Bible at all!

To claim the biblical authors 'believed in the supernatural' is simply stating the obvious, but that is not my point. My point is a cultural one. My purpose here, remember, is to draw your attention to the world behind the words and to see how often the assumed norms and knowledge of the ancient Hebrews differed to those held by many of us today.

Simply put, the more scientifically advanced our world has become, with increased reliance on natural explanations and solutions to life's challenges and concerns, the less inclined we are to be cognisant of the spirit realm. In turn, the less we consider the supernatural as part of our everyday lives, the more prone we are to read over the portions of Scripture that speak to this reality—especially those that do so discreetly.

Case in point: the book of Ephesians. As with almost all of Paul's letters, Ephesians contains many understated insights into the supernatural realm. For example, the opening passage begins with the apostle praising the Father for bestowing upon us 'every spiritual blessing in the **heavenly places**'. This term is used five times in this epistle and denotes the realm where God's throne is located, together with whom, says Paul, both Christ and believers are 'seated'. Further, these so-called heavenly places are also inhabited by other spiritual rulers, including a scheming devil, powers of darkness and named forces of evil who carry dominion, authority, power and various forms of weaponry.[134]

Yep, it's all there in black and white.

In the most casual manner, Paul provides little more than a passing mention of these spiritual beings and the space in which they operate. As with all biblical authors, use of supernatural terms and talking points are simply par for the course. He senses no need to provide evidence of these realities, define their distinctives or explain the nature of their existence. After all, Paul and his audience share a common culture, and when communicating within a common culture, certain concepts are simply left unsaid.

In ancient times, it was widely accepted that the cosmos comprised multiple realms and dimensions, both seen and unseen, with each populated by various creatures and characters. In the broadest sense, this included 'the heavens, the earth and under the earth' (Phil. 2:10; Rev. 5:13). Simply put, the heavens served as the abode of the gods, the earth as home to man and the underworld as the dwelling place of the dead.

From as early as Abraham, the Old Testament describes physical death as a time when God's people were gathered to their ancestors in Sheol. Contrasted with the 'land of the living', the realm of the dead was understood to be where Hebrews descended at their passing, a place characterised by darkness, silence and rest.[135] Some hold that Sheol was nothing more than a philosophical concept, or simply an alternate way of describing the burial of a biological body. Others claim the Hebrews viewed Sheol as a very real spiritual dimension wherein the souls of the departed were kept, awaiting resurrection and relocation to heaven. In the mysterious story of the medium in Endor, the deceased prophet Samuel apparently rises from Sheol, before appearing in spirit form and speaking to King Saul. This eyebrow-raising incident draws many questions from modern audiences, but is little explained by the author. Behind the text lies the undeniable reality that King Saul believed it possible that a dead man could be called and consulted. Clearly, his cosmology included the existence of an underworld—a realm inhabited by the deceased (1 Sam. 28:3–20).

However, in Ephesians, Paul's main concern is those living on and above the earth. According to Hebrew thought, the occupants of the heavenly realms operated within a system of hierarchy in which they carried varying degrees of responsibility and authority. They included angels of various stripes, animal-like creatures and a company of divine beings referred to as *Elohim*: that is, 'gods' with a lower-case 'g'.[136]

Yahweh, the greatest of all gods, had apparently assigned these divine beings to rule over particular nations from the time of early Genesis, with Israel uniquely chosen as His own: 'The Most High ... assigned to each nation a heavenly being, but Jacob's descendants he chose for himself' (Deut. 32:8–9

GNB).[137] While many of these heavenly beings remained loyal to Yahweh, at times acting as His messengers and even consulting with Him in an apparent 'council' situation, it seems that others neglected their holy duties, defied His supreme authority and were themselves condemned to suffer the indignity of demotion and ultimately, death: 'God has taken his place in the divine council; in the midst of the gods he holds judgment ... I said, "You are gods, sons of the Most High, all of you; nevertheless, like men you shall die, and fall like any prince"' (Ps. 82:1–7 ESV).[138]

Some of these rulers are named in the Scriptures, perhaps the most infamous being Molek, Baal-zebub, Gog, the Princes of Persia and Greece and, of course, the devil known as Satan.[139] Here in Ephesians, Paul refers specifically to 'the prince of the power of the air' but provides no further detail on this particular being's name or backstory (Eph. 2:2). Perhaps he simply doesn't sense the need to do so—yet another indication of assumed knowledge shared between the author and his original audience.

Regardless of their names, titles, influence or jurisdiction, the New Testament is clear on this: Jesus Christ, the Most High Incarnate, is in every way superior to all such personalities and powers. Indeed, so too are those humans who, as members of His new-covenant body, have been raised, united and seated with Him in heavenly places. In fact, it seems that right from the first verse, Paul's supernatural worldview is woven into the most unassuming of terms when he refers to the Ephesians as 'saints' or 'holy ones' (Greek: *hagios*), a word used in both testaments to describe heavenly beings.[140] By calling believers 'holy ones', Paul is doing more than claiming we are special and set apart—we are also, by very nature, *supernatural*. Declared holy by His redemptive work, the new-covenant believer is no longer a 'mere mortal', but an entirely new creation—precious, powerful and purposed to participate in the divine nature of the Great God of all gods (2 Peter 1:4)![141]

Cultural Context—Closing Comments

The cultural influences of the biblical writers pervade most everything they wrote. As modern readers tasked to discover the author's intended meaning, it is important that we appreciate some of the fundamental differences between our worldview and that held by the ancient Hebrew people. We have just explored four of these: collectivism, ethno-nationalism, parochialism and supernaturalism.

Regarding collectivism, be prepared to hear the Bible 'in the key of we'. The Scriptures were written by men for whom the collective was paramount— put yourself in their sandals and think more in terms of 'we' than of 'me' as you read. As you do this, be aware of the emphasis on ethnicity in collective language. In the New Testament, the term 'we' may not be referring to 'we-Christians', but rather, 'we-Jews'. From their founding under Moses, the Hebrew nation was to view itself as God's chosen people, distinguished from others by virtue of their unique relationship with Yahweh. While you may proudly consider yourself colourblind to the race of other people, this was not the case for those in the ancient world.

Third, when it comes to geography, think smaller. When biblical authors speak of 'the earth', do not assume they are referring to planet Earth; when they reference 'the entire world', ask yourself *which world* they have in mind. Remember, the goal of exegesis is to draw out what the author meant by the words he used, regardless of what those words may mean to you.

Finally, Tammy, I leave you with this.

Earlier I stated that the science of hermeneutics, and exegesis particularly, requires you to keep your head and approach the Bible intelligently. Please know that one of the most intellectually honest things we can do is acknowledge the reality of the unseen realm. Like Elisha's young servant who became aware of the angelic hosts surrounding him, we also should be willing for our eyes to be opened in this regard (2 Kings 6:15–17). After all, God Himself 'is spirit' and His words 'spirit and life' (John 4:24; 6:63). A true student of the Scripture is simultaneously a student of the Spirit. So, since 'you have been raised with Christ, seek the things that are above, where Christ is, seated at the right hand of God. Set your minds on things that are above' (Col. 3:1–2 ESV).

Just as Paul encouraged the Ephesian saints to be actively engaged in the supernatural strength and authority bestowed upon them as sons and daughters of God, so do I to you. In fact, I pray:

> [That] the God of our Lord Jesus Christ, the Father of glory, may give you the Spirit of wisdom and of revelation in the knowledge of him, having **the eyes of your hearts enlightened**, that you may know what is the hope to which he has called you, what are the riches of his glorious inheritance in the saints, and what is the immeasurable greatness of his power toward us who believe, according to the working of his great might that he worked in Christ when he raised him from the dead and seated him at his right hand in the heavenly places, far above all rule and authority and power and dominion, and above every name that is named. (Eph. 1:17–21 ESV)

Amen.

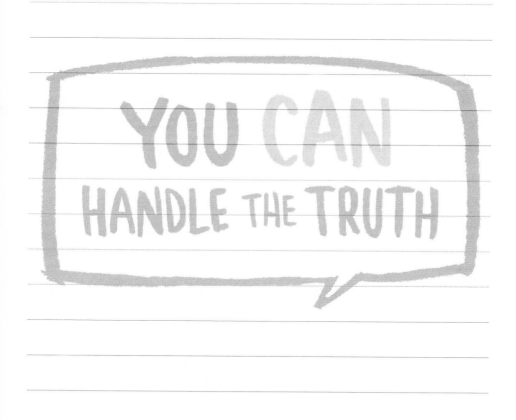

Corroborating Content

Be they in novels, television, comic books or film, from Sherlock Holmes to Veronica Mars, Nancy Drew to Scooby Doo, in the world of fiction, everybody loves a 'whodunnit hero'. During my childhood years I wanted nothing more than to be part of Enid Blyton's Famous Five gang, running around with friends collecting clues, solving crimes and drinking ginger beer. Today, my favourite fictional sleuth is Agatha Christie's Hercule Poirot. A strange little Belgian with a tell-tale moustache, this private detective is renowned for his curious mind, attention to detail and employment of logic, order and method as he pieces together the most complex of crimes, leaving no stone unturned in the pursuit of truth.

At a philosophical level, crime-solving and criminal justice is based on the idea that truth itself is objective and can be exposed, confirmed and tested through the collection of data. On the path to a verdict, many theories may be entertained and speculations considered, but to arrive at a correct

conclusion, a good detective is consumed with just one thought: where does the evidence lead? In a judicial system committed to justice, this is also the primary concern of those entrusted with ultimately deciding a case.[142]

These foundational ideas find their beginnings some 3,500 years ago as part of Israel's judicial system, courtesy of Moses: 'You must not convict anyone of a crime on the testimony of only one witness. **The facts of the case must be established by the testimony of two or three witnesses**' (Deut. 19:15 NLT). When judging serious matters, it was not enough to consider a conviction based solely on a single accusation. Evidence would need to be brought forward and witness testimony scrutinised and substantiated. The higher the stakes, the heavier the burden of proof. In the New Testament, both Jesus and Paul adopt this principle of 'two or three witnesses', applying it to various aspects of Christian life and ministry.[143]

I encourage you to do the same with your exegesis.

Before reaching a conclusion on the meaning of a text, especially in situations in which the subject matter is of a serious nature, make a habit of corroborating your evidence with two or three reliable sources. While those alternate sources may at times include the wisdom and insight of other saints, or the personal witness of the Spirit to your heart and mind, in this section, I am concerned primarily with interpreting Scripture with Scripture.

In short, use the Bible as its own interpreter. Allow the Scripture to explain itself.[144]

When you are unclear on the meaning of Scripture or encounter a passage that appears inconsistent with another, you must refrain from jumping to conclusions or allowing the obscure to trump the clear. This is your opportunity to keep your head and employ the scientific method of testing for truth. More often than not, clarity will come as you compare, cross-reference and corroborate your content.

Having taken a step back, we will now begin the process of zooming in on the Bible's detail. Following are some practical case studies from Jesus and Paul, highlighting eight aspects of Scripture that you may need to compare in the pursuit of clarity:

> Themes and Motifs
>
> Accounts, Incidents and Stories
>
> Rules, Guidelines and Commands
>
> Quotations, Citations and References
>
> Phrases, Symbols and Figures of Speech
>
> Allusions and Echoes
>
> Grammar and Sentence Structure
>
> Individual Words

As we continue our investigation into the meaning of the biblical text, it's time to take a closer look, collect some clues, and corroborate our content.

CHAPTER 24

Themes and Motifs

He went on to tell the people this parable: '**A man planted a vineyard**, rented it to some farmers and went away for a long time. At harvest time he sent a servant to the tenants so they would give him some of the fruit of the vineyard. But the tenants beat him and sent him away empty-handed' … The teachers of the law and the chief priests looked for a way to arrest him immediately, because **they knew he had spoken this parable against them**. (Luke 20:9–19)[145]

At first glance, it may seem that these religious leaders were being hypersensitive when they concluded that Jesus' story specifically referred to them. You know the type—always taking what the preacher says personally! However, a little detective work will demonstrate that in this case, their instincts were correct. This was absolutely His intention. After all, the vineyard metaphor was a well-established theme in the Hebrew Scriptures when speaking of the old-covenant community and its leadership. The evidence for this is not difficult to find.

The first appearance of the 'Israel as God's vine/vineyard motif' is found in the Song of Moses, in which he likens apostate Israel to the 'vine of Sodom' (Deut. 32:32). It is later appropriated and expanded upon by both the psalmists and the prophets. Indeed, Isaiah has an entire chapter dedicated to his so-called Song of the Vineyard, in which he states plainly, 'The vineyard of the LORD Almighty is the nation of Israel, and the people of Judah are the vines he delighted in' (Isa. 5:7). Here in the Gospels, Jesus simply continues this time-honoured tradition and does so multiple times, notably, during His final journey into Jerusalem, the Jewish capital.[146]

The fact that vines and vineyards feature so frequently in Jesus' teaching is no indication that our Lord is an avid viticulturist. Nor is it simply a preacher's attempt to find a relatable illustration for an agrarian audience. Jesus purposefully borrowed, and built upon, a pre-existing theological concept drawn straight from the pages of the Old Testament, and the biblically literate priests recognised it immediately.

On another occasion, Jesus turned this motif upon Himself, claiming: 'I am the true vine, and my Father is the gardener'. He explained that each believer, like individual branches, is dynamically connected as members of the one plant under the care and husbandry of God (John 15:1–8). I'd suggest most Christians today understand this point quite easily.

However, there's another aspect to this teaching often missed by those who neglect to cross-reference this Scripture with other vineyard-themed passages. In John 15, Jesus identified Himself, thus, the community united in Him, not simply as 'the vine', but as the '**true** vine'. In doing so, He drew a distinction between His new-covenant community—that which is true—and the prevailing vine of the old-covenant community. Christ takes this collective metaphor and makes it comparative, contrasting one vine to another, Himself to Israel. This subtle, but intentional, inference would be lost on us were we to not consider and compare its Old Testament usage.[147]

 Pay attention, Tammy.

The Bible is littered with recurring motifs, repeated and redeveloped by different authors in different contexts throughout the scope of Scripture, and often, in a manner far more circumspect than that given here. Watch out for them, because the full depths and meaning of the truths these motifs reveal will remain lost to us should we not embrace an 'all-Bible' view, cross-reference our content and compare how these themes are communicated over time.

CHAPTER 25

Accounts, Incidents and Stories

You know it was because of **a bodily ailment** that I preached the gospel to you at first, and though my condition was a trial to you, you did not scorn or despise me ... For I testify to you that, if possible, you would have gouged out your eyes and given them to me. (Gal. 4:13–15 ESV)

Popular English Bibles vary widely when translating the term Paul employs for 'bodily ailment' (Greek: *astheneia*). Some prefer 'weakness' or 'infirmity of the flesh', while others strongly infer a medical condition, employing the phrase 'bodily illness' or simply 'I was sick'.[148] These varied translations have given rise to widespread speculation over the precise nature of Paul's condition, one that appears to have affected his eyes. Is it possible to ascertain the identity of this ailment? Is the answer best found in an ophthalmology journal or can we discover further detail of this same account elsewhere in the Bible?

I believe we can.

The book of Acts documents Paul's first ministry visit to the Galatians as part of his apostolic travels with Barnabas. As was often the case with Paul, on this particular leg of his tour, he encountered fierce opposition. In Lystra, his persecutors pelted him with rocks and dragged him outside the city, believing him to be dead. With help from his friends, Paul managed to pick himself up and, the next morning, begin the 95 km (60 mi) walk to the city of Derbe in Galatia's south-east. One can only imagine what the apostle must have looked like the day he arrived, battered, beaten, bloodied and bruised from a death-defying stoning! With only the most basic form of medical treatment available, little time to rest or heal, and no makeup to conceal his wounds, Paul took to the pulpit and began to preach (Acts 14:1–23).

According to this comparative account, the only physical ailment Paul experienced when he first ministered in Galatia was the head-to-toe injuries sustained from this brutal attack. Despite a plethora of theories and speculations from Bible students over the years, the apostle was not carrying some debilitating strain of conjunctivitis, ocular allergy or macular degeneration when he first preached to the Galatians. His eyes were bloodshot and his face swollen from the bludgeoning he suffered during that stoning. Thus, Paul closes his Galatian letter reminding them of what they had seen firsthand: 'I bear on my body the marks of Jesus' (Gal. 6:17).[149]

There. Mystery solved.

The Bible is full of occasions like this—the same incident is recounted in another book, by another author, offering another perspective on the identical story.[150] Whenever possible, I urge you to compare these varying accounts to reach a more complete understanding of the story. Use Scripture to interpret Scripture.

CHAPTER 26

Rules, Guidelines and Commands

> I do not permit a woman to teach or to assume authority over a man; she must be quiet. (1 Tim. 2:12)

Well, that seems quite to the point doesn't it? No beating around the bush here. Way to create endless contention and confusion within future generations of Bible readers, Paul. Well done to you, sir!

Alright, sarcasm aside—what is the apostle's *intent* here? Is he issuing a blanket rule to be applied to all women in all situations, everywhere, across all cultures, for all time? Is this a permanent and universal prohibition? Or is it a limited prescription, specific to a particular person and place, as was his instruction to the Corinthian believers in avoiding marriage?[151]

On the matter of women teaching, the Gospels and Acts demonstrate multiple occasions in which women inform and instruct men in the truth of Christ, including Mary Magdalene, the Samaritan woman and Priscilla, not to mention those who evidently prophesied.[152] In regard to exercising authority, the Old Testament describes God ordaining Miriam and Deborah to govern over large groups of men, while Paul himself uses leadership terms when naming Junia and Phoebe as apostles and deacons in their respective churches.[153]

These comparative examples indicate that the scope of the biblical text—and

Paul specifically—has no issue with females leading and serving as ministers of God and His Gospel. Why, then, would Paul preach one rule, when the evidence shows he practised another? Is he being dishonest and inconsistent? What did Paul mean when he claimed, 'I do not permit a woman to teach'?

When it comes to this particular challenge, multiple approaches and theories exist. Some highlight the historical attitudes and practices related to gender-based learning in Ephesian and/or Jewish society at the time. Others focus on Paul's peculiar choice of Greek words, his use of present tense and his shift from men and women (plural) in Verses 9–10, to '*a woman*' and '*a man*' (singular) in Verses 11–12. Some dismiss apostolic authorship altogether, claiming this entire epistle is *pseudonymous*, that is, written by someone else entirely!

Unsurprisingly, there is much debate and a variety of views on this text's original intended meaning. As always, I encourage you to do your own research.[154] We can safely conclude, however, through a basic text comparison, that Paul was not advocating for a blanket ban on women teaching the Gospel or operating in positions of authority. The reality is, while it may be difficult to nail down the precise point an author is making in a given text, it is often quite simple to dismiss what he is *not* saying. As for Paul's comments further on in this passage about women only being saved through childbearing … again, I'll leave that for you to investigate.

 Timothy—take my advice. When you come across a command, guideline or rule in Scripture, avoid drawing significant conclusions in the absence of clear and consistent corroborating evidence from elsewhere in the Bible.

Again, I say: 'Let every serious matter be established in the presence of two or three reliable witnesses'. Compare Scripture with Scripture and allow the Bible to explain itself.

YOU CAN HANDLE THE TRUTH

CHAPTER 27

Quotations, Citations and References

As he says in Hosea: 'I will call them "my people" who are **not my people**; and I will call her "my loved one" who is **not my loved one**,' and, 'In the very place where it was said to them, "You are **not my people**," there they will be called "children of the living God."' … What then shall we say? That **the Gentiles**, who did not pursue righteousness, have obtained it, a righteousness that is by faith. (Rom. 9:25–30)

In Romans Chapters 9–11, Paul confronts yet another set of contentious issues, including one we touched on earlier—predestination and election. In my experience, it would seem that most Christians, and many pastors for that matter, would be happy to skip this section of Romans entirely! After all, Chapters 8 and 12 contain so many truths near and dear to us, whereas the discourse in-between tends to illicit more confusion and controversy than it does comfort. So, let's take a look.

Place of Origin

In proposing his argument here, Paul relies heavily on Moses and the Prophets. In fact, these three chapters contain no fewer than 30 separate citations from a dozen Old Testament books! To gain clarity on his process, it's important to note these references and their original contexts. Paul is not simply cherry-picking random passages to support his case. His theology on election, and particularly of God predestinating non-Jewish peoples, is deeply rooted in the prophetic promises of the Hebrew Bible, literally, from Genesis all the way to Malachi.[155]

In the passage above, Paul argues that the prophets, and Hosea specifically, predicted the day that Gentile nations would be gathered into covenant with God. That is, non-Jewish peoples are among those predestined to be saved. Follow these quotations back to their place of origin; you'll notice they were first spoken to the northern kingdom of Israel, just prior to its destruction by Assyria. Hosea, and subsequent prophets, explain how, at this point in history, God decided to annul His marriage covenant with this kingdom, meaning the peoples of the 10 northern tribes effectively became indistinguishable 'among the nations' (Hos. 8:8; 9:17). The divine penalty imposed on the northern kingdom was that they, from a covenantal perspective, became 'Gentile'. In other words, God's promises to *re-covenant* with the northern kingdom at some point in the future were effectively made to Gentile people. Those who were considered 'not my people' would one day be declared 'children of the living God' (Hos. 1:9–10).[156]

Back to the Future

> Then one of them, named Caiaphas, who was high priest that year, spoke up, 'You know nothing at all! You do not realize that it is better for you that one man die for the people than that the whole nation perish.' He did not say this on his own, but as high priest that year he prophesied that **Jesus would die for the Jewish nation, and not only for that nation but also for the scattered children of God, to bring them together and make them one.** (John 11:49–52)[157]

Teachers of the law agreed that in the age of Messiah, God would regather the 10 lost tribes into one kingdom, united with the Jews under a Davidic king, with a new and everlasting covenant. However, precisely *how* He would perform this grand and implausible task remained a mystery to them, but not to Paul: 'the mystery made known to me by revelation … which was not made known to other generations as it has now been revealed by the

Spirit ... is that through the gospel the Gentiles are heirs together with Israel, members of one body, and sharers together in the promise of Christ Jesus' (Eph. 3:3–6).[158]

As Paul witnesses non-Jewish people in his day coming into covenant relationship with God through Christ, he interprets this as a fulfilment of the long-awaited prophetic promises to re-covenant with the dispersed, dead and divorced northern tribes. God had elected Gentile nations to enter into covenant with Him, and this was coming to pass in dramatic fashion right before the apostle's eyes! While controversial among Paul's rabbinical contemporaries, it was a conviction that he was willing to give his life for, courtesy of revelation by the Spirit, confirmation from the saints and corroboration from the Scriptures.[159]

Here's the takeaway: when you encounter an Old Testament citation in the New, imagine it as a hyperlink. Click on the quotation, see where it takes you and consider its original placement within the Bible's big picture. Then ask yourself, what was taking place in Hebrew history when the prophet first spoke these words, and how is that original context comparable to the situation of God's community as the apostle was writing? In referring back to an Old Testament passage, what kind of thoughts, truths or themes is the author hoping to 'trigger' in his New Testament audience?

When you come across a quotation, citation or any other form of explicit scriptural reference, clarify its use by considering its original context.

CHAPTER 28

Phrases, Symbols and Figures of Speech

> Therefore, in order to keep me from becoming conceited, I was given **a thorn in my flesh**, a messenger of Satan, to torment me. Three times I pleaded with the Lord to take it away from me. But he said to me, 'My grace is sufficient for you, for my power is made perfect in weakness.' (2 Cor. 12:7–9)

As with Paul's infirmity in Galatia, there have been countless theories on the true identity of his infamous 'thorn in the flesh'. All manner of diseases, disorders, deformities and demons have been suggested, as Bible students the world over apply their wildest imaginations. But does the Bible itself shed light on the meaning of this phrase? Is it found elsewhere in the Scriptures?

Quite simply, yes.

It occurs at least twice in the Old Testament. First, when God spoke to Moses by the Jordan river: 'But if you do not drive out the inhabitants of the land, those you allow to remain will become barbs in your eyes and **thorns in your sides**. They will give you trouble in the land where you will live'. It was spoken again by an angel of the Lord in the book of Judges: 'you are not to make a covenant with the people of this land … they will be **thorns in your sides**, and their gods will be a snare to you' (Num. 33:55; Judg. 2:2–3).[160]

In both cases, the phrase refers to *human* troublemakers—people who shared the same geography as Israel but did not share the same god or core values. When Paul employed this symbolism, he did so to communicate the same thing in his situation. His thorn in the flesh was harassment from *people* who were close to him in proximity, but far from him in purpose. This is further confirmed just two verses later when he describes his hardships as including 'persecutions, troubles and insults'. Further, it harmonises perfectly with the narrative of Acts, in which Paul is constantly depicted as harmed, harassed and harangued by *human* adversaries.[161]

Almost every society has well-known colloquialisms unique to their culture through which communicators utilise the power of symbolism and imagery to support their point. The biblical authors are no different.

The point is, when you come across a phrase that seems a little ambiguous, investigate if and how it is used elsewhere in the Bible before drawing conclusions. The intended meaning behind such figures of speech becomes clearer when you compare their use elsewhere. After all, the Bible is its own best interpreter.

CHAPTER 29

Allusions and Echoes

Occasionally, you will come across a phrase or statement that harks back to a significant biblical event but does not explicitly say so. Without quoting a verse, repeating an expression or providing a precise reference, certain authors discreetly echo and allude to biblical concepts in the hope that their audiences will catch their meaning and make the connection, albeit an inferred one.

However, the problem with allusions is that they often elude us, especially when we are not paying close enough attention to the trail of subtle clues provided in such nuanced communication. Case in point: the thief in the night, and its parallels to Passover:

> [For] you know very well that the day of the Lord will come **like a thief in the night**. While people are saying, 'Peace and safety,' destruction will come on them suddenly, as labor pains on a pregnant woman, and they will not escape. But you, brothers and sisters, are not in darkness so that this day should surprise you like a thief. You are all children of the light and children of the day. We do not belong to the night or to the darkness. So then, let us not be like others, who are asleep, but let us be awake and sober … For God did not appoint us to suffer wrath but to receive salvation through our Lord Jesus Christ. (1 Thess. 5:2–9)

Collecting Clues

The phrase 'thief in the night' and its association with the day of the Lord did not originate with Paul. It first appears in Matthew 24, when Jesus delivers His famous Olivet Discourse and urges His audience to keep watch, be ready, and thereby not allow one's house to be broken into (Matt. 24:42–44).[162]

In the passage above, Paul echoes this encouragement by contrasting those who are prepared for this thief and those who are not. Some will be surprised by this coming, but others will be ready. The prepared ones, those appointed to salvation, are awake, sober and 'of the light'. The unprepared ones, those 'in darkness', are instead found sleeping and unprotected when the thief comes to their homes. For these, the thief's arrival is unexpected and, consequently, a day of great suffering, but for others, including the believers in Thessalonica who 'know very well' that the thief is on His way, the day of the Lord is one of salvation.

The parallels between this thief-coming and the story of Passover are striking. In Exodus, immediately prior to the killing of the firstborn was the plague of supernatural darkness, in which God made a distinction between His chosen people—those in the light—and the Egyptians, who were literally left in the dark for three consecutive days. When the Destroyer of the firstborn came through the land, he did so while the people were sleeping. The unprepared Egyptians were caught completely off guard and suffered a swift and irreversible judgment that night. Conversely, the Israelites were up, dressed and ready. After all, their prophet had warned them the thief was on his way: 'When the LORD goes through the land to strike down the Egyptians, he will see the blood on the top and sides of the doorframe and will pass over that doorway, and he will not permit the destroyer to enter your houses' (Ex. 12:23). Alert, awake and anticipating his coming, the people of faith were spared destruction. As promised, the thief had come to steal, kill and destroy, but the blood of the Lamb had provided salvation.[163]

In light of these powerful correlations, it seems to me that Jesus and Paul are alluding to Passover when employing the 'thief in the night' metaphor. Unlike our previous examples, the phrase itself is not explicitly found in the Old Testament, nor does any New Testament author directly cite the exodus in conjunction with it. However, the parallels strongly suggest an *inferred association*. One simply needs to look a little closer to notice that the fingerprints of Passover are all over it.

Catch My Meaning?

Identifying this correlation helps us understand the apostle's meaning and, just as importantly, avoid false conclusions that the metaphor may otherwise suggest. Paul does not want his Thessalonian audience to be fearful of Christ's coming, or to see Him as a common criminal, a brash law-breaking burglar sneaking into homes and stealing valuable assets from unsuspecting innocents as they sleep! His purpose in employing the 'thief in the night' imagery is the same as that of Moses at Passover: 'Christ Himself, the Great Prophet, has warned us that a day of the Lord is soon coming! Have faith in the Lamb. Be alert, awake, dressed and ready—for salvation is on its way to the children of the light, to those who place their trust in His covenant blood!'.

Allusions like this may be discreet, but they are detectable just under the surface, waiting to be discovered. Your discernment in this area will increase as your familiarity with the Scripture grows. Have your feelers out, be prepared to dig a little deeper and don't let allusions elude you.

CHAPTER 30

Grammar and Sentence Structure

Grab a magnifying lens from your toolkit Tammy; it's time to zoom in close and consider some of the finer details of the biblical text as we continue to corroborate its content. Pay attention, this is going to require some focus:

> For what I received I passed on to you as of first importance: that Christ died for our sins according to the Scriptures, that he was buried, that **he was raised** on the third day ... But if it is preached that Christ has been **raised from the dead**, how can some of you say that there is no resurrection of the dead? (1 Cor. 15:3–4, 12)

On the surface it would seem that the two statements—'he was raised' and 'raised from the dead'—communicate the same thing, but a closer examination reveals a noteworthy variance in the apostle's linguistics. I'd like to propose that these verses communicate two complementary, but clearly different, truths. Permit me to explain.

More than Meets the Eye

Like a two-sided coin, the resurrection of Christ contains two distinct realities, one physical and the other spiritual. The resurrection of Jesus' biological body from physiological death is a truth attested to by multiple first-century witnesses and Gospel writers, who go to great pains to explain how the body killed at Calvary was the self-same body alive again days later.

Without question, Jesus' resurrection had a visible and tangible component to it.[164] Equally true is the fact that Jesus' resurrection contained a critical *non-visible* component, a reality that occurred in the spirit realm outside the reach and range of natural human senses. While His physical body lay dead in Joseph's tomb, Jesus ventured into the unseen realm where, among other things, He 'descended to the lower parts of the earth' and 'made proclamation to the imprisoned spirits—to those who were disobedient long ago when God waited patiently in the days of Noah' (Eph. 4:9; 1 Peter 3:19–20).

In the natural realm, Christ's physical body was laid in a garden tomb and raised back to biological life. Simultaneously, in the unseen realm of the spirit, Christ descended to Sheol (Greek: *Hades*), the place where the dead ones were bound, before being raised from *that* realm 'through the glory of the Father' and the working of His 'mighty strength' (Rom. 6:4; Eph. 1:19). The seen and unseen, two complementary sides of Jesus' one resurrection coin: for 'he was not abandoned to the **realm of the dead**, nor did **his body** see decay' (Acts 2:31).

Take a Closer Look

Back to 1 Corinthians 15. In the first case—'he was raised [Greek: *egēgertai*] on the third day'—Paul is highlighting the *physical* nature of Christ's resurrection, as evidenced by the statements immediately surrounding it. The context makes this clear. However, zoom in a little closer and you'll see that subsequent references to Jesus' resurrection, in Verses 12 and 20, employ a distinctly different grammatical structure, with more elements added to the mix. Here, Paul applies the conjunctive *ex*, a preposition meaning 'out from' (from which comes 'exodus') and connects it with *nekrōn*, literally 'the dead ones'. By adjusting his grammar Paul appears to be drawing the reader's attention to the unseen nature of Christ's resurrection—His raising-up *out from among the dead ones*.[165] By identifying this variance, we realise that Paul's focus in this passage of teaching is fixed largely on the invisible aspect of this miraculous event. The author's intent is to have his readers set their eyes on what was *not* seen. This brings us to the question of how the so-called dead ones were said to be raised:

But someone will say, "How are **the dead** raised up? And with **what body** do **they** come?" (1 Cor. 15:35 NKJV)

There are a couple points of interest in this verse. First, 'the dead' (Greek: *hoi nekroi*) is plural, while 'body' (Greek: *sōmati*) is presented as singular. The question here is not 'with what bodies' do the dead ones come, but 'with what body', singular. Second, the verbs 'raised' and 'come' are both in a tense known as the present indicative passive. It is not future tense, but a form of *present* tense. Used no fewer than five times throughout this chapter in relation to the dead being raised, it is identical to this statement from Luke: 'And he answered them, "Go and tell John what you have seen and heard: the blind receive their sight, the lame walk, lepers are cleansed, and the deaf hear, **the dead are raised up**, the poor have good news preached to them"' (Luke 7:22 ESV). These passages intentionally employ a form of present, not future, tense. What is Paul getting at here?

Is he appealing to the truth of Christ's *physical* resurrection to claim that at some point in the future a myriad of dead corpses will be raised from their graves to experience biological life again? Or is he drawing attention to the *invisible* aspect of Christ's resurrection, claiming that dead ones were presently being raised, as part of a single body, and experiencing a form of life that was beyond biological? Was this resurrection to occur at some point in the future, or was it already underway at the time of Paul's writing? Did Paul believe the dead would be resurrected with their own individual bodies,

or was he using the word in a collective sense so that the imperishable body in view here is a covenant body—that is, 'the body of Christ'?[166]

As you can see, a close look at something as seemingly innocuous as grammar opens up wildly different theories regarding the intended meaning of this passage. So, which one is correct?

Again, I'll leave that to you for further investigation and personal study. Just remember, seek two or three corroborating evidences before reaching a final conclusion on this matter.[167]

Merely Semantics?

My point is simply this: each jot and tittle of the biblical text is both inspired by God and intentionally employed by its author. While I stress again the importance of not becoming lost in the finer details of the Scripture, every detail holds significance. This includes the author's choice of grammar, including conjunctives, pronouns, inflections and the like. These should not be dismissed as 'merely semantics'.

When seeking to discover a text's intended meaning, be prepared to consider these finer details and compare their use elsewhere. Formal word-for-word translations and especially your *something-blue* Bible will prove particularly useful in this regard.[168]

CHAPTER 31

Individual Words

I am the true vine, and my Father is the vinedresser. **Every branch in me that does not bear fruit he takes away** [Greek: *airó*], and every branch that does bear fruit he prunes, that it may bear more fruit. Already you are clean because of the word that I have spoken to you. Abide in me, and I in you. As the branch cannot bear fruit by itself, unless it abides in the vine, neither can you, unless you abide in me. I am the vine; you are the branches. Whoever abides in me and I in him, he it is that bears much fruit, for apart from me you can do nothing. If anyone does not abide in me he is thrown away like a branch and withers; and the branches are gathered, thrown into the fire, and burned. (John 15:1–6 ESV)

Timothy, we've come full circle. We are back at the vineyard motif. Only this time, we are focused closely on the meaning of one tiny word in this passage: *airó*. Let's take a look.

As outlined previously, the basic elements of this 'I am' statement are pretty straightforward—individual believers are likened to individual branches of the collective vine of Christ, with God the Father as the vinedresser or husbandman. Although the details aren't entirely spelt out here, Jesus claims that somehow, at some point in time, the Divine Gardener would consider the productivity of individual members. The fruitful He would prune, while the fruitless He would *airó*.[169]

What does *airó* mean? What was Jesus intending to communicate?

When Words Have Multiple Meanings

A common meaning of *airó* is 'remove' or 'take away'. The New Testament, including the following passages in John, contains many occasions in which this appears to be the most obvious interpretation: 'The next day John saw Jesus coming toward him and said, "Look, the Lamb of God, who **takes away** the sin of the world!" ... To those who sold doves he said, "**Get these out of here!** Stop turning my Father's house into a market!" ... No one **takes it** from me, but I lay it down of my own accord ... If we let him go on like this, everyone will believe in him, and then the Romans will come and **take away** both our temple and our nation' (John 1:29; 2:16; 10:18; 11:48).

However, on other occasions, the same word communicates something quite different, when something is not taken *away*, but rather taken *up* from a lower to a higher place. In these cases, *airó* is commonly rendered 'to bear', 'carry' or 'pick up'. Again, from elsewhere in John: 'At once the man was cured; he **picked up** his mat and walked ... the Jewish leaders said to the man who had been healed, "It is the Sabbath; the law forbids you **to carry** your mat" ... At this, they **picked up** stones to stone him' (John 5:9–10; 8:59). This same word is also used by Luke when the disciples 'picked up' 12 basketfuls of food, when Jesus encouraged them to 'take up' their cross daily, when the 10 lepers 'lifted up' their voices, and when the sailing crew 'hoisted' a lifeboat back into their ship to ensure its safety (Luke 9:17; 9:23; 17:13; Acts 27:17).

In fact, in the story of Lazarus, *airó* is used twice in one verse, with both meanings inferred one after the other: 'So they **took away** the stone. And Jesus **lifted up** his eyes and said, "Father, I thank you that you have heard me"' (John 11:41 ESV). When Jesus prayed here, He did not 'take away' His eyes, nor did the funeral goers somehow 'lift up' the stone. True, the word can mean both these things, but to translate *airó* in these ways would be nonsensical and misleading. The stone was taken *away*, and Jesus' eyes were taken *up*. The one word has different meanings, depending on the context.

Evaluating the Options

This brings us back to John 15:2. The text here plainly states that the farmer of the true vine, God the Father, would *airó* every fruitless branch in Christ. We know that's what this Scripture says, but what does it *mean*?

Does it mean that God will *take away* these branches, removing them from Christ, their place in His community and—as a result—from the promise of life that is only to be found in union with Him? Or does it mean that He will *take up* these branches, lifting them from a lower to a higher place? After all, there are two things vine branches require to bear fruit: connection to a healthy vine and plenty of sunshine. This is one of the reasons grapevines are often splayed across a trellis. Without support, growing branches end up collapsing on the ground, in the dirt and under shade. They may be connected well enough, but without consistent exposure to the summer sun and proper aeration, vine branches have no hope of producing a healthy cluster of grapes. In this case, a fruitless branch does not need to be killed, but cared for. Not cut off, but coached—lifted up out of the dirt, given support and pointed towards the light.[170] Here is an alternate translation of the same passage:

> I am a true sprouting vine, and the farmer who tends the vine is my Father. He cares for the branches connected to me by **lifting and propping up** the fruitless branches and pruning every fruitful branch to yield a greater harvest. (John 15:1–2 TPT)[171]

Quite a different picture there, isn't it?

When it comes to the word *airó*, both 'take away' and 'take up' are accurate renderings, but only one of these accurately communicates the intended meaning of the author. So, which is it? What does the word *mean* in this context? Which message was the author hoping to communicate? That the Father would kill these branches, removing any hope of them ever bearing fruit into the future, where they are destined to be piled up and burnt with other deadwood? Or, that He would respond to their barren condition by caring for them, providing them with strength, guidance and hope for a better season to come? Which interpretation is most consistent with everything else the Bible has to say concerning the nature of the Father, His Gospel and what it is to be in covenantal union with Christ?

Consistency is Crucial

As I see it, the answer is elementary, my dear Timothy. On this particular issue, I will not leave you hanging. The consequences of your conclusions in this matter are far too critical for me to leave open to speculation. By all means, investigate it for yourself (that's the point, after all!), but in the meantime, after careful consideration of the Bible's corroborating content, here is Chad's current conviction. Permit me to enter preacher-mode.

Jesus delivered this true vine teaching as part of a lengthy departure speech, just prior to His death, to a group of committed Jewish disciples who would soon become the founding members of His new-covenant community. Later in this chapter, Jesus draws on the exodus motif, explaining how He had called them 'out of' the bondage of the old-covenant world to belong to Him (John 15:18–25). You see, at this time in history, believers like these had a choice as to which vine they would belong: the vine of Christ or the prevailing vine of old-covenant Israel; the new-covenant body of Christ, or the old-covenant body of Moses, in which they had previously been held as slaves to the law of sin and death. It was one or the other. They could not be joined to both. To be part of the new, they had to consider themselves dead to the old and, as when Lot left Sodom and as Israel passed through the Red Sea, refuse to turn back. As demonstrated that evening by Judas Iscariot, the temptation to turn would be real but needed to be resisted. After all, the old vine was on its way out. There was no life left for them there. As long as the option to return to the old was standing, these disciples would need be resolute in their commitment to 'abide' in the new. By choosing to remain identified with Christ, they were assured of a fruitful future and a faithful farmer-Father who would care for them in times of struggle, holding them in His hands and lifting them up towards the light.

As Paul articulates so clearly in Romans 8, I too am convinced that there is now no condemnation for those who are in Christ Jesus. God is for us, gave up His Son for us, and now—together with Christ—graciously provides us with all we need for life, godliness and fruitfulness. Who shall separate us from such a love? Nothing and no-one. Who shall condemn us or bring any charge against us? Certainly not Christ, who died for us. Nor the Father, who gladly justifies us. Indeed, nothing can cut us off from the love of God that is in Christ Jesus our Lord, including our seasons of apparent fruitlessness (Rom. 8:1–2, 31–39).

 Timothy, be assured today that He is a good, good farmer who tends to both His sheep and His branches with a compassionate heart and caring hands.

Allow Him to lift you up out of the dirt and darkness, attach you to supportive structures and point you towards the ever-shining light of the Son! Next time you're feeling down, discouraged or disheartened by your seeming lack of fruitfulness, rest assured that the Father will *airó* you. You may feel dejected, but you will not be rejected! Step out of the shade … and let the sun shine on you again!

Corroborating Content—Closing Comments

The Bible is a cohesive book containing complex but consistently compatible truths, awaiting discovery by your inquisitive investigation. However, before reaching a conviction on a critical theological concern, clarify and confirm your conclusions by compiling considerable corroborating evidence, drawn from a collection of comparable and complementary biblical content.

Let everything be established by the testimony of two or three witnesses. Allow the Scripture to explain itself. Use the Bible as its own interpreter.

Style of Speech

We complete our study on the ABCS of exegesis by addressing the all-important matter of *sensus literalis*, the consideration of the *style of speech* employed by the biblical authors.[172] Here we acknowledge that parables are to be read as parables, prose as prose, poetry as poetry and prophetic symbols as prophetically symbolic. The Bible is, after all, a work of literature in which the various authors employ various literary genres and various literary devices to deliver various truths to their various audiences. Therefore, readers are to approach the Bible like they would any other form of literature. The Scriptures are to be understood in the sense in which they were written.

Thankfully, most Bible content is presented in a plain, straightforward and matter-of-fact manner. By and large, the biblical authors simply say it as it is. When we are told that Jesus was born in Bethlehem, baptised in the Jordan, betrayed by Judas and beaten by the Romans, there is little doubt that the Gospel writers intended these truths be taken at face value. Similarly, when He is said to have healed the sick, walked on water, fed the multitudes and risen from death, we are to understand these stories as literal, historical

and factual accounts and interpret them in accordance with the plain and obvious sense.

Yet often, the biblical authors deviate from so-called plain-speak to communicate with *non-literal language*, utilising forms and figures of speech that were never intended to be taken literally.

In this section we discuss the following:

> Interpreting the Text Literarily
>
> Jesus' Parabolic Propensities
>
> How to Detect Non-Literal Language

My repeated refrain throughout, is this: you can take the Scriptures *seriously* without having to take them all *literally*. In many cases, a non-literal reading is precisely what the biblical authors intended.

CHAPTER 32

Interpreting the Text Literarily

Consider this selection of outlandish statements from David's Psalms:

> Do all these evildoers know nothing? They devour my people as though eating bread … men whose teeth are spears and arrows, whose tongues are sharp swords … My heart has turned to wax; it has melted within me … I am a worm and not a man … Keep me as the apple of your eye; hide me in the shadow of your wings … He makes me lie down in green pastures … the hills are clothed with gladness. The meadows are covered with flocks and the valleys are mantled with grain; they shout for joy and sing. (Ps. 14:4; 57:4; 22:14, 6; 17:8; 23:2; 65:12–13)

Allow me to state the obvious here—these evildoers were not cannibals with swords for tongues. David's heart did not literally turn to wax, nor was he, at any point, transformed into a worm. God is not a bird, nor does His eye contain apples. Hills cannot be happy, meadows cannot shout and valleys cannot sing. Even if they could, God never forced David to lie down in one.

No matter what is said on the surface, neither God nor David ever intended for these statements to be taken literally. Songwriters throughout history and across all cultures are famous for employing emotive, metaphoric and overstated language to communicate their point and affect their audiences, using poetic words to paint powerful pictures. King David is no exception.

The content of his psalms is to be understood in accordance with the sense in which they were written—not literally, in many cases, but rather *literarily*. We are to interpret these statements *according to the style of literature* in which they are presented.

Our Bible contains many types of non-literal verbiage, including euphemism, colloquialism, conundrum and riddles, allegory, typology, poetry and idioms, metaphor, irony, rhetoric and pun, parables, paradox and exaggeration. Combine these with the use of literary devices such as chiasm and inclusion, anthropomorphism and personification, atbash, gematria, acrostic alliteration and poetic parallelism and before long, one can easily feel overwhelmed by this task!

 Tammy, let's keep this simple. Taking the Scriptures seriously does not necessarily mean we must take the Scriptures literally.

At times, the biblical authors communicate in a very matter-of-fact style, in which they say what they mean and mean precisely what they say. However, at other times, they deliberately use figures of speech, by which what they say is not intended to be taken literally. Your task is to discern the difference, and the more you grow familiar with the Bible and the basic lessons we will learn here, the easier this will become.

At this point, many books on hermeneutics begin to detail the Bible's varied literary categories, such as poetry and wisdom, prophecy and apocalypse, Hebrew narrative and court tales, first-century Gospels, Epistles and many, many more. The ability to recognise such genres and understand their distinctives, primary purpose and typical characteristics can prove invaluable to the exegetical success of the serious Bible student, especially when it comes to awareness of non-literal communication. That said, I am not about to reinvent that wheel.[173]

The fact is, non-literal speech is used *all through the Bible*, even in books that consist predominantly of historical narrative and straightforward prose. Figures of speech are woven throughout the full scope of the Scripture in every book, from every author, within every genre. And Jesus—the Word of God Himself—is one of the biggest culprits.

CHAPTER 33

Jesus' Parabolic Propensities

Jesus' consistent use of non-literal language created a great deal of trouble for Him during His earthly ministry. Even today, it is the cause of many a misunderstanding. In this chapter we'll take a brief look at some examples from John's Gospel in which Jesus' audiences, from all persuasions, clearly mistook His meaning, not realising He was using figures of speech.[174]

Rebuilding in Record Time

> Jesus answered them, '**Destroy this temple, and I will raise it again in three days**.' They replied, 'It has taken forty-six years to build this temple, and you are going to raise it in three days?' (John 2:19–20)

This statement, or variations of it, was later used against Jesus during both His trial and crucifixion (Matt. 26:61; 27:40). Considering the temple of first-century Jerusalem was one of the great wonders of the ancient world—the construction of which took decades, was financed by Rome and required a labour force of thousands—Christ's claim that He, a solitary carpenter's son, could rebuild it within 72 hours was delusional! Providing He was speaking literally, of course.

Only after His resurrection did the disciples understand what He had actually meant—that '**the temple he had spoken of was his body**' (John 2:21).

This case also shows us that the Bible's use of figurative language is not necessarily an all-or-nothing affair. While the reference to 'this temple' was clearly figurative, the term 'three days' literally meant three days.[175]

Rebirthing a Full-Grown Man

> Jesus replied, 'Very truly I tell you, **no one can see the kingdom of God unless they are born again.**' 'How can someone be born when they are old?' Nicodemus asked. 'Surely they cannot enter a second time into their mother's womb to be born!' (John 3:3–4)

It is unclear whether Nicodemus was being sarcastic or truly serious when providing this preposterous proposition. Either way, I would so love to have been there to witness Jesus' response! Was our Lord amused or bemused at the Pharisee's reply? Did He restrain Himself from laughing or perhaps offer a discreet eye-roll to His disciples, outwardly polite, no doubt, but internally 'face-palming' Himself at Nicodemus' ridiculous reaction?

O, the possibilities!

Sadly, however, Nicodemus was unable, or perhaps unwilling, to see beyond the physical realm and appreciate the profound spiritual realities Christ was attempting to communicate. Jesus' exhortation to be 'born again' was lost on this esteemed teacher, who failed to think beyond the realm of the flesh. But Nicodemus was certainly not alone in this. Time and again, the religious leaders and teachers of the day, despite being trained in the language of Hebrew idiom and metaphor, were often clueless when Jesus spoke to them:

> Jesus used this **figure of speech**, but the Pharisees did not understand what he was telling them. (John 10:6)

There are several reasons the Jewish leaders often missed Jesus' point, but for our purposes, the takeaway is this: if these men, living at the same time, within the same culture, speaking the same language and educated in the same religious system could so easily misunderstand the teachings of Christ, how much more today are those within the Bible-believing community at risk of mistaking His metaphorical meaning?

A Water to Quench All Thirst

Now to someone outside the Jewish community—a woman from Samaria. How would she fare with Jesus' propensity to speak parabolically?

> Jesus answered, 'Everyone who drinks this water will be thirsty again, **but whoever drinks the water I give them will never thirst**. Indeed, the water I give them will become in them a spring of water welling up to eternal life.' The woman said to him, 'Sir, give me this water so that I won't get thirsty and have to keep coming here to draw water.' (John 4:13–15)

While her response obviously exposes this lady's misreading of Jesus' point, I do admire her respectful tone towards Him. Consider the audacity of a man asking this poor woman to draw water for Him in the heat of the day, only to tell her that He already had an endless self-supply!

That aside, again we see Jesus reference a physical reality to illustrate a mystical truth. The water Jesus promised was not two-parts hydrogen, one-part oxygen. Rather, 'by this he meant the Spirit whom those who believed in him were later to receive' (John 7:37–40).

Not quite grasping His meaning at first, this Samaritan woman experienced a piercing clarity in Jesus' words as He proceeded to read her mail in regards her personal life, marital history and current living arrangements. At this, she declared Him to be a prophet.[176]

And just to be clear, when I say Jesus 'read her mail', I mean that figuratively.

Feeding on God's Work

> Meanwhile his disciples urged him, 'Rabbi, eat something.' But he said to them, '**I have food to eat that you know nothing about**.' Then his disciples said to each other, 'Could someone have brought him

food?' 'My food,' said Jesus, 'is to do the will of him who sent me and to finish his work'. (John 4:31–34)

Here is an example in which Jesus immediately *explains* His use of figurative language when it is obvious His friends have not understood Him. We observe something similar a few chapters later, when the disciples mistakenly thought that Jesus' statement, 'Lazarus has fallen asleep; but I am going there to wake him up', meant that Lazarus had simply taken a nap (John 11:11–14).[177]

Wrong again, lads.

Jesus employs this same modus operandi repeatedly in the Synoptics, in which He is noted as speaking parabolically in public, to 'those on the outside', but then plainly to those in private. To those nearest to Him, Jesus would often explain His parables to ensure they understood the point.[178]

However, not everyone was privy to such commentary. In fact, it seems that for most of His audience, Jesus was very much at peace with having them misunderstand His style of speech.

Christ's Call to Cannibalism

I am the living bread that came down from heaven. Whoever eats this bread will live forever. This bread is my flesh ... **unless you eat the flesh of the Son of Man and drink his blood, you have no life in you** ... [for] my flesh is real food and my blood is real drink. (John 6:30–66)

Advocating for cannibalism now, Jesus? That's going to go down well!

Understandably, these statements caused a great ruckus among the congregation in Capernaum that day, and deeply unsettled a great number of Jesus' so-called disciples. In fact, many disavowed Him because of this message, or rather, because they *misunderstood* this message.

Jesus, clearly, did not intend these words to be taken literally, and yet neither did He feel the need to explain Himself to these fickle followers. In fact,

He seemed quite content with having this particular group misinterpret this 'hard teaching' and, as a consequence, 'no longer follow him' (John 6:60–66). Here stands a man whose confidence does not lie in the praises of the mob.

Fast forward to the end of His ministry and Jesus says to His friends over a Passover meal, 'Though I have been speaking figuratively, a time is coming when I will no longer use this kind of language but will tell you plainly about my Father'. To which His disciples replied, 'Now you are speaking clearly and without figures of speech' (John 16:25, 29).

After all the problems His parabolic propensities had caused them, I am sure this news was received that night with a great sigh of relief! However, these disciples still had time to wait before the coming of the straight-talking Spirit—the 24 hours preceding His death would be loaded with non-literal lingo.

A Passion Pop Quiz

Alright Tammy, it's time for a pop quiz, and a little change of pace. Grab a pen, and let's get cracking.

Below are 10 statements spoken by Jesus towards the end of Passion Week, in the lead up to His death.[179] Your task is simple: mark each statement as literal or non-literal. Did Jesus mean precisely what He said, or was He employing a figure of speech?

1. 'As you enter the city, a man carrying a jar of water will meet you. Follow him to the house that he enters … He will show you a large room upstairs, all furnished.'

   Literal / Non-Literal

2. While they were eating, Jesus took bread, and when he had given thanks, he broke it and gave it to his disciples, saying, 'Take and eat; this is my body.' Then he took a cup, and when he had given thanks, he gave it to them, saying, 'Drink from it, all of you. This is my blood.'

   Literal / Non-Literal

3. While they were reclining at the table eating, he said, 'Truly I tell you, one of you will betray me—one who is eating with me.'

   Literal / Non-Literal

4. 'Simon, Simon, Satan has asked to sift all of you as wheat.'

   Literal / Non-Literal

5. Jesus answered, 'I tell you, Peter, before the rooster crows today, you will deny three times that you know me.'

   Literal / Non-Literal

6. Going a little farther, he fell with his face to the ground and prayed, 'My Father, if it is possible, may this cup be taken from me.'

   Literal / Non-Literal

7. Again the high priest asked him, 'Are you the Messiah, the Son of the Blessed One?' 'I am,' said Jesus. 'And you will see the Son of Man sitting at the right hand of the Mighty One and coming on the clouds of heaven.'

   Literal / Non-Literal

8. Jesus turned and said to them, 'Daughters of Jerusalem, do not weep for me; weep for yourselves and for your children. For the time will come when you will say, "Blessed are the childless women, the wombs that never bore and the breasts that never nursed!" Then they will say to the mountains, "Fall on us!" and to the hills, "Cover us!" For if people do these things when the tree is green, what will happen when it is dry?'

   Literal / Non-Literal

9. Jesus answered him, 'Truly I tell you, today you will be with me in paradise.'

   Literal / Non-Literal

10. When Jesus saw his mother there, and the disciple whom he loved standing nearby, he said to her, 'Woman, here is your son,' and to the disciple, 'Here is your mother.'

Literal / Non-Literal

Pens down. Time's up. Tell me, how did you go?

I'll be releasing the answers sometime soon. Of course, don't take my promise of 'soon' too literally. I may take longer than you think.

Fun aside, I trust my point here is clear enough. None of the examples provided above are considered parables or poetry, nor do they appear in what would be deemed prophetic books. While non-literal language is certainly more prevalent in some genres over others, the fact remains that figures of speech can be found throughout the entire Bible, as the Word made Flesh frequently demonstrates.

 Be alert, Tammy, and remember, you can take God's Word seriously, without taking it all literally.

In the next chapter, we'll explore five helpful ways to detect and discern the difference.

How to Detect Non-Literal Language

In this section—*Style of Speech*—we are discussing the importance of understanding the Bible's content literarily: that is, in accordance with the sense and style of the literature in which it is presented. While, for the most part, the biblical authors speak plainly, there are many instances in which they employ non-literal language as part of their communication. Our job is to detect and discern when this is the case. Here are five practical ways we can do just that.

1. The Bible Says So

> By faith Abraham, when he was tested, offered up Isaac ... He considered that God was able even to raise him from the dead, from which, **figuratively speaking, he did receive him back**. (Heb. 11:17–19 ESV)

We'll start with the easy one.

At times, the Bible itself will issue a warning that non-literal language is on its way. It is common for the Gospel writers, for instance, to prepare you in advance with the caveat: 'Jesus told them another parable' (Matt. 13:3, 24, 31, 33–34). Similar precursors are found occasionally in the Prophets: 'The word of the Lord came to me: "Son of man, **set forth an allegory** and tell it to the Israelites as a parable. Say to them, 'This is what the Sovereign Lord says'" (Ezek. 17:1–3).

Old and New Testaments frequently employ the use of *simile*, a figure of speech by which two things are compared using the words 'like' or 'as'. While similar to a *metaphor*, similes have the added benefit of explicitly presenting themselves as illustrative. For example, when David declares in Psalm 22: '**Roaring lions** that tear their prey open their mouths wide against me', it is not immediately clear whether he is speaking literally or figuratively. Did David really have a run-in with roaring lions? Conversely, in Psalm 17, he employs the preposition 'like', removing all doubt that in this case, the ravenous lions were wicked men: 'They are **like a lion** hungry for prey, **like** a fierce lion crouching in cover … rescue me from **the wicked**. By your hand save me from such **people**' (Ps. 22:13; 17:12–14).

That said, sometimes an author will use metaphor (or its expanded form, *allegory*) and plainly tell you so. This from the apostle Paul:

> For it is written that Abraham had two sons, one by a slave woman and one by a free woman … **Now this may be interpreted allegorically: these women are two covenants** … Hagar is Mount Sinai in Arabia; she corresponds to the present Jerusalem, for she is in slavery with her children. But the Jerusalem above is free, and she is our mother. (Gal. 4:22–26 ESV)

Since the apostle is addressing a group of primarily Gentile believers whose familiarity with the Old Testament stories would have been somewhat negligible (and who had a reputation for not being too bright!), Paul wisely explains his use of allegory before launching into the illustration. Thus, he prepares them to receive his point.

In a somewhat related text in Revelation, a book awash with apocalyptic allegory, John also makes clear his use of metaphoric language: 'And their bodies will lie in the main street of Jerusalem, the city that is **figuratively called** "Sodom" and "Egypt," the city where their Lord was crucified' (Rev. 11:8 NLT). While a great deal of the symbolism in Revelation is left open for reader interpretation, in this case, John makes it clear that his reference to

Jerusalem as 'Sodom' was figurative.[180]

Who knows? Perhaps he thought it would soften the blow a bit: 'No offence, but you're kind of like Sodom. You know … *figuratively* speaking'.

2. Use Common Sense

Seems to me like common sense is becoming increasingly less commonplace, and the Christian community is certainly not exempt from this phenomenon. As a member of the so-called charismatic evangelical wing of the church, I've witnessed many a believer kiss their brain goodbye and leave it at the proverbial door! Jokes aside, this is a serious issue. Too many precious people have been unnecessarily deterred from Christ and His Gospel in response to the weird conduct and wild claims of Christians who have neglected to apply rationality and logic to their Bible reading. While Jesus encouraged His disciples to 'become like little children', Paul later clarifies that principle: 'stop thinking like children. In regard to evil be infants, but **in your thinking be adults**' (Matt. 18:3; 1 Cor. 14:20). There's a big difference between childlike innocence and childish ignorance. Remember that, Timothy.

Common sense demands that Jesus' instructions to cut off one's hands or gouge out a wandering eye were *hyperbolic* statements intended to be taken seriously, but not literally. His claim that a left hand could 'know' what a right hand was doing is anatomically impossible, but illustratively, it is powerful. Christ claimed to be a gate, and yet had no hinges; a shepherd, who owned no sheep. He called Peter 'Satan' and Judas a 'devil', the Syrophoenician woman a 'dog', King Herod a 'fox' and the Pharisees 'snakes' who 'strain out a gnat but swallow a camel'. Each of these statements is undeniably metaphoric, as the Teacher communicates a point with imagery commonly understood by the audience of the day.[181]

When the psalmist declared that the sun 'knows when to go down', that rivers 'clap their hands … the mountains sing together for joy', and Isaiah that 'the mountains and hills will burst into song … and all the trees of the field will clap their hands' (Ps. 104:19; 98:8; Isa. 55:12), they were not claiming that rivers and trees possess hands, mountains a literal voice or the sun knowledge of its descent!

Similarly, when the prophets foretold a day when the moon would be turned to blood, devour the people and be brought to shame by God's glorious reign, common sense demands a non-literal interpretation of these claims. That big old rock in the night sky does not feel emotion nor does it have an appetite for humans. It is no more reasonable to take these predictions literally than it is to suggest that the moon would be placed under a woman's feet or bow down to the dreamer Joseph.[182] This is prophetic language, rich in symbolism and hyperbole, designed to engage the imagination of one's audience while pointing them towards another reality altogether.

At Mount Carmel, when the prophets of Baal failed to call down fire on the altar, Elijah did not genuinely believe the god they worshipped was daydreaming, on holiday or stuck on the toilet. Saul's daughter Michal did not really think David had 'distinguished himself' by dancing exuberantly before the Lord, nor did Amos truly want the Israelites to go to Bethel and sin—'to Gilgal and sin yet more' (1 Kings 18:27; 1 Sam. 6:20; Amos 4:4). Yes, that's what they *said* … but it's clearly not what they *meant*. As Homer Simpson once famously quipped, 'O, by the way, I was being sarcastic'.

Believe me, when it comes to interpreting the Scriptures, a little common sense can go a long way.

3. Query Coincidence and Recurrences

> Know therefore that the LORD your God is God; he is the faithful God, keeping his covenant of love to **a thousand generations** … May the Lord, the God of your ancestors, increase you **a thousand times** … Finding a fresh jawbone of a donkey, he grabbed it and struck down **a thousand men** … for every animal of the forest is mine, and the cattle on **a thousand hills** … Better is one day in your courts than **a thousand elsewhere** … With the Lord a day is like **a thousand years**. (Deut. 7:9; 1:11; Judg. 15:15; Ps. 50:10; 84:10; 2 Peter 3:8)

I'm just going to come right out and say it: I like numbers. Whether it's a natural part of my temperament, or a result of childhood tutoring by Sesame Street's Count von Count ('I love to count!'), numbers grab my attention.

My office phone number ends in '6-7-8-9'. My wife's number includes a '7-7-7' and mine a '1-2-3-4'. Believe me, this is no accident. I requested these sequences! When I registered my current motor vehicle, I had the customer service agent hand me the box of identity plates. I chose one ending in '1-1-2', a constant reminder of one of my favourite psalms.

Numbers matter to me. And not in a superstitious or pseudo-spiritual way. I just like them. And so too, it seems, does God.

When constructing ways to communicate divine mysteries to man, God decided to include numerals in His vocabulary. The Bible is full of them and a good number of those numbers are not intended to be interpreted literally. While there is no foolproof formula to determine which equations

Gematria: Does the Bible Speak in Code?

Ever noticed how the New Testament opens with a strange numeric coincidence? 'This is the genealogy of Jesus the Messiah the son of David … there were fourteen generations in all from Abraham to David, fourteen from David to the exile to Babylon, and fourteen from the exile to the Messiah' (Matt. 1:1–17). Compare this Gospel list with the Old Testament genealogies and you will soon discover a discrepancy in accounts. The numbers don't match. Which begs the question: what was Matthew trying to achieve by presenting the genealogy of Christ in three sets of 14? Could this number hold significance and meaning beyond straightforward maths?

There are two ways in which we English speakers write our numerals. We either use number names (e.g., twelve) or digits (e.g., 12). Likewise, the biblical languages employed either number names (e.g., Hebrew: שְׁנֵים-עָשָׂר / Greek: δώδεκα), or digit-equivalents—the Hebrews used hieratic and Aramaic numerals, the Greeks, acrophonic symbols (e.g., ΔΙΙ).

But both cultures also employed a *third* method: alphabetic numerals. In this system each letter of the existing alphabet was issued a corresponding numerical value (e.g., A=1, B=2, C=3 etc). When communicating a number, scribes would simply add a tiny accent-stroke above the letters. For compound numbers a series of letters were written together, much like a word. It was then the task of the reader to add up each of the letter-values and arrive at a total figure (e.g., 'cab' would mean '6': 3+1+2).

Which brings us back to Jesus' genealogy. It has been suggested that the author

YOU CAN HANDLE THE TRUTH

are literal and which are not, my advice here is simple: when you encounter a numerical coincidence or recurring sequence, stop and consider whether the author is communicating something other than straightforward maths:

> Later Peter approached Jesus and said, 'How many times do I have to forgive my fellow believer who keeps offending me? Seven times?' Jesus answered, 'Not seven times, Peter, but **seventy times seven times**!' (Matt. 18:21–22 TPT)

I trust you don't need a calculator to work this one out but just in case you missed it, Jesus here instructs Peter to forgive his offending brother a total of 490 times. Not 5 or 6 times, not 28, 114 or 372 … no. For brotherly forgiveness to truly count, the mandated number from our Lord is precisely 490. No more, and certainly no less. This is providing of course, that Jesus was intending to be understood literally.

here is employing a somewhat clandestine form of communication known as Jewish *gematria* (or Greek *isopsephy*), where the conspicuous presentation of a number is intended to draw the reader's attention to a word or phrase with the same value. If this be the case, Matthew's repeated use of 'fourteen' is most likely a reference to the name 'David'. In Hebrew script, David contained three letters (דוד) with the values four, six and four (4+6+4=14). The number 14 was David's name-number, and a Jewish audience would not have missed it.

The most speculated application of this practice, whether John intended it or not, concerns the book of Revelation: 'This calls for wisdom: let the one who has understanding calculate the number of the beast, for it is the number of a man, and his number is 666' (Rev. 13:18 ESV).

Over the centuries, keen Bible interpreters have turned to gematria in order to identify a hidden name behind this notorious number. Early proposals vary widely from Roman Caesar Nero, whose Hebraic letters add up to 666; Emperor Diocletian, when calculated in Latin; and the Roman people, with Greek. Even Martin Luther and the Catholic Pope have been offered as candidates, using Roman numerals. A fascinating product of the Reformation's war-of-words.

One doesn't need to read far beyond Moses to realise that certain numbers receive frequent and conspicuous airplay in our Bibles, in particular 3, 4, 5, 7, 10, 12 and combinations thereof. The Torah explicitly and repeatedly associates these numbers with Israel's creation story, genealogies, tribes, festivals and calendar, her tabernacle, law, religious rites, offerings, sacrifices and wilderness wanderings. Engrained in Hebrew culture by recurring sets and sequences, these numbers gained special significance in the psyche of God's covenant community.

So, later, when we read that Job, for example: 'had seven sons and three daughters ... seven thousand sheep, three thousand camels, five hundred yoke of oxen and five hundred donkeys', we can either marvel at the profound coincidence of these neatly presented figures, or alternatively pause to consider whether they serve an other-than-literal purpose (Job 1:2–3).[183] When we note the significant quantity of Israel's leaders who were said to have governed for a 'forty year' period (including Moses, Othinel, Deborah, Gideon, Eli, kings Saul, David, Solomon, and Joash in Judah), it is not unreasonable to query whether 40 in these cases is presented as a round figure, associated perhaps with the idea of a 'generation', rather than as a precise dating mechanism.[184] Recurring number patterns like these are present throughout the entire scope of the Scripture, literally, from Genesis to Revelation.

Genesis 5 presents the genealogy of Adam through to Noah and contains 26 unique numbers, each a multiple of 5 or a multiple of 5 + 7. What are the chances of that! Is this mere coincidence? Did Enoch literally live to 365 (a number associated with a solar year), Lamech to the remarkable age of 777 and Adam to 930, precisely 70 years short of 1,000? Or is Moses attempting to communicate something other than a literal biological lifespan?[185] And what of John's '1000-year' reign of Christ, his redeemed company of 144,000 (12^2 by 10^3) and the so-called heavenly Jerusalem with her 12 gates of 12 pearls guarded by 12 angels, a wall 12-squared cubits thick with 12 foundations made of 12 precious stones, defining a space 12,000 stadia high, 12,000 wide and 12,000 long, and housing the Tree of Life as it bears 12 crops of fruit 12 months of the year.[186]

What are we to make of these recurring sequences? Are these measurements supposed to be understood as literal and physical, or is John employing symbolic language to communicate something of theological, spiritual or covenantal significance? Is the new Jerusalem truly a golden cube, or is this merely God's way of associating it with the most holy place in Solomon's temple, built as a cube and overlaid with pure gold (1 Kings 6:20)?

Perhaps I should clarify that I am by no means encouraging you to view every number in Scripture as somehow symbolic, cryptic or indicative of something else, nor am I asking you to question whether the numbers in the Bible are accurate or doubt the inerrancy of the Holy Text. My point is that numbers, like any other words, can be used to communicate other-than-literal meanings. At times, numbers are intentionally employed for non-numeric purposes.[187]

 Tammy, if I've said it once, I've said it a thousand times: you can take the Scriptures seriously, without having to take them all literally.

Our task is to interpret the Bible's facts and figures according to the sense in which they were written. Should any of the examples provided above have unsettled you, please forgive me.

Then, forgive me again ... 489 times more.

4. Compare the Poetic with the Plain

> **He rebuked the Red Sea**, and it became dry, and he led them through the deep as through a desert ... God, when the waters saw you, they were afraid ...The sea looked and fled ... the deep gave forth its voice; it lifted its hands on high ... **At the blast of your nostrils the waters piled up**. (Ps. 106:9; 77:16; 114:3; Hab. 3:10; Ex. 15:8 ESV)

It is said that there are many ways to skin a cat and, so it seems, there are many ways to recount a story. I'm not sure exactly how *you* believe Yahweh went about parting the Red Sea, but according to Moses, God simply blew

His nose. Can't argue with Moses now, can we? He was there to witness it firsthand.

Earlier, we examined the importance of collecting and corroborating biblical content, allowing that which is clear to bring clarity to the obscure. When it comes to discerning non-literal lingo in the biblical text, the same principle applies. Allow the plain to shed light on the poetic. Allow the obvious to explain the outlandish. Case in point, David's Song of Deliverance:

> In my distress I called to the Lord; I called out to my God. From his temple he heard my voice; my cry came to his ears. The earth trembled and quaked, the foundations of the heavens shook; they trembled because he was angry. Smoke rose from his nostrils; consuming fire came from his mouth, burning coals blazed out of it. He parted the heavens and came down; dark clouds were under his feet. He mounted the cherubim and flew; he soared on the wings of the wind. He made darkness his canopy around him—the dark rain clouds of the sky. Out of the brightness of his presence bolts of lightning blazed forth. The Lord thundered from heaven; the voice of the Most High resounded. He shot his arrows and scattered the enemy, with great bolts of lightning he routed them. The valleys of the sea were exposed and the foundations of the earth laid bare at the rebuke of the Lord, at the blast of breath from his nostrils. He reached down from on high and took hold of me; he drew me out of deep waters. (2 Sam. 22:7–17)[188]

The Bible says that David wrote this psalm to commemorate the Lord's delivery of him from his enemies, including King Saul (2 Sam. 22:1). These wars, together with the persecution and trouble he experienced from Saul and his supporters, are presented plainly in the books of Samuel and Chronicles. Read David's battle stories in these narrative books and you'll discover something quite significant: nowhere do they mention God delivering David by parting the heavens and coming down on a cloud. There is no mention at all of angelic activity, earthquakes, thundering voices or burning coals. The narrative accounts make no reference whatsoever to God riding on wind, spewing fire, blasting His nostrils, shooting arrows or blazing bolts of lightning from the brightness of His presence. Nowhere do they mention David ever drowning.

The reason for this is that *these things never actually happened.* Not literally at least, and certainly not physically, audibly or visibly. This psalm, like many from King David, is replete with vivid, dramatic and exaggerated language. As a Hebrew prophet, he draws on the Songs of Moses and the language of God's appearance at Sinai to describe how God worked behind the scenes to conquer his political opponents. In other words, God would move heavens and earth to secure His king's success.[189]

As time progresses, the language of *cosmic disruption* becomes part and parcel of prophetic poetry, particularly when announcing the downfall of one nation at the hands of another. In the Prophets, it is common to see a military defeat, or destruction of a city, described in terms of the sun being darkened, the moon losing its light, the stars falling or no longer shining and the heavens and earth trembling.[190] When Jeremiah foresees the Babylonian destruction of Jerusalem, he draws on the language of Genesis 1 to describe how the Kingdom of Judah would be returned to a pre-creation state:

> Look! He advances like the clouds, his chariots come like a whirlwind … **I looked at the earth, and it was formless and empty; and at the heavens, and their light was gone**. I looked at the mountains, and they were quaking; all the hills were swaying. I looked, and there were no people; every bird in the sky had flown away. I looked, and the fruitful land was a desert; all its towns lay in ruins. (Jer. 4:13–26)

When compared with the straightforward narrative accounts of these military conquests in Kings and Chronicles, it is clear that none of these colossal cosmic catastrophes ever literally happened. These prophecies proved accurate and their predictions were fulfilled, but they were never intended to be understood literally. This kind of language is essentially the Prophets' way of declaring 'lights out!' for a particular regime.

The point is, once you establish a precedent differentiating 'poetic-speak' and plain-speak, you will find yourself better positioned to recognise similar language elsewhere. This is especially helpful where the Bible does not have a corresponding narrative that can bring clarity to a particular prophecy.

For example, when Jesus predicts a time when '"the sun will be darkened, and the moon will not give its light; the stars will fall from the sky, and the heavenly bodies will be shaken" … when they see the Son of Man coming on the clouds' (Matt. 24:29–30), your mind should be alert to the possibility that He is foretelling some kind of military defeat, not the obliteration of our earth and its solar system as a literal reading would suggest.[191] Similarly, when we see John witness the opening of the sixth seal resulting in an earthquake, a darkened sun and blood-red moon, the stars falling to earth, receding heavens like a scroll and the removal of 'every mountain and island' from its place (Rev. 6:12–16), your symbolic language detector should be going wild!

Knowing what we do from the Old Testament, it seems likely that in both cases, John and Jesus are borrowing terms straight from their prophetic forebears. Observing how this kind of language was used in the past could prove invaluable as we consider whether these similar-sounding predictions in the New Testament are intended to be understood literally or figuratively. After all, if every mountain was removed from its place, why would the kings of the earth seek to find solace in them? And how would our planet even survive a darkened sun or the impact from falling stars in the first place?

The Bible says what it means, but it doesn't always mean what it says. If you come across a text that seems overstated or outlandish, allow the plain to explain.[192]

5. Learn from Others

> Then Philip ran up to the chariot and heard the man reading Isaiah the prophet. 'Do you understand what you are reading?' Philip asked. 'How can I,' he said, '**unless someone explains it to me?**' So he invited Philip to come up and sit with him. (Acts 8:30–31)

I cannot think of a better way to close this discussion than by encouraging you to engage your second toolkit—*The Saints*. When it comes to detecting the Bible's use of non-literal language, make it your business to draw on the expertise of others.

Without doubt, your personal ability to discern figures of speech will improve as your familiarity with the Bible increases. Identifying literary genre is, for the most part, an intuitive exercise, especially when it is one common to your own culture. For example, when a story begins with the phrase, 'Once upon a time', you recognise immediately that what follows is most likely a work of fiction directed to children. When a line of text reads with a discernible rhythm and rhyme ('There was a young lady of Niger, who smiled as she rode on a tiger'), the English speaker realises instinctively that humour and hyperbole are on the horizon. These styles of speech are well known to us.

Conversely, the Bible, as a work of ancient literature, contains forms, fashions and figures of speech unfamiliar to the modern reader. To succeed in your exegesis, sometimes you'll need to consult the experts—those who have dedicated the best part of their lives to learning the language of the Bible and studying the world from which it emerged. Commentators and professors, both Jewish and Christian, formally trained theologians, academics and dedicated students of the Scriptures have published articles, papers, doctorates, books and commentaries exploring and explaining these issues. Allow their studies to inform and enhance your own.[193] Purchasing a good study Bible is the best and simplest place to begin.

This is particularly the case with the Bible's use of *idiom*. A colloquial phrase communicating figurative meaning, idioms use words and terms entirely unrelated to the subject matter. English contains thousands of idioms and are par for the course in everyday communication. Were a friend to tell me to 'break a leg' before I was to preach, I would take that as a word of encouragement. Afterwards, were they to claim that I 'was on fire, totally killed it, knocked the ball out of the park and brought the house down', I would accept these comments as complimentary. On the surface, none of these statements seem to have anything to do with the art of preaching. If interpreted literally, I would be deeply concerned as to my friend's opinion of both myself and my ministry, but, understood in the sense in which they were given—idiomatically—I would feel greatly supported by these sentiments.

A few biblical idioms are still in use today, so we tend to read over them without a second thought: 'See, I have placed before you an open door ... pray for us, too, that God may open a door for our message' (Rev. 3:8; Col. 4:3).[194] An open door speaks, of course, of an opportunity or positive possibility.

Some biblical idioms, despite not being commonplace today, are simple enough to discern on our own with a little thought. When the Lord said of Israel at Sinai: 'they are a stiff-necked people' (Exo. 32:9), He coined what would become a common Hebrew idiom, denoting stubbornness.[195] How may a stiff neck communicate stubbornness, you may ask? The Bible itself does not explicitly say, but knowing this was spoken in an age in which farmers would drive animals, requiring them to turn the animals' necks to change direction, we can deduce that perhaps this is what God had in mind. Like a stubborn mule or obstinate ox, Israel's defiant refusal to turn their behaviour around, face another direction and change course would become known as them being 'stiff-necked'.

Speaking of oxen, consider this obscure reference from the testimony of Paul:

> About noon, King Agrippa, as I was on the road, I saw a light from heaven, brighter than the sun, blazing around me and my companions. We all fell to the ground, and I heard a voice saying to me in Aramaic, 'Saul, Saul, why do you persecute me? **It is hard for you to kick against the goads.**' Then I asked, 'Who are you, Lord?' 'I am Jesus, whom you are persecuting,' the Lord replied. (Acts 26:13–15)

Tell me, when was the last time Jesus brought up the futility of goad-kicking in conversation with you? I'd say ... likely never. Idioms like these are so entirely foreign to our culture that they remain largely undetected by the average Bible reader, or we just read over them dismissively, immediately recognising it is something we will simply never understand. This is when the input of others is invaluable.

Were it not for somebody else putting in the hard yards researching first-century Jewish culture, I would never have known that Jesus was employing an everyday idiom on generosity when He claimed that if 'your **eyes are healthy**, your whole body will be full of light' (Matt. 6:22).[196] Had others not told me that the priests who served in the temple would take imperfect salt from the storehouse, deemed unworthy of being used on the holy offerings, and throw it on the steep ramps leading up to the altar to stop their feet from slipping, I may never have understood what Jesus meant when He claimed that if His followers became salt that was tasteless (a play on words from the Greek for 'foolish': *mórainó*), they would be 'trampled underfoot'. This metaphor indicated that if His disciples remained committed to Him, they would have the honour of giving their life as a burning sacrifice for His glory, but if instead they turned dull, they would suffer the indignity of simply being ignored (Matt. 5:13).[197]

I am especially indebted to our modern Bible translators who, particularly with the thought-for-thought varieties, not only research but then *remove* certain colloquialisms altogether, replacing them with phrases that convey a comparable modern meaning. In this way, 'I will cut off from Ahab him that **pisseth against the wall**' from the KJV, becomes 'I will destroy every one of his **male** descendants' in the NLT (2 Kings 9:8).

Translators frequently take the same approach to *euphemisms*—figures of speech used to soften the edges of a subject considered socially awkward or unpleasant, such as those related to the bedroom, bathroom and bereavement. Thus, 'Saul went in to cover his feet' becomes 'Saul went into a cave to relieve himself'; 'Adam knew Eve' becomes 'Adam had sexual relations with his wife'; while Rachel's 'the custom of women is upon me' translates to 'I'm having my monthly period' (1 Sam. 24:3; Gen. 4:1; 31:35). In the tender case of Elisha and the Shunammite's son: 'there was neither voice, nor hearing' becomes 'there was no sign of life' (2 Kings 4:31).[198] As we might say today, the dear child had 'passed on' and 'was no longer with us'.

The point is, some of the work required to discern and decipher the Bible's figures of speech has been done for us by others, including our translators.

As discussed previously, study the Scriptures *for* yourself, but don't study the Scriptures *by* yourself. I am convinced that almost anyone can read the Bible and understand its basic message, just as anyone can appreciate and enjoy the music of an orchestra. However, a professionally trained musician will discern nuance, detail and intricacies in the complexity of symphonic production that the average music lover will never hear or understand. The same applies for those trained in biblical history, culture and linguistics.

When determining the style of speech employed by a biblical author, draw on the experience and expertise of others. As for what it means to 'kick against the goads' ... I'll leave that to you to research on your own.

Style of Speech—Closing Comments

We have previously established that the Bible is a work of history and, therefore, must be read intelligently. But equally true is this: the Bible is a work of art through which the Creator has painted powerful pictures to make an indelible imprint on our internal world. This artistic masterpiece has been presented to us through a variety of literary expression and devices.

The books of both Old and New Testaments, through the pen of each author and within every genre they employ, are richly imbued with figurative language. In His sovereign wisdom, God has chosen to communicate truth in metaphor, symbols, idioms and imagery designed to catalyse emotion and capture the imagination of His people. The idea that prose equals fact, while poetry equals fiction, is to be dismissed once and for all, as is the thought that figurative speech is somehow inferior to language more literal—God has chosen them both.

For us to catch the artist's message and meaning, we are to understand the words of Scripture according to the sense in which they have been presented to us. As good Bible interpreters, we are responsible to discern between the literal and figurative so that we may correctly handle the Word of Truth.

SUMMARY REMARKS—STEP 2

Time to sum up Step 2.

The second step in the process of healthy hermeneutics is to answer the following question of the biblical text: *What does it mean?* This critical task is known as exegesis, the aim of which is to draw out the author's intended meaning. Having read the text (Step 1), we are now required to reflect, research and reason our way to discover its meaning, giving particular consideration to the ABCS of exegesis: author and audience, big-picture background, corroborating content and style of speech employed.

Some portions of Scripture are more difficult to exegete than others. At times, this task requires discernment, determination and attention to detail. However, with the presence of the Spirit, the perspectives of other saints and plenty of practice, you *can* handle it! Once our exegesis is complete and we have established a confident sense of authorial intent, we may move forward to our third and final step.

 Timothy, Tammy, it's time to bring this thing home.

Step 3

What Does it Matter?

As Paul closes out his letters to Timothy, he calls to attention that fundamental reality every believer knows to be true: the Scriptures matter. Every book from every author, every jot and every tittle hold special significance to the lives of God's people today, forming our beliefs and fashioning our behaviours. The Bible shapes our convictions and speaks to our conduct, providing eternal principles for everyday practice. For our sake and for others, we are to give close watch to our life and doctrine, allowing the Scriptures to dictate our dogma and direct our deeds.

Be diligent in these matters; give yourself wholly to them, so that everyone may see your progress. **Watch your life and doctrine closely**. Persevere in them, because if you do, you will save both yourself and your hearers … All Scripture is God-breathed and is **useful for teaching, rebuking, correcting and training** in righteousness, so

that the servant of God may be thoroughly equipped for every good work. (1 Tim. 4:15–16; 2 Tim. 3:16–17)

We come now to the third and final step in our hermeneutic process. Our *observation* (Step 1) and *interpretation* (Step 2) of the ancient text has led us to consider the *implications* and *applications* for the modern reader. We know what the Bible says, we have a fair idea as to what it means, but what on earth does it matter? How exactly is the revelation given to 'them then and there' relevant to 'us here and now'? What are we to do with the information we have acquired and how should it influence our thinking, feeling and doing?

Here in Step 3, we examine five cutting considerations when responding to biblical truth, before circling back to Nehemiah 8, where I will encourage you to find 'JOY' in biblical revelation. Before then, a brief word on hermeneutics

CHAPTER 35

The Art of Hermeneutics

It is here—in Step 3—that hermeneutics becomes more of an artform than a science. It is also here that I have experienced my biggest struggle in writing this book. After all, performing a work of art is largely an intuitive exercise. It is difficult to articulate the process in precise terms. An artist may operate by a set of broad principles and established norms, but to fill in the details and bring a work to life, one largely feels their way through. In some respects, it is a skill that is more caught than taught. In fact, I have wondered whether this may be the reason that many books on hermeneutics, and a good number of Bible commentaries, give little place to contemporary application at all.[199]

Regardless, this step in our process, as with the previous two, must be approached with thoughtfulness and intentionality. In the same way a triple-jump athlete would fall far short of their goal should they neglect to pay attention to the critical last step, so it is with those of us who handle the Word of Truth. Here, we launch ourselves into the present reality of God's potent and powerful Word—where His eternal truth is brought to bear upon our everyday living and allowed opportunity to have its desired effect on the earth.

So, let's jump right in.

Believe and be Baptised

To this point in the process, when we sought to discover what the Scriptures say and mean, we have been pursuing an objective goal. Ideally, the conclusions reached should not fundamentally differ from reader to reader. The results of our exegesis are either right or wrong—we hit the mark or miss it, according to how well we observed the text and applied interpretive principles. However, when it comes to application (i.e., how those truths are to be outworked in the lives of believers today), a much broader scope of valid possibilities is presented. Answers to *What does it matter?* often vary person-to-person, and for the most part, this is how it should be. Case in point: the ministry of John the Baptiser:

> In those days John the Baptist came preaching in the wilderness of Judea, **'Repent, for the kingdom of heaven is at hand'** … Jerusalem and all Judea and all the region about the Jordan were going out to him, and they were baptized by him in the river Jordan, confessing their sins. But when he saw many of the Pharisees and Sadducees coming to his baptism, he said to them, 'You brood of vipers! Who warned you to flee from the wrath to come? **Bear fruit in keeping with repentance.'** (Matt. 3:1–8 ESV)

Establishing the meaning of John's message here is not difficult. Certainly, the target audience, primarily Jewish, appeared to have understood his point clearly enough. The coming of God's rule and reign was fast approaching and with it, an impending wrath for His enemies. Israel's promised King was on His way and His people were to be prepared for His arrival. The question was, 'so what?'.

The implications were twofold. First, this revelation called for a turnaround in their thinking. Repentance literally means to 'change the way you think' (Greek: *metanoeó*)—one performs a deliberate shift from one line of thought to another. Whatever this audience had in mind regarding the timing of kingdom-come, their beliefs now had to align with the truth John was presenting. The arrival of the Kingdom was imminent, his was a 'now-word' and demanded an immediate change of mind.

As a result, this change of conviction was to outwork itself in a change of conduct—a call to bear fruit in accordance with their repentance. Here, we witness the second implication—'What then, should we believe?' turns to 'How then, should we behave?'. Again, we see revelation speaking to one's doctrine and lifestyle, with external evidence resulting from an internal adjustment.

This is where *application* comes in, and these crowds responded en masse! First, John's message carried a general, or universal, application: water baptism. This, it seems, was a one-size-fits-all response to the truth he proclaimed. According to Mark, 'all the people' of Jerusalem and Judea 'were baptized by him in the Jordan River' (Mark 1:5).

Yet Luke's Gospel details a variety of applications, differing from listener to listener. When the people asked, 'What should we do then?', those with food and clothing were instructed to 'share with the one who has none', tax collectors were told to be truthful in their dealings, and soldiers to quit exploiting their authority and find contentment in an honest day's work (Luke 3:10–14). John even brought a very personalised application to Herod Antipas, who had violated Torah by marrying his brother's wife (Luke 3:19–20; Mark 6:17–18).

In short, the message to 'repent and produce' may have had a single meaning, but it carried *multiple applications* according to the specific circumstances of the individuals in view. It is the same with us today.

One Word, Many Outworkings

At times, the Bible issues a one-size-fits-all instruction for its target audience. In other cases, a plethora of possibilities is presented. Therefore, determining 'what it matters' is not an exact science. The art of hermeneutics requires us to draw on the promptings of the Spirit, the perspectives of other saints and our own common sense, as we seek how best to outwork God's will, wisdom and ways revealed in His written Word.

 Grab your toolkits, Tammy, we're about to create something beautiful.

YOU CAN HANDLE THE TRUTH

NOTES

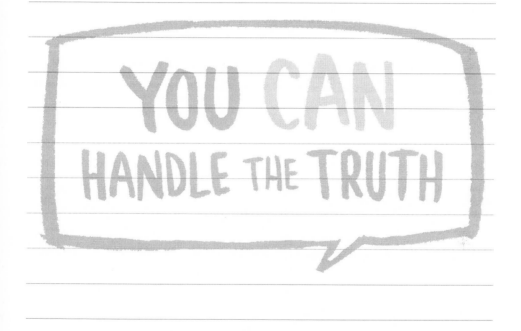

Cutting
Considerations

Let's return, once again, to our title text—2 Timothy 2:15.

> Be diligent to present yourself approved to God, a worker who does not need to be ashamed, **rightly dividing** the word of truth. (2 Tim. 2:15 NKJV)

The Greek word here for 'rightly divide' is *orthotomeō*, which simply means to 'cut straight'.[200] There are two possible reasons Paul chose this particular term. First, he may have had in mind the practice of cutting a straight path in a field, as per the exhortation in Hebrews 12:13: 'make straight [Greek: *orthós*] paths for your feet'. In other words, Timothy should provide a correct 'line of thought' for his listeners as they walk through the biblical narrative, an idea we considered previously when discussing the Bible's big picture.

Alternatively, the imagery here may be drawn from his personal experience as a tradesman, when Paul cut cloth and timber poles for constructing tents. By associating *cutting right* with being a 'worker', a term commonly used

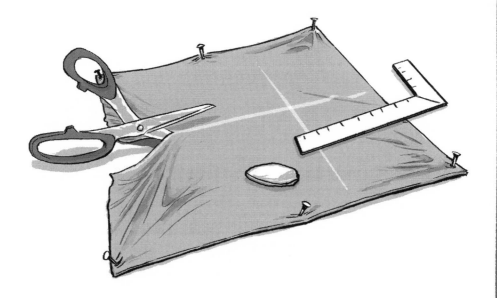

to denote those in the labour force, it would seem this is the most likely meaning.[201] A house literally rises or falls on the execution of a builder's blade! A dodgy cut from a tent-maker could place the entire construction in jeopardy.

When pondering the implications of biblical truth on the beliefs and behaviour of the modern-day audience, my advice is to consider these five critical cuts:

What is Major | What is Minor

What is Clear | What is Cloudy

What is Descriptive | What is Prescriptive

What is Theirs | What is Yours

What is the Practice | What is the Principle | What is the Purpose

Sharpen your blade, Timothy, it's time to start cutting.

CHAPTER 36

What is Major | What is Minor

> Hearing that Jesus had silenced the Sadducees, the Pharisees got together. One of them, an expert in the law, tested him with this question: 'Teacher, which is the greatest commandment in the Law?' Jesus replied: '"Love the Lord your God with all your heart and with all your soul and with all your mind." **This is the first and greatest commandment.** And the second is like it: "Love your neighbor as yourself." All the Law and the Prophets hang on these two commandments.' (Matt. 22:34–40)

On this first point, we take our lead from none other than Christ Himself.

The idea that God's commandments somehow vary in value was not rejected by our Lord. Indeed, He seems to reinforce it. Of the 600+ instructions issued in Torah, to 'love the Lord your God' was both the first (Greek: *prótos*) and greatest (Greek: *megas*) of them all. Search the pages of the entire Hebrew Bible and any command you find will be smaller in significance and second in importance to those contained in Deuteronomy 6:5 and Leviticus 19:18.[202]

Like crossbars holding up a suspended mobile, every Old Testament principle and directive, encouragement and correction hangs on these two commands. In other words, it is God's purpose for *relationship* that holds up all other biblical revelation. Relationship with God is what matters most. According to Jesus, this is the Old Testament's entire thrust, and every teaching stems from this divine priority.[203] Living out a love relationship with God, and then others, is the main thing.

As my church hears me say often, I am convinced that our great purpose in life is to know Him, and to show Him. This, from the Lord's Prayer in John 17:[204]

> **Now this is eternal life: that they know you**, the only true God, and Jesus Christ, whom you have sent. I have brought you glory on earth by finishing the work you gave me to do … **I have revealed you** to those whom you gave me. (John 17:3–6)

Stop and think about that for a moment. Eternal life is communion with God. Surely nothing is more important than that!

In this prayer, Jesus explains that His mission on earth was fundamentally twofold: to portray a true representation of God's nature and provide the means for people to be reconciled to Him in right-standing relationship, that humankind may know God. As the Father sent Him, so He also sends us, with a ministry of revelation and reconciliation (John 17:18; 2 Cor. 5:18–21). The divine mandate given first to Israel and fulfilled by Christ now becomes the mission of the church: to know Him and to make Him known to others. To know Him and to show Him.

Ultimately, the purpose of all revelation is to have us relate properly to God, others and ourselves, a point we shall discuss in further detail soon. In the meantime, back to the 'greatest commandment'.

Not All Truths are Created Equal

There is a timeless principle behind Jesus' claim here: *not all truths are created equal.* Some biblical subjects are simply more important than others. When it comes to both the convictions we profess and the conduct we pursue, it is incumbent upon us to major on the majors and minor on the minors—to make a clear divide between the issues central to our life and doctrine, and those that are peripheral.

Jesus brings specific application to this principle in the chapter following as He rebukes these same Pharisees: 'You give a tenth of your spices—mint, dill and cumin. But you have neglected **the more important matters** of the law—justice, mercy and faithfulness. You should have practiced the latter, without neglecting the former' (Matt. 23:23). As is so often the case, an out-of-balance belief system produced out-of-order behaviour in these men. Failure to prioritise what lay at the very heart of the commandments ('love God, love people') resulted in hypocrisy of the worst and most damaging kind. While called to be stewards of heavenly wisdom, these religious leaders became blind guides leading both themselves and others astray.

My point here is this: our challenge as Bible students is to find, focus, feed on and follow the teachings of greatest importance.

All Scripture may be equally true, but not all Scripture is equally significant. Some truths warrant less attention than others. It's that simple. While it may feel uncomfortable to admit this, it's something you already know to be true. And you're about to prove it to me.

This Week's Memory Verse

Time for another game. Timothy, fill in the blanks:

> For God so loved the _____ that he gave his one and only
> _____ that whoever believes in him shall not _____ ,
> but have _____. (John 3:16)

Well done. I am sure you managed that one easy enough. Moving on to the next:

> Now Ehud had made a _____ about a _____
> long, which he strapped to his right _____ under his
> _____. (Judg. 3:16)

Hmmm … not quite as easy is it? Don't worry, I won't make you wait for the answer sheet on this one. Head to the endnotes if you are stumped.[205]

In the meantime, here's the point:

While both John 3:16 and Judges 3:16 are equally true, they are not equally important. Knowing that God's great love for the world resulted in the gift of Jesus Christ and the offer of eternal life to all who would believe in Him is one of those absolutely essential truths. For me, the realities revealed in John 3:16 shape my worldview, relationship with God and purpose on this planet. As is the case for countless other believers over the past 2,000 years, I am willing to give my life for the revelation presented in this passage and am committed to doing all I can to make others aware of its powerful reality!

Conversely, to learn that there once was a man named Ehud who fashioned himself an 18-inch sword that he conceal-carried underneath his robe by his right leg … I'm sure you can identify the difference here. While the information in this verse may be true, it's clear to see that its value and relevance to the life and doctrine of the average Bible reader is negligible. I highly doubt Judges 3:16 will appear on a bumper sticker or Christian T-shirt anytime soon. I know of nobody who'd give their life for such a truth.

That Which is Most Important

There is a clear difference between teachings that are fundamental to our faith, essential to our eternity and vital to establishing relationship with God, and those that, while equally true, are not nearly as important to the life of the church. The apostle Paul demonstrates this in his letter to the Corinthians. Having addressed countless issues pertaining to their warped beliefs and whacky behaviour, listing them one-by-one, chapter after chapter,

Paul begins to draw his epistle to a close by sharing that which he deemed of highest worth:

> Dear friends, let me give you clearly **the heart of the gospel** that I've preached to you—the good news that you have heartily received and on which you stand ... For I have shared with you what I have received and what is of **utmost importance: The Messiah died for our sins**. (1 Cor. 15:1–3 TPT)

Healthy hermeneutics involves finding out the things that matter most, prioritising the weightier matters of biblical revelation as we keep the main things the main things. Our first cutting consideration when seeking to implement the Bible's teaching is to distinguish between the important and the incidental, that we may put first things first, major on the majors and minor on the minors.

> But what does it matter? **The important thing is ... Christ is preached**. And because of this I rejoice. (Phil. 1:18)

CHAPTER 37

What is Clear | What is Clouded

But when Peter came to Antioch, I opposed him in public, because he was **clearly wrong** … You foolish Galatians! Who put a spell on you? Before your very eyes you had a **clear description** of the death of Jesus Christ … Now, **it is clear** that no one is put right with God by means of the Law, because the scripture says, 'Only the person who is put right with God through faith shall live.' (Gal. 2:11; 3:1, 11 GNB)

If there's one thing to be learnt from the Galatian epistle, it's this: don't mess with Paul's Gospel!

The most passionate of all his letters, in Galatians, Paul comes right out the gate expressing how astonished he is that the church, having been thrown into a state of bewitchment and confusion, is so quickly 'deserting' Christ by embracing a false, perverted, no-gospel-at-all gospel, the propagators of which, be they angelic or human, he denounces as deserving of divine curse (Gal. 1:6–9). To assure the Galatians that he is not singling them out with such a rebuke, Paul tells his readers of a similar confrontation he initiated with Peter, publicly calling out the apostle's hypocrisy when he was clearly in the wrong and 'not acting in line with the truth of the gospel' (Gal. 2:14).

Perhaps more than any other, this epistle demonstrates Paul's no-nonsense approach to maintaining the purity of his Gospel message. After all, it wasn't fundamentally *his* Gospel, it was 'the Gospel **of God**' (Rom. 1:1). The message of Christ was not to be toyed with—this was God's story, not any man's. Therefore, no man had the right to change its content or cloud its clarity. As a steward entrusted with heavenly revelation, Paul took very seriously his responsibility to proclaim God's Word correctly, courageously and clearly.[206]

Indeed, Paul would literally give his life for this cause. He would bend and buckle for no-one. Like many others of his day, Paul was ceremoniously executed for his confession of these unwavering convictions.

Open to Discussion

There are many issues on which the teaching of Scripture is both clear and consistent throughout: the character of God and the nature of Christ, moral virtues and vices, the existence of an invisible realm and more. When convinced of such, we, like Paul, should hold these truths tightly, especially in times of testing. And trust me, every truth you claim to embrace will at some point be tested!

Other matters are not so clear. On some issues of life and doctrine, the Bible seems a little cloudy, with not so much black and white, but various shades of grey. In these cases, developing a conviction is fine and living by that conviction is commendable, but opinions such as these should be held a little lighter. Consider this, from Paul's letter to the Romans:

> Accept the one whose faith is weak, without quarreling over **disputable matters**. One person's faith allows them to eat anything, but another, whose faith is weak, eats only vegetables … One person considers one day more sacred than another; another considers every day alike. Each of them should be fully convinced in their own mind … I am convinced, being fully persuaded in the Lord Jesus, that nothing is unclean in itself. But if anyone regards something as unclean, then for that person it is unclean … **So whatever you believe about these things keep between yourself and God**. (Rom. 14:1–22)

The difference in Paul's tone and tenor here is quite something to behold. In Galatians, he is willing to fight tooth-and-nail in defence of his convictions, calling down curses, confronting esteemed apostles and commanding false teachers to take a knife to their delicates! Yet, in this passage, he seems unphased that certain people in the church of Rome believed differently than him. Playing the role of peacemaker, Paul encourages the members of this congregation to avoid quarrelling, agree to disagree and push on with living their lives.

Why such a change?

Simply put, Paul knew what it is to distinguish between issues that are clear as day and those that are more cloudy. Some areas are non-negotiable, set in stone, a matter of undeniable fact. Other topics, however, are open to discussion. Here, a healthy dose of disagreement, doubt, dispute, deliberation, debate and dialogue are simply natural outcomes of life in a diverse community, so long as such differences are respected, and individuals remain free to live according to their own conscience.[207]

When it came to the sacredness of certain days or the sinfulness of particular foods, Paul was confident that his convictions were correct and, insofar as it caused no undue distress to genuine believers who viewed things differently, he conducted himself in accordance with his personal views. In doing so, he demonstrated that it is possible to disagree without becoming disagreeable, to hold an opinion, yet not be opinionated. Sadly, this is a skill lacking in too many and, as church history demonstrates, has led to innumerable (and largely unnecessary) divisions in the body of Christ.

Stepping Off Your Soapbox

On a personal note, I hold to a number of doctrinal perspectives that would be deemed unconventional by many believers. In some areas of theology, I lean towards particular views with which many of my church members and ministry friends would likely disagree. According to my interpretation of particular passages, I have encouraged certain practices in the congregation I pastor that run counter to broad swaths of the church-world today. On certain issues, I stand in the minority, yet I am not about to detail any of these topics here. I don't have need to. After all, none are all that important and many of them remain opinions I hold to rather loosely and privately. Some views I hold simply do not warrant worldwide broadcast. Frankly, I'd rather give my time to things that unify us than to those that highlight our differences.

As I see it, our personal persuasions on clouded issues should neither divide us nor define us. Sure, I may be inclined to believe that Lazarus (and not the apostle John) is 'the disciple whom Jesus loved', that the thief in the night metaphor alludes to Passover and that the genealogies in Genesis are not recording precise biological ages, but these are not beliefs I am willing to go to war for, lose friends over or build my reputation upon. Subjects like these make for interesting discussions, not solid foundations. The Gospel of Christ is what matters most and the fundamentals of that message are crystal clear.

So, if you believe that the 'sons of God' in Genesis 6 were angelic beings who interbred with human women, that Ezekiel's temple is still yet to be built, that snake-handling is a legitimate Christian practice or that 666 is a numeric code for Emperor Nero … fine. Good for you. Just be sure that issues like these never become your pet cause and never take priority over the place of peace in your relationships. Do not be one of those who develops 'an **unhealthy interest in controversies** and quarrels about words' because often, doing so leads to nothing but strife (1 Tim. 6:4).

In the same way that 'all Scripture is equally true, but not all Scripture is equally important', so it is that all Scripture is equally *correct*, but not all Scripture is equally *clear*. Some areas of biblical theology, interpretation of prophecy, meanings of teachings and intended applications will always remain a mystery to us or, at best, ongoingly subject to debate. Once more, we should take the lead from the apostle Paul, who said humbly:

> Now we see things imperfectly, like puzzling reflections in a mirror, but then we will see everything with perfect clarity. **All that I know now is partial and incomplete**. (1 Cor. 13:12 NLT)

Tammy, when it comes to formulating your response to God's Word, focus your energies on the main things and the plain things.

Strengthen your stance on the clear, soften your stance on the cloudy and always be certain to 'keep [your] eyes fixed on Jesus' (Heb. 12:2 GNB).

CHAPTER 38

What is Descriptive | What is Prescriptive

> Then have them make a sanctuary for me, and I will dwell among them. Make this tabernacle and all its furnishings **exactly like the pattern I will show you**. (Exo. 25:8–9)

There is no way I would have found the grace or space to pioneer a church at age 23 were it not for the influence of the church we planted out from, in particular, its strong emphasis on leadership. The global network to which we belonged was also big on leadership concerns, particularly pertaining to church structure. Messages on how to 'build according to the pattern' were commonplace, as leaders within the movement insisted we implement the 'New Testament model' of church, as witnessed in Acts. Were we to get the wineskin right, the wine would surely follow. Build it correctly and He would come.

This approach was predicated on the idea that the book of Acts somehow provides a *prescription* for how 'God wants His church to be'. After all, God is a builder and the Bible His instruction manual, right? If it's in the book, it is there to be followed. If we too would devote ourselves 'to the apostles' teaching and to fellowship, to the breaking of bread and to prayer', then signs, wonders and daily salvations would result (Acts 2:42–47). Of course, the part about selling property for the poor wasn't nearly as important as being at the prayer meeting!

Unfortunately, this brand of poor hermeneutic is commonplace in many pulpits. Taking a Bible story and insisting it reveals a universal prescription believers *must* employ today demonstrates a lack of discernment regarding authorial intent. By all means, be encouraged, inspired and instructed by the example set when Joseph forgave his brothers (for example), but please understand that nowhere does the Bible insist that his is somehow 'the pattern' to be followed for forgiveness to truly count today. There is a difference between the way things *should* be and the ways things simply *could* be. A biblical hero like Joseph serves as a model we *may* follow, but it is Jesus who is explicitly described as *the* model we *must* follow: 'as the Lord has forgiven you, so you also must forgive' (Col. 3:13 ESV).

What Did Happen ≠ What Should Happen

Distinguishing between what is *descriptive* (what the Bible says *did* happen) and what is *prescriptive* (what the Bible says *should* happen) is our next critical cut. For the most part, this distinction is not that difficult to make, especially when one avoids the temptation to jump to conclusions, by sufficiently exegeting the passage or subject matter first. Observing the text well and discovering the author's meaning and original intent should show us the difference without much added effort.

Take marriage as an example. The fact that Abraham slept with Hagar as a kind of proxy-wife to bear him a son is not evidence of God endorsing (no less prescribing!) either polygamy or polyamory (Gen. 16:1–4). Similarly, nor is the patriarch's insistence that a daughter-in-law be found only from among 'my own relatives' an indication that mixed-race romance is somehow unbiblical or against God's pattern for marriage (Gen. 24:4). Here, Genesis is not giving a prescription for all marriage match-ups throughout all of history, it is simply describing the standalone stories of these men and their wives, in their unique and particular circumstances. Relationships that cross cultural divisions such as class or ethnicity may cause discomfort to some, as when Moses married a well-to-do North African woman (Num. 12:1–3), however, this is no excuse for taking a descriptive text and insisting it prescribes God's universal will for all.

Similarly, when Isaac's son, Jacob, laboured two sets of seven years for the hand of Rachel, it should be quite obvious that this is not presented as 'God's pattern' for prospective husbands the world over! This story is simply a description of what it was for him, not what it should be for others (Gen. 29:16–30). Although, for my daughters … who knows? Perhaps I'll find a way to manipulate this story to my personal advantage when the time comes.

That said, the Bible certainly does contain prescriptions for important relationships, including marriage, with basic patterns and principles that Christian believers are explicitly, and repeatedly, instructed to follow.[208] This begs the question, how exactly do we spot the difference?

Tell Me Straight—Tell Me Again

In my experience, there are two things to watch for when making this critical cut. Generally speaking, New Testament prescriptions are both directly stated and repeatedly demonstrated. When differentiating between what is instructive and what is simply informative, watch for imperative statements and (where possible) consistently repeated responses.

Think back to John the Baptiser. His call for repentance and baptism in first-century Judea was obeyed by literally thousands of adherents. Jewish people of all persuasions heeded his command by being submerged (Greek: *baptizó*) in the Jordan river. Even Jesus followed this prescription, to 'carry out all that God requires' (Matt. 3:13–15 NLT). However, the preaching and practice of water baptism continued well beyond the ministry of John, the borders of Judea and the ethnicity of the Jews, largely because it featured within Christ's Great Commission: 'Therefore go and make disciples of all nations, baptizing them in the name of the Father and of the Son and of the Holy Spirit' (Matt. 28:19).

The book of Acts tells us that following the baptism of 3,000 Jews at Pentecost, Philip immersed new converts in Samaria and an Ethiopian while on route to Gaza, Ananias baptised Saul after his Damascus road encounter, Peter dipped the family of an Italian soldier, while Paul dunked synagogue officials in Corinth, disciples of John in Ephesus and entire households in Philippi, including in the dead of night![209] Further inferences to water baptism and its implications are found throughout the epistles of both Paul and Peter.[210]

Unlike baptism, many practices appear as one-offs, with no record of them being repeated or revisited. Be it eating locusts and wild honey or cursing out-of-season fruit trees, praying in the dark of early morning or for precisely one hour in the evening, casting demons into pigs, drinking deadly poison or handling snakes, spitting on people with disabilities, selling off one's possessions for the poor or evangelising two-by-two with nothing more than a staff and sandals, a wide examination of the Scripture demonstrates that incidents and instructions like these carry no sense of universal insistence.[211]

Conversely, with the New Testament repeatedly presenting water baptism as both an imperative instruction and a widely followed practice for believers in Jesus, it is safe to consider it a prescription for all. More than a mere description of what happened to 'them then and there', the command to be baptised in water is one that should accompany the repentance and faith of all those who come to Christ 'here and now'.

 Timothy, if you have committed yourself to be a follower of Jesus but are yet to have taken the sacred plunge—I encourage you to delay no more. Dive in.

Methods are Many

Failing to distinguish between what is unique and what is universal, what is a description given to encourage or a prescription there to enforce, is the cause of many a rift in the body of Christ. This is especially so when it comes to issues related to that mysterious third member of the Trinity! While our Lord's command to be 'baptized with the Holy Spirit' provides the basis of perhaps the most prevailing theme in the book of Acts (Acts 1:5), the many examples of this experience demonstrate that there is no prescribed pattern as to *how exactly* this should take place, or what precisely it must look like. Manifestations vary from blowing winds to burning fires, prophetic utterances to foreign tongues, shaking buildings to drunken behaviours. The methods surrounding such outpourings include unexpected baptism during times of prayer and preaching and intentional baptism by the laying on of hands, accompanied at times by extensive explanation, while at others by very little at all.[212] Whatever it looks like and however it happens, there is only one prescription here of universal import:

> **Repent and be baptized, every one of you**, in the name of Jesus Christ for the forgiveness of your sins. **And you will receive the gift of the Holy Spirit**. The promise is for you and your children and for all who are far off—for all whom the Lord our God will call. (Acts 2:38–39)

As the old saying goes, 'Methods are many; principles are few. Methods always change; principles never do'.

So, if, as I did in my young adult years, you sense a call to leadership in a local church context, by all means take the requirement lists of 1 Timothy 3 and Titus 1 as serious prescriptions to follow. Just don't expect your name to be drawn from the casting of lots, or that a signs-and-wonders-working apostle will immediately take you under their wing, invite you on global ventures and personally mentor you as a 'dearly loved son' in the Lord. Sure, the New Testament may contain accounts of these things, but that's not to say they are intended to serve as 'the pattern of biblical leadership' for time immemorial.

When rightly dividing the Word of Truth, make a clear cut between things that are prescriptive and those that are merely descriptive.

CHAPTER 39

What is Theirs | What is Yours

Do your best to come to me quickly, for Demas, because he loved this world, has deserted me and has gone to Thessalonica. Crescens has gone to Galatia, and Titus to Dalmatia. Only Luke is with me. Get Mark and bring him with you, because he is helpful to me in my ministry. I sent Tychicus to Ephesus. When you come, bring the cloak that I left with Carpus at Troas, and my scrolls, especially the parchments. Alexander the metalworker did me a great deal of harm. The Lord will repay him for what he has done. You too should be on your guard against him, because he strongly opposed our message. (2 Tim. 4:9–15)

 Timothy, answer me truthfully. Have you ever obeyed this Scripture?

Have you visited Paul in his Roman prison and taken him his scrolls and parchments? Have you ever watched for an objectionable metal worker named Alexander, requested Carpus to hand over Paul's cloak or sought John Mark to accompany you as you travel? Of course not. You have not obeyed these instructions. And it's not because you are dismissive of the written Word, neither are these verses confusing or complicated. You know what this Scripture *says* and have no problem discerning what this Scripture *means*. The struggle here is to determine how, if at all, this passage *matters* to you. After all, despite the fact I've been calling you 'Timothy' throughout

CHAD M. MANSBRIDGE   265

STEP 1

STEP 2

3. WHAT DOES IT MATTER?

this book, it is quite obvious that these instructions were not written to you.

This next critical cut relates to an issue touched on earlier when discussing the 'A' in the ABCS of exegesis—ascertaining the text's author and intended *audience*. To rightly divide the Word of Truth, we must identify that which is theirs and that which is yours. After all, what was required of them may never be required of you. Similarly, what was true of them may not be true of you.

Case in point, the dreadful depravity of your dirty rotten heart.

How's Your Heart?

> The LORD saw that the wickedness of man was great in the earth, and that every intention of the thoughts of his heart was only evil continually … **[the] heart is deceitful above all things, and desperately sick**; who can understand it? (Gen. 6:5; Jer. 17:9 ESV)

Houston, we have a problem.

I'm sure you'd agree that whether it is physiological or, in this context, an issue of the soul, heart disease is not something to be taken lightly. King David famously demonstrated the deeply personal nature of these concerns when the confronting condition of his heart, and the consequences of the conduct that followed, inspired him to write Psalm 51:

> For I know my transgressions, and my sin is always before me … Surely I was sinful at birth, sinful from the time my mother conceived me … **Create in me a pure heart, O God**, and renew a steadfast spirit within me. Do not cast me from your presence or take your Holy Spirit from me. (Ps. 51:3–11)

I'd guess that after Psalm 23 ('The Lord is my shepherd'), this could well be the most frequently referenced of all Davidic songs within the Christian community, as sincere and self-reflective believers echo the king's sober sentiments and express their desire for a pure heart, pleading with God to not remove us from His holy presence, despite the confronting reality of our wretched, warped and wicked internal world.

The question is: are we right to do so?

These may be accurate assessments of the original author and audience, but are they true of us Christians today? As a beneficiary of the eternal and superior covenant, should I be concerned that God may cast me from His presence or remove His Spirit from me? As a new creation in Christ, is it true that my heart is deceitful and desperately sick, its every intention continually evil?

When speaking of unbelievers, the prognosis of the apostles mirrors that of the Old Testament authors. Paul describes hearts that are foolish, unrepentant and hardened (Rom. 1:21; 2:5; Eph. 4:18). Peter tells of those whose hearts have been 'trained in greed' and Stephen of hearts 'uncircumcised' (2 Peter 2:14; Acts 7:51 ESV).[213] Yet, when describing the salvation experience of those in Cornelius' household, Peter claimed that the giving of Holy Spirit to these new believers was evidence that God had **'purified their hearts** by faith' (Acts 15:9). No matter how filthy their internal condition may have been prior to Peter's ministry, it seems that in receiving the Gospel, a supernatural cleansing had taken place. God had cleaned house and moved in.

It is no surprise then that Paul believed his heart to be 'pure' (1 Tim. 1:5; 2 Tim. 2:22) and claimed that the heart circumcision prophesied by Moses was being fulfilled in both Jewish and Gentile Christians of his day (Rom. 2:29).[214] In other words, these new-covenant believers had received the 'new heart' promised by the prophets:

> Then I will sprinkle clean water on you, and you will be clean. Your filth will be washed away, and you will no longer worship idols. **And I will give you a new heart, and I will put a new spirit in you. I will take out your stony, stubborn heart and give you a tender, responsive heart.** And I will put my Spirit in you so that you will follow my decrees and be careful to obey my regulations … And I will give them one heart and one purpose: to worship me forever, for their

own good and for the good of all their descendants. And I will make an everlasting covenant with them: I will never stop doing good for them. I will put a desire in their hearts to worship me, and they will never leave me. (Ezek. 36:25–27; Jer. 32:39–40 NLT)

Jesus claimed that 'out of the heart of man, come evil thoughts, sexual immorality, theft, murder, adultery, coveting, wickedness, deceit, sensuality, envy, slander, pride, foolishness. All these evil things come from within' (Mark 7:21–23). With this in mind, perhaps His instruction to 'cut off' appendages that cause us to sin was not hyperbolic at all! One's eyes, feet and hands may certainly be *instruments* of immoral behaviour but, as this passage proves, they are never the *cause* of it.[215] Immorality stems from within. The solution to a life of victory over sin begins with the removal, and replacement, of one's heart. A life-saving transplant, His heart for ours, is just one of many benefits granted in the Gospel. Spiritual transformation is, first and foremost, an 'inside job'.

Tammy, far be it from me to tell you what you should and shouldn't pray, but, as I see it, the answer to David's cry has been provided in the new-birth experience. Personally, I see no point in asking God to create in me a new and pure heart. He has already done so (2 Cor. 5:17). Likewise, I see no point in pleading with Him to not remove His Spirit from me. Holy Spirit may have left people under the old covenant, such as King Saul, but Jesus promised His disciples that the Advocate would 'never leave' them (1 Sam. 16:14; John 14:16 NLT).

My point is this: when rightly dividing the Word of Truth, be prepared to acknowledge that what was true of them, may not be true of you.

To Me or Not to Me?—That is the Question!

Consequently, what was *required* of them, may not be required of you. As followers of Christ, we have committed ourselves to building our lives on the revelation of His Lordship: what He says, goes (Matt. 7:24). We desire to be doers of the Word, not just hearers, and to experience the blessedness that follows such obedience (Luke 11:28; James 1:22). Yet, clearly, not all Bible commands are addressed to us. Not every instruction is ours to follow.

Simply put: all Scripture is given for our information, but not all Scripture is for our application.[216]

Paul did not tell Timothy that all Scripture is God-breathed and *applicable*, but rather, that all Scripture is 'God-breathed and **useful**'. Everything in the Bible is useful for you to learn, but not everything in the Bible is intended for you to live out. The question is, since none of us are the original audience of the Bible's decrees and directives, how do we find application at all?

When coming across a biblical command, consider this. Generally speaking, the more common ground you share with the original intended audience, the more directly applicable that instruction will be for you today. The further apart you are, the less the likelihood of one-for-one application.

Your task then, is to imagine yourself in the biblical story by discerning the characters you most closely identify with. Do this by considering the two most important features of biblical revelation: your covenant with God and relationship with others.

For example, the commands '**you must** be circumcised', '**you must** observe my Sabbaths' and 'as I have loved you, so **you must** love one another' were each spoken directly from God, to His people, at different times in biblical history.[217] Each instruction functions as a vital sign of covenant relationship with Yahweh. However, only one has direct application for you and me. The question is, with which covenant community do you identify? Are you a natural descendant of Abraham (male circumcision), an Israelite bound to Torah (Sabbath observance) or a follower of Christ (love one another)?

Broadly speaking, there is a greater chance of us finding application from instructions to the Bible's *Christian communities* than from Old Testament directives issued to the ancient Israelites. From a covenant perspective, we simply have more in common. It's not difficult to see how the 'one-another commands' of Romans, for example, are just as relevant for churches today:

Be devoted to one another in love. Honor one another above yourselves

... Share with the Lord's people who are in need. Practice hospitality ... Live in harmony with one another ... Accept one another, then, just as Christ accepted you ... Greet one another with a holy kiss. (Rom. 12:10, 13, 16; 15:7; 16:16)

Okay, perhaps we should examine that kissing command a little later.

Finding Common Ground

The point is, many instructions issued to the Bible's new-covenant community are more easily applied to us than those given in the old-covenant Law. But what are we to make of more obscure New Testament directives within narrative accounts, like Paul's 'fetch me my cloak' instructions to Timothy, quoted previously? In these cases, a little more imagination and the guidance of Holy Spirit is required.

For example, imagine yourself as identifying with Timothy in this passage. Then, ask the Good Teacher to speak to you: 'Lord, is there anything here you want to tell me?'. Upon reflection, you may sense Holy Spirit challenge you to personally visit inmates at your local prison, or somehow support a ministry to persecuted Christians. Perhaps these verses serve as a reminder to make yourself available to practically assist your ministry leaders, or visit a father-figure who has played a significant role in your spiritual development.

Alternatively, place yourself in the shoes of Paul. In this case, this passage may provide reassurance that the loneliness, opposition and betrayal you are currently experiencing is a common struggle, even to the greatest of God's generals. Just as Paul was willing to ask for Timothy and Mark to help him, so you too, perhaps, should recognise your need to have loyal people around you in times of emotional difficulty.

Even identifying with the Demas character, a former companion to Paul, could prove helpful. Here, you may sense Holy Spirit's warning that while you belong to an effective and supportive ministry environment, it is your personal commitment to the Lord that will see you last the distance. Since the pull of 'this world' was strong enough to sidetrack Demas, you too should take note and keep guard.

The key to placing yourself in the story is to make a connection to whatever common ground you share with the biblical characters then and there, while asking your ever-present Bible tutor, Holy Spirit, to guide you in how best to respond in the here-and-now.

Let me reiterate that seeking appropriate responses to biblical instruction is more of an art than a science. There is often a degree of subjectivity involved and multiple applications may present themselves. While strictly speaking none of the Bible was written directly to you, all of it exists to benefit you. As a general principle, when you find a community or character to whom you closely resemble, an instruction from God to them may very well bring a corresponding application for you. At the very least, even if no instruction exists, observe closely their relationship with the Lord and with others and take a lesson from their example:

> **These things happened to them as examples** and were written down as warnings for us, on whom the culmination of the ages has come … **For everything that was written in the past was written to teach us**, so that through the endurance taught in the Scriptures and the encouragement they provide we might have hope. (1 Cor. 10:11; Rom. 15:4)

CHAPTER 40

What is the Practice | What is the Principle | What is the Purpose

When he had finished washing their feet, he put on his clothes and returned to his place. 'Do you understand what I have done for you?' he asked them. 'You call me "Teacher" and "Lord," and rightly so, for that is what I am. Now that I, your Lord and Teacher, have washed your feet, **you also should wash one another's feet. I have set you an example that you should do as I have done for you** … Now that you know these things, you will be blessed if you do them … A new command I give you: Love one another. As I have loved you, so you must love one another.' (John 13:12–34)

It was December 1998. At 20 years of age, I had just completed my third-year bachelor studies and summer had begun. It was Saturday morning. The sun was out, the skies were calm and there was only one thing on my mind. Placing a small but significant item into my backpack, I picked up my girlfriend and drove her to the beach. Climbing onto the granite rocks by the water's edge, we sat down by a rockpool: 'Jaye, I've brought you here for a reason. I have something to ask you'. She had no idea what was coming. Kneeling in front of her, I took her feet and began washing them in the seawater. If she would permit me, I promised that day to love her as Christ loved His church.

She said yes.

This would be the first and only time I'd wash my wife's feet. In fact, except for an awkward exercise during a church leadership camp a couple of years later, it would be the last time I would wash *anybody's* feet! To date, anyway. Jesus may have commanded it at the Last Supper, but it's not something that forms part of my everyday Christian living. I'm perfectly happy leaving that one to the podiatrists.

The Why Behind the What

When asking *What does it matter?*, one of the frequent challenges we encounter is that of cultural contextualisation—finding contemporary ways to implement ancient biblical practices in keeping with the intent of the original instruction. To do this, we need to discover *the why behind the what*, making a clear cut between the specific practice and the broader principle, and purpose, behind it.

A background study into John 13 shows us that foot-washing before a meal was a common practice in first-century Judaism. Despite what is depicted in Leonardo's *The Last Supper* painting, it is likely that Jesus and His companions were seated on the floor (or possibly low-lying Roman couches) in a three-sided-square formation, the banquet laid in the middle. With sandals kept at the entry, their filthy feet were just inches away from both the guests next to them and the food they were sharing. Before eating commenced, a servant would be brought in with a basin and a standard feet-and-handwashing procedure would begin.

Discerning the why behind the what here is quite simple. Foot-washing for mealtime was an essential, everyday exercise performed primarily for the purpose of good hygiene. While the commanded *practice* is 'wash one another's feet', the underlying *principle* is 'serve one another with practical and menial tasks' and the *purpose* is 'to love one another as Christ has loved you'.

I may not wash my wife's feet before mealtimes, but I do make her a coffee each morning before she starts her day. Believe me, everybody benefits from that!

No matter how obscure they may seem to us, every edict issued by God has a reason behind it. There is purpose behind every command. Each expression of His will and manifestation of His ways is underpinned by His divine wisdom. We may not always see it, but when we do, we do well to implement God's principles in a manner equivalent and relevant to our contemporary culture.

What, Why and How-Now?

Here are some further examples of this *what*, *why* and *how-now* process:

What: 'If a soldier demands that you carry his gear for a mile, carry it two miles' (Matt. 5:41 NLT). *Why*: you'll demonstrate the nature of a God who both recognises authority and generously exceeds expectations. *How-now*: when your boss asks you to fetch her a coffee, grab her a muffin as well. Go the extra mile.

What: 'Greet one another with a holy kiss' (Rom. 16:16). *Why*: displaying familial affection to your fellow Christians is a useful way to demonstrate love. *How-now*: a high five, hug or handshake is probably more appropriate so long as it's warm and genuine. In most modern cultures, it would be better to keep your lips to yourself.

What: 'If the ox had a reputation for goring, yet its owner failed to keep it under control, he must pay full compensation' (Exo. 21:36 NLT). *Why*: it is not right that others pay the price for the irresponsible management of your powerful possessions. *How-now*: if the tyres on your car are bald, either take it off the road or replace them quickly! If not, you should be held fully responsible for any injury your vehicle inflicts.

In fact, I implemented the 'goring ox' principle this week for my Honda. Better safe than sorry.

Speaking of oxen, watch how Paul unpacks an agricultural principle in

Old Testament Law before applying it to his financial relationship with the Corinthian Church. Yep, we've made it this far and I'm only now going to talk about giving. Not bad for a pastor, hey?

> Who serves in the military at his own expense? Who plants a vineyard and does not enjoy the grapes for himself? Who would nurture and shepherd a flock and never get to drink its fresh milk? Am I merely giving you my own opinions, or does the Torah teach the same things? For it is written in the law of Moses: '**You should never put a muzzle over the mouth of an ox while he is treading out the grain**'. **Tell me, is God only talking about oxen here? Doesn't he also give us this principle so that we won't withhold support from his workers? It was written so that we would understand that the one spiritually 'plowing' and spiritually 'treading out the grain' also labors with the expectation of enjoying the harvest.** So, if we've sowed many spiritual gifts among you, is it too much to expect to reap material gifts from you? And if you have supported others, don't we rightfully deserve this privilege even more … Don't you know that the priests employed in sacred duty in the temple are provided for by temple resources? And the priests who serve at the altar receive a portion of the offerings? In the same way, the Lord has directed those who proclaim the gospel to receive their living by the gospel. (1 Cor. 9:7–14 TPT)

It's Offering Time!

As we saw with the 'two or three witnesses' principle in *Corroborating Content*, Paul cites a specific Old Testament prescription, finds the principle behind it and applies it to an analogous situation in his here-and-now. In this case, the giving of finance to feed the oxen who serve in the temple. Gee, way to mix metaphors Paul!

The Mosaic law contains numerous prescriptions for voluntary and non-voluntary offerings. Of the obligatory ones, the tithe is perhaps the best known and everyone seems to have their own take on it. Here's mine.

The specific *practice* of tithing is modelled first by the patriarchs, then mandated by Moses. Abraham and Jacob tithed (it seems) by their own initiative, whereas those under Torah tithed by direct instruction. The underlying *principle* to tithing is stewardship. The Israelites' tithe was never something they owned—it 'belonged' to the Lord. This is why they never *gave* a tithe; they *brought* the tithe. A steward, after all, is one who handles the property of another, who has something *in* their possession that is *not* their possession. The tithe was a sacred portion of one's produce, special and set apart for a specified task.

The ultimate *purpose* of the tithe was to empower ministry in the context of community worship, ensuring the effective operation of God's house. As the nature of God's house changed over time, so did the specifics of how the tithe was administered to fulfil its mission. During Israel's wilderness wanderings, the tithes exclusively supported the Levites in their tabernacle service. In the promised land, tithes supplied what was needed for a family to worship at the Jerusalem temple, and to empower ministry in the local community, where one's tithe supported the Levites and were shared among those in need. Under King David, temple singers and gatekeepers were also among those financed by tithing, a practice Nehemiah reinstates centuries later at the second temple. In the Gospels, Jesus Himself endorses tithing as a dutiful discipline for His fellow first-century Jews.[218]

The question is: what about the Christian community? *What does it matter to us?*

The new-covenant Scriptures do not specifically mandate tithing as a practice for followers of Christ. However, the purpose of tithing and the principle undergirding it are clearly expounded in the Epistles. The principle of obligatory giving is stated explicitly in Romans, in which Paul explains how the believers in Macedonia and Achaia gave money to the church in Jerusalem, in part because 'they owe it to them' or, more literally, because 'debtors they are' (Rom. 15:27 YLT). This is the same turn of phrase Paul uses of himself when he states: '**I am obligated** both to Greeks and non-Greeks' (Rom. 1:14). Paul owed a message, while the church owed money. The financial blessings given them by God were not theirs alone—they were obligated to share their material gifts with those who had benefitted them with spiritual ones.

In the passage above, Paul speaks of financial support as something he 'rightfully deserved' (1 Cor. 9:12 TPT), the implication being that since the apostle had a God-given right to receive, the Corinthians had a God-given *duty* to provide. He employs the same rationale in light of the local church elders in Ephesus, citing both Moses (Deut. 25:4) and Jesus (Luke 10:7) to support his claim:

> The pastors who lead the church well should be paid well. They should receive double honor for faithfully preaching and teaching the revelation of the Word of God. For the Scriptures have taught us: 'Do not muzzle an ox or forbid it to eat while it grinds the grain.' And also, 'The one who labors **deserves** his wages.' (1 Tim. 5:17–18 TPT)

As shepherds, pastors have a responsibility to both lead and feed their flock. As oxen, pastors have a right to be paid for their work from the community their ministry benefits.

While the practice may not be specifically or directly taught in the New Testament, the *purpose* of tithing (ensuring the effective operation of God's house) and the underlying *principle* behind it (faithful stewardship) clearly are.

 Timothy, believe me when I say your consistent financial support will do far more for your pastor than offering a kiss on the cheek or a foot-wash before dinner. Take good care of your ox.

Remember, when you come across a command that appears to have cultural overtones or specificities, avoid the temptation to simply dismiss it as 'irrelevant today'. Instead, seek to discover the why behind the what and—just as importantly—ask the Spirit and the saints to help you find an equivalent, contemporary application.

Cutting Considerations—Closing Comments

When constructing a life in keeping with the pattern of God's Word, as we seek to correctly contextualise its implications and applications for Christians today, the competent Bible student will find themselves making several critical cuts. These include distinguishing between the major and minor; clear and cloudy; descriptive and prescriptive; theirs and yours, and discerning the abiding purpose and still-relevant principles behind the then-and-there practice of the original audiences.

Rightly dividing the Word of Truth should be done with care-filled consideration and from a heart committed to bringing honour to its Divine Architect. After all, ultimately, the purpose behind every act of responsive obedience to the truth of Scripture is that we may know Him and make Him known to others. While the greatest commandment given under Torah was to 'love the Lord your God with all your heart, all your soul, all your mind, and all your strength' (Mark 12:30 NLT), the coming of the *greater* Moses brought about a new and more pressing command: 'to believe in the name of his Son, Jesus Christ, and to love one another as he commanded us ... As I have loved you, so you must love one another' (1 John 3:23; John 13:34).

His love *for* us has come *to* us. Now let what's *in* us flow *through* us:

> This is how God showed his love among us: He sent his one and only Son into the world that we might live through him. This is love: not that we loved God, but that he loved us and sent his Son as an atoning sacrifice for our sins. Dear friends, since God so loved us, we also ought to love one another ... We love because he first loved us. (1 John 4:9–19)

The Scriptures matter, so watch your life and doctrine closely. Rightly divide the Word of Truth and, in all things '[Let] love be your highest goal!' (1 Cor. 14:1 NLT).

Find 'JOY' in Biblical Revelation

In the first part of our *What does it matter?* discussion, we examined one of the most critical issues to the human experience: the question of life's *purpose*. This, I argued, is 'to know Him and to show Him'.

Here, I will address a related and equally pivotal concern: the question of *identity*. Certainly, in my cultural context, these appear to be among the most significant concerns for modern-day audiences: *who am I and why do I exist?* One of the reasons I am convinced the Bible matters to the modern reader is because it provides clear and accurate answers to these critical existential issues.

In this section we begin with some insights into the foundational importance of identity. I will then share with you one of my personal truth-discovery techniques, a helpful way to find relevancy and personal significance in

JESUS   OTHERS   YOU

most every Bible passage. It is here I will be encouraging you to *find 'JOY' in biblical revelation*, as we walk our way through the following:

A Rock-Solid Identity

Identify Yourself

Identify Others

Identify Jesus

Let the discovery begin.

CHAPTER 41

A Rock-Solid Identity

Father's Day Sunday, 2002, was a particularly significant one for me. To begin with, it was my first as a father. Our son was 10 months old and while I don't remember receiving a decent gift from him that particular day (he typically gave me disrupted sleep and a dirty nappy most mornings), I do recall the joy of becoming a parent for the very first time. When Jesse was born, I received one of God's greatest gifts and, with it, a significant and irreversible identity shift. I was now a father. Both literally, as I held my baby in my hands, and legally, as my name was placed on his birth certificate. Chad was now 'Dad'.

Yet, that first Father's Day was unique for another reason. That morning, just a week after being ordained into pastoral ministry, I would deliver my very first Sunday morning sermon to our newly planted church community. I had become a pastor and one of the primary responsibilities attached to that new identity was to feed God's flock.

The title of my maiden message consisted of five simple words: *I Will Build My Church*.

A Heavenly Revelation

> When Jesus came to the region of Caesarea Philippi, he asked his disciples, 'Who do people say the Son of Man is?' They replied, 'Some say John the Baptist; others say Elijah; and still others, Jeremiah or one of the prophets.' 'But what about you?' he asked. 'Who do you

say I am?' Simon Peter answered, '**You are the Messiah, the Son of the living God**.' Jesus replied, 'Blessed are you, Simon son of Jonah, for this was not revealed to you by flesh and blood, but by my Father in heaven. **And I tell you that you are Peter, and on this rock I will build my church**, and the gates of Hades will not overcome it. I will give you the keys of the kingdom of heaven; whatever you bind on earth will be bound in heaven, and whatever you loose on earth will be loosed in heaven.' (Matt. 16:13–19)

I chose to preach that day from this particular portion of Scripture for obvious reasons. The truth this text reveals is foundational to the life of the Christian community and fundamental to her ongoing health, growth and effectiveness. While this passage makes passing mention of the purpose and activity of the church (e.g., exercising the victorious authority of heaven on earth), it is first and foremost concerned with the importance of identity.

More than anything else, this passage speaks to the eternal identity of Jesus, the new identity of Simon-Peter and the collective identity of His called-out community (Greek: *ekklésia*).[219]

It is the rock-solid foundation of identity—the truth of who we are and Whose we are—that forms the bedrock of the house of God on earth. The revelation from heaven of who Jesus truly is and the revelation of who we are because of Him is the rock on which the new-covenant community stands and spreads.

Identity Precedes Activity

Since our great purpose in life is found in relationship (to know Christ and to show Him to others), it follows that we must give ourselves to discovering precisely who *Jesus* is, who *we* are and who are the *others* to which we are called. Knowledge of identity empowers us to fulfil our purpose.

Similarly, to love others as Christ has loved you, you must first *know* others, *know* Christ and *know* your true self! After all, we cannot love what we do not know.

In other words, identity precedes activity. I am, therefore, I do.

This divine order is demonstrated powerfully by the apostle Paul, particularly in the way he structures his epistles. While the bulk of his Corinthian correspondence consists of commands and corrections (and for good reason!), Paul opens his letter to this divided, fornicating, immature and selfish community, by first *affirming them in their blood-bought identity* as sons, servants and saints:

> [To] the assembly of God that is in Corinth, to **those sanctified in Christ Jesus, called saints,** with all those calling upon the name of our Lord Jesus Christ in every place—both theirs and ours: Grace to you and peace from **God our Father and the Lord Jesus Christ!** (1 Cor. 1:2–3 YLT)

Before instructing the Ephesians in Chapters 4–6 in how to 'live a life worthy of the calling' they had received (Eph. 4:1), the apostle first grounds them in the Gospel through Chapters 1–3, declaring what Christ had done for them and *who they now were* in light of His work. Romans 12 begins similarly, 'Therefore I urge you, brethren ... present your bodies a living and holy sacrifice ... your spiritual service of worship' (Rom. 12:1 NASB). However, this exhortation is only to be received in view of the passionate mercies of God as articulated in the previous eleven chapters. This, after all, is why 'therefore' is there for.

My advice here is simple. As you read your Bible and seek personal significance in its pages, I encourage you to ask yourself three questions: what does God's Word reveal about me, about others and about Him?

In other words: seek to identify *yourself*, identify *others* and identify *Jesus*.

We begin with you.

CHAPTER 42

Identify Yourself

And I tell you that **you are Peter**, and on this rock I will build my church. (Matt. 16:18)

Arguably, the most insecure of all the disciples, and certainly the most impetuous, Simon's heart was crying out to discover a true sense of his personhood, purpose and place in the world. Perhaps, like his Old Testament namesake Simeon, the fisherman feared that his propensity to impulsive behaviours would consign him to a future of lost opportunity, forfeited inheritance and the shame of not measuring up to the success of his brothers (Gen. 49:5–7). The Gospels demonstrate clearly that Simon knew what it was to live below his best-self and what it was to experience the overwhelming disappointment of such failures (Matt. 26:69–75).

 Sound familiar, Tammy?

But where Simon viewed himself as a self-doubting, erratic and sword-swinging fisherman, Jesus saw something else. By changing his name to Peter, which literally means 'a piece of rock' (Greek: *Petros* / Aramaic: *Cephas*), Jesus made it known that He saw something of Himself in this disciple. This man was more like His Master than he gave himself credit for. According to Jesus, Simon-Peter was a 'chip off the old Rock'.

Years later, no doubt with greater confidence in his rock-solid identity, Peter penned the following:

So keep coming to him who is the Living Stone—though he was rejected and discarded by men but chosen by God and is priceless in God's sight. **Come and be his 'living stones'** who are continually being assembled into a sanctuary for God. For now you serve as holy priests, offering up spiritual sacrifices that he readily accepts through Jesus Christ. (1 Peter 2:4–5 TPT)

Finally, Jesus' message seems to have sunk in! Christ was the 'Living Stone' of God's spiritual house, chosen, holy and precious in His sight. So too was Peter, and, as the student himself became a teacher, he desired the next generation of disciples to know they too were 'living stones'. These believers were more like their Master than they realised. The apostle wanted nothing more than for them to be secure and confident in their newfound identity in Christ:

But **you are God's chosen treasure—priests who are kings, a spiritual 'nation' set apart as God's devoted ones**. He called you out of darkness to experience his marvelous light, and now he claims you as his very own. He did this so that you would broadcast his glorious wonders throughout the world. For at one time you were not God's people, but now you are. (1 Peter 2:9–10 TPT)

The Old and New Testaments are replete with examples of God announcing identity over His people. In some cases, as with Simon-Peter, this literally involved a change of somebody's name: Abram to Abraham, Sarai to Sarah and Jacob to Israel (Gen. 17:5, 15; 32:38). 'What's in a name?' you may ask. Apparently, in cases in which it concerns identity, a great deal. Though they struggled with fertility issues, Sarai and Abram were to refer to themselves as 'mother and father of nations', and this before their first child was ever born! The point is: if God has called you something, if He has spoken concerning your identity *as He sees it*, no matter how unreasonable it may seem to you, who are you to disagree? Embrace what He says about you and change your speech to suit.

Make the Good Confession

Fight the good fight of the faith. Take hold of the eternal life to which you were called and about which you made **the good confession** in the presence of many witnesses. I charge you in the presence of God, who gives life to all things, and of Christ Jesus, who in his testimony before Pontius Pilate made **the good confession**. (1 Tim. 6:12–13 ESV)

The notion of 'making confession' in a religious context conjures varying thoughts depending on one's background. For many, however, it would most certainly include acknowledging sinfulness and admitting to error, disclosing deeds of darkness and professing one's depravity. However, this is not the type of confession Paul has in mind here. 'Confession' literally means 'to speak the same conclusion',[220] and is precisely what Jesus did while testifying before Pilate. Let me assure you, no matter what your preconceived ideas of confession may be, Jesus certainly did not confess His sin or shortcomings at that time! So, what confession did Messiah make?

Turns out He said very little, but what He did speak was profound. Jesus declared His identity:

Pilate asked Jesus, 'Is this true? Are you their king and Messiah?' Jesus answered, '**It is true**.' (Luke 23:3 TPT)[221]

When it didn't look like Jesus was King, when circumstances seemed to be stacked against Him, Jesus made the good confession. He spoke 'the same conclusion' that the Father had made regarding His identity. Jesus was indeed King and Messiah and He knew that to fight the good fight of faith, He would need to stand in agreement with heaven's revelation and speak the same word concerning His God-given identity and calling.

I encourage you to do the same. Having come to know who Christ is, lend your ear to truths that speak to who *you are* because of Him. Discover your identity and allow your lips and lifestyle to agree with that heavenly revelation: 'I am who I Am says I am'.

I Am Who I Am Says I Am

While the Bible contains occasional 'identity statements' over individuals, it is far more common to see God pronouncing an identity over His people *collectively*. The passage above from Peter, for example, famously draws from the announcement of God at Sinai when He called the nation of Israel His 'own special treasure', His 'kingdom of priests' and His 'holy nation' (Exo. 19:5–6 NLT).

Sadly, this same generation failed to enter their promised land when they cowered in fear at the thought of facing the giants who lived there. How could this be? Hadn't Yahweh just destroyed the mighty armies of Egypt before them, the most powerful nation known at the time? Did the Israelites think this same God was incapable of defeating the inhabitants of Canaan? No. God's ability was not in doubt here. The question was not whether Yahweh was big enough to defeat the giants; the challenge was 'are *we* big enough?'. The doubt did not lie in the issue of *God's* identity. What they doubted was their *own*. Listen to how the 10 unfaithful spies reported back to the community:

> But the men who had gone up with him said, '**We can't** attack those people; they are stronger than **we are** … **We seemed like grasshoppers in our own eyes**, and we looked the same to them.' (Num. 13:31–33)

In contrast to these unbelieving 10, Joshua and Caleb were of 'a different spirit'. Like Jesus before Pilate, these men stood face-to-face with the giants and the naysayers to declare the same word God had spoken: '**We should** go up and take possession of the land, for **we can** certainly do it' (Num. 14:24; 13:30). Centuries later, another young man from Judah, a humble shepherd boy, would stand before his giant and confidently say the same: 'This day the LORD will deliver you into my hands, and I'll strike you down and cut off your head. This very day I will give the carcasses of the Philistine army to the birds and the wild animals, and the whole world will know that there is a God in Israel' (1 Sam. 17:46).

Tammy, standing firm in your God-given identity is something future generations will thank you for and take great inspiration from.

To fight the good fight of the faith, take firm hold of the sword of the Spirit, the Word of God, which He has placed in your hands (Eph. 6:17). Know what God says about you and stand on that unshakeable testimony. For the most part, the New Testament Epistles will serve you best in this discovery, for these books speak most directly to the identity of those who are beneficiaries of Christ's life and covenant work. That said, when reading the Gospels, remember that, like Peter, you have more in common with Jesus than you likely appreciate.

See Yourself in Him

What I mean is this. In reading the story of the feeding of the 5,000 you may identify instinctively with the hungry crowds, the 'send them away' disciples or the little boy who shared his lunch. These are valid approaches, with unique lessons to be taken from each. Alternatively, gain a truly 'Christian' perspective by imagining yourself as Jesus in that situation and consider

 the potential *you* possess as a multiplier of resources to serve a world in great need. Rather than viewing yourself as Zaccheus, clambering desperately to catch a glimpse of Messiah in heavily crowded spaces, put yourself in the sandals of Jesus, and contemplate how you too are an *anointed one*, tasked to grant dignity to the outcast and call out the treasure within those stunted by shame. Although you may note some

similarities between yourself and the demonised boy, his doubting father, disbelieving Pharisees or despondent disciples, remember, *it is Christ*—the One who provides solutions when others cannot—in whose image you have been created and into whose image you are continuously being conformed.[222] Put simply: make a habit of finding yourself in Him.

Like a mirror, the Scriptures reveal *the real you* and urge us to apply that true identity in our everyday life. Your mission, should you choose to accept it, is to *discover* your identity, *delight* in what God says about you and *display* your true self to others. After all, the best way to re-present Christ, is to simply be yourself—a true chip off the old Rock:

> **Don't just listen to the Word of Truth and not respond to it, for that is the essence of self-deception.** So always let his Word become like poetry written and fulfilled by your life! If you listen to the Word and don't live out the message you hear, you become like the person who **looks in the mirror of the Word to discover the reflection of his face in the beginning.** *You perceive how God sees you in the mirror of the Word,* but then you go out and forget your divine origin. But those who set their gaze deeply into the perfecting law of liberty are fascinated by and respond to the truth they hear and are strengthened by it—they experience God's blessing in all that they do! (James 1:22–25 TPT)

CHAPTER 43

Identify Others

Since that first Father's Day Sunday in 2002, I have grown a great deal as a parent and pastor. While challenges have been plentiful, and no doubt there are more to come, as I begin to move into my 40s, I am certainly more 'comfortable in my own skin' than I was back then. Prioritising the truth of God's Word, spoken and written, has been a significant key to any success I have achieved in these spaces. This is not only because I have learnt a great deal about *myself*. Both life and the Logos have taught me a great deal about *others*:[223]

> Elijah was a man **with a nature like ours**, and he prayed earnestly that it would not rain … But when the apostles Barnabas and Paul heard of it, they tore their robes and rushed out into the crowd, crying out and saying, 'Men, why are you doing these things? We are also men **of the same nature as you.**' (James 5:17; Acts 14:14–15 NKJV)

The grumpy old philosopher was right. Insofar as the nature of people is concerned, 'there is nothing new under the sun' (Eccl. 1:9).

One of the reasons the characters of the biblical narrative serve as 'examples for us' (1 Cor. 10:6–11 NLT) is that in almost every significant way, human nature remains the same today as it was then. Be it the Bible's great heroes, such as Elijah, Barnabas and Paul just mentioned, or its notorious villains such as Haman, Abimelech and Jezebel, the Scriptures contain the tales and testimonies of people just like us. Specifically, for our purposes right now, their stories serve as wonderful aids to help us relate well to those significant 'others' in our life.

Whether you are connected to others in the context of family, friendship, politics or business, to those in places of struggle or success, poverty or power, the Bible provides insight into understanding how people work and how you can work best with them. After all, understanding others is vital to the health of all interpersonal relationships. Jesus modelled this for us: '**He understands humanity**, for as a Man, our magnificent King-Priest was tempted in every way **just as we are**' (Heb. 4:15 TPT). By understanding us 'just as we are', Jesus was able to empathise, and thereby effectively serve, those to whom He was called.

As Habit 5 in his bestselling *The 7 Habits of Highly Effective People*®, Stephen Covey phrases it this way: 'Seek first to understand, then to be understood'.

In seeking to understand others in my personal and pastoral life, I have found great benefit in studying the stories of David in particular. Here are a few things I've observed.

David's Father Wounds

Before becoming king, David faced the significant challenge of rejection from those in his own family, most notably his father and brothers, who quite openly expressed no belief in him (1 Sam. 16:5–11; 17:28–29). Further, he received constant rejection (even abuse) from his mentor-come-spiritual-father Saul, despite having proved himself a loyal and successful servant in both contexts (1 Sam. 18:28–30).

I can thankfully say this is not my experience, but such is not the case for many, and this has been something I have had to understand when dealing with others. This is especially so when those who have been hurt by father-figures in the past struggle to trust even the most faithful of fathers (or mothers) in the present.

One of the great pains of pastoral ministry is to watch people whom you have loved, believed in and even fought for, turn their hearts away from you, no longer trust your counsel and question the purity of your intentions and commitment towards them. This is a struggle Paul the apostle knew too well in his dealings with the Corinthians.[224]

Reading through David's rejection experience has helped me sympathise with those who struggle with this, even when their turning away from me has pained my heart in the process. Rather than reacting to such rejection, 'seeking first to understand' has helped me as a pastor to remain kind and compassionate towards those who, like David, experience ongoing injury from historical father-wounds.

Jonathan's Naivety

Jonathan provides fascinating insight into the dangers of unsanctified naivety and over-extended loyalty. Read his story and you'll observe a man who continued to believe the best about his dad despite Saul demonstrating over and again that he was entirely untrustworthy.

Through 1 Samuel 18–26, King Saul makes attempts on David's life no fewer than 15 times! Whether he was hurling his trusty spear or orchestrating death by foreign fighters, sending men to abduct him from his house or assembling armies to chase him through the desert, time and again Saul makes concerted efforts to kill David, repents and apologises when unsuccessful, then changes his mind and seeks out David once more. Saul was seemingly obsessed with destroying God's chosen leader, demonstrating a classic case of 'David derangement syndrome'.

Despite his repeated offending, despite witnessing Saul explode in fits of rage and even threaten his own life in a fanatical frenzy, Jonathan naively believed the best of his father: "'Never!" Jonathan said. "If I had the least inkling that my father was determined to harm you, wouldn't I tell you?'" (1 Sam. 20:9). Sadly, though he had opportunity to join David's growing army and play a part in the kingdom he would soon lead, Jonathan died on the battlefield while playing for a losing team. His over-extended loyalty cut short his destiny and broke David's heart (2 Sam. 1:26).[225]

On a personal level, I struggle to identify with Jonathan on this issue. While I certainly endeavour to see the best in all people, it is clear that there comes a point at which it is foolish to continue entrusting yourself to those who have proven themselves un-trust-worthy. Jesus may have taught His followers to 'turn the other cheek' (Matt. 5:39), but once both those cheeks have been callously and intentionally struck, it is likely time to consider a *full* turn and ensure you are not struck again!

Throughout my pastoral life, I have met people who remain committed to dangerous and damaging relationships. At times, these are personal relationships, at others, professional ones. In some cases, they are even pastoral, when naïve Christians repeatedly grant their spiritual seniors 'room for doubt' despite clear evidence to the contrary. In my counsel to them, I have remembered Jonathan and empathised with the very real pull he must have felt between his loyalty to a friend and his loyalty to a father.

Absalom's Cunning

One of the primary responsibilities of a pastor to their people, as with a parent to their child, is to offer protection. Paul warned the Romans to 'watch out for those who cause divisions' and the Ephesian elders of 'savage wolves' who would seek to destroy their flocks (Rom. 16:17; Acts 20:29). Jesus said the wolf's purpose was to attack and scatter, and warned against 'ferocious wolves' subtly dressed as innocent sheep (John 10:12; Matt. 7:15). Like it or not, there are some who, for whatever reason, are out to harm God's people. Like the serpent in the garden, they do so cunningly.

While very rare, there have been moments in my pastoral career when I have had to pull out the shepherd's rod and drive a dangerous wolf away. The most memorable occasion happened soon after three separate people in our congregation had vivid dreams concerning dangerous animals attacking our church. We shared them with a ministry friend experienced in dream interpretation. It was his opinion that Holy Spirit was warning us to be alert to an attack of the kind demonstrated by Absalom. I am so thankful we were issued that warning.

Reading the story of Absalom is heartbreaking. His little sister had been raped by her half-brother, Amnon, and while David was apparently angered by this heinous act, he did nothing about it. David refused to confront his rapist son. After two long years harbouring hatred towards his brother, Absalom murdered Amnon and fled to the land of a foreign king. David, again, did nothing about it. He made no contact with his murderous son for five years (2 Sam. 13–14).

Although the Bible does not say, it is likely the king's silence was evidence of crippling shame. Not only did David have cause to be embarrassed by the sordid behaviour of his boys, he too had performed the very same crimes: raping Bathsheba and then murdering her husband (2 Sam. 11).[226]

Having returned to Jerusalem, Absalom began to stage a deliberate and devious takeover of the kingdom by winning the hearts of the people to himself with lies, flattery and seductive promises. Under great intimidation, David fled in fear of his own son. The once-courageous shepherd who had fought off lions, bears and giants had now been reduced to a cowardly king, who deserted his God-given post and allowed the cunning conspirator to move in (2 Sam. 15–16).

If there's one thing I've learnt in pastoral ministry it's this: hurt people hurt people. In extreme cases (e.g., Absalom), they do so intentionally and with intense intimidation tactics. To love people, we do well to develop our understanding of the subtle strategies and manipulating manoeuvrings of those who are out to deliberately harm God's flock. We also do well to understand the proclivity in certain personalities to suffer debilitating shame (e.g., David) in the hope that we can avoid creating Absaloms in the first place.

Over the years, each of these life lessons have proved invaluable to me, and all three come from just one book! The Bible is full of such stories and every one matters. After all, the Bible is written about people just like us.

The Scriptures teach us about *others*, that we may understand them and thereby love them, just as Christ has commanded.

CHAPTER 44

Identify Jesus

Philip found Nathanael and told him, '**We have found the one Moses wrote about in the Law, and about whom the prophets also wrote--Jesus of Nazareth**, the son of Joseph' ... And beginning with Moses and all the Prophets, he explained to them what was said in all the Scriptures concerning himself ... 'Everything must be fulfilled that is written about me in the Law of Moses, the Prophets and the Psalms ... These are the very Scriptures that testify about me.' (John 1:45; Luke 24:27, 44–45; John 5:39)

And so, we have saved the best until last!

The Scriptures reveal the true identity of Jesus Christ. More than any other reason, this is why they truly matter.

The Big Reveal

Today, my wife and I are proud parents to four amazing kids—our eldest is now an adult with two others close behind. In this season of parenting, I am finding great enjoyment in sharing cultural influences from my young adult years with my growing brood. For the most part, this includes music, film and sitcoms from the nineties and early noughties. Fashion ... not so much. My favourite brand of movie (and this era seemed to produce a good number of these) are those that build to a big reveal at the end. The suspense created by a well-crafted and executed storyline, together with the genuine surprise of an unexpected ending, provides a great formula for films that stand the test of time. To witness my kids experience their own 'I did not see that coming!' moment is somehow deeply satisfying. On a personal level, watching these films again, fully aware of the big reveal coming, is likewise a satisfying experience. There is something about knowing the end from the beginning that makes you appreciate the story even more.

In many ways, the Bible does the very same thing.

The Bible is the self-revelation of God in written form, presented within the framework of an unfolding narrative. A suspense-building storyline leads the reader to a big reveal at its end. And that big reveal is Christ—the final piece in the puzzle Who holds all the others together:[227]

> Throughout our history God has spoken to our ancestors by his prophets in many different ways. **The revelation he gave them was only a fragment at a time, building one truth upon another. But to us living in these last days, God now speaks to us openly in the language of a Son** ... The Son is the dazzling radiance of God's splendor, **the exact expression** of God's true nature—his mirror image! (Heb. 1:1–3 TPT)

The main reason the Bible *matters* to us, what makes it most significant of all, is that it reveals Jesus and Jesus is the greatest self-revelation God has ever provided. In hermeneutic terms, Jesus is the exegesis of the Father: '**He has explained** [Greek: *exēgēsato*] **Him**' (John 1:18 NASB).

Back to the movies. My kids and I recently watched the *Karate Kid* sequel series, *Cobra Kai*. Predictably, and I guarantee this happened with fathers my age everywhere, this gave me a great excuse to insist they first sit through the original 1984 film from my childhood. The storyline is simple. Japanese karate instructor Mr Miyagi takes young Daniel LaRusso under his wing to coach him for a tournament in which he can face against a notorious group of bullies. Mr Miyagi's training methods, which mostly involved menial chores around the yard and performing a one-legged balancing act at the beach, were far from conventional. For most of the movie, until the day of the tournament, the Karate Kid performs no karate at all.

Were you to switch this film off at the 100-minute mark, you would be left with a desperately deficient view of both the ability of Daniel LaRusso and the wisdom of Mr Miyagi. Sure, you may draw *some* accurate assessments about them, but your conclusions would certainly be incomplete. After all, it's not until the final five minutes that the Karate Kid is revealed in his full glory. Only then is the mystery behind Mr Miyagi's seemingly mad methods made known. Towards the end of the film, all the pieces come together, leaving the audience awestruck by the master's grand plan, celebrating the victory of a wounded hero and revelling in the humiliation of a villain who had no idea what hit him.

Progressive Revelation

The primary purpose of all Scripture is to make God known to us, and it does so in what is often called *progressive revelation*.[228] God's self-revelation has come in stages, progressively, as part of an unfolding sequence of ever-increasing clarity and certainty. Simply put, the further along in the Bible you read, the fuller the picture you will develop of God's true nature. Like Karate Kid, the big reveal comes right towards the end.

As you read through the Old Testament particularly, remember this: every character, conflict, communication and command build towards a culmination and climax in the unveiling of Christ:

> **He is the exact living image** [the essential manifestation] **of the unseen God** [the visible representation of the invisible] ... Anyone who has seen Me has seen the Father. (Col. 1:15; John 14:9 AMP)[229]

While there are parts and portions of Scripture that are perplexing, and at times obscure (to say the least), somehow all of it serves to reveal something of the name and nature of God. It is not always easy to find contemporary significance in each story, psalm, passage or prophecy. It is not always clear where biblical application can be made to us today.

But this I know: Christ is the clearest and most precise picture we have of the otherwise invisible God. All Scripture is designed to point us to Him, that we may know Him as He truly is, draw near to Him in unfettered assurance, participate in His unshakeable Kingdom and worship Him 'with reverence and awe, for our "God is a consuming fire"' (Heb. 12:28–29).

You see, ultimately, true knowledge of God should lead us to true worship of God. In other words: theology produces doxology.[230]

Through the Torah, Yahweh reveals Himself as a God of promise, power and purity, while in the histories, He is a conquering yet kind covenant-keeping King. The books of wisdom display His passion, prudence and praise, while the Prophets declare One who is faithful, fair and future-there. The Gospels give manifestation, the book of Acts brings multiplication, the Epistles explanation and Revelation sees consummation. As you read through the 66 books of our Bible, know that while you may not be clear on all the detail, you will always have cause to declare His praise:

> Now to the King eternal, immortal, invisible, the only God, be honor and glory for ever and ever. Amen. (1 Tim. 1:17)

The Endgame

I have spent considerable time in this book encouraging you to grow in your understanding and comprehension of Scripture. To ask questions of the text, embrace curiosity, employ good sense and logic as you intelligently read, research and reason your way to discover the meaning of God's Word. With all that said, please remember that increasing our understanding of the Bible is not an end in itself. *Knowing God* as He has revealed Himself to be, and responding accordingly, is what matters most.

As we handle the Scriptures well, sometimes the best response we can offer is not to ask 'why?', but simply to say 'wow!', not to pose a query, but to issue a 'glory!'. In your search for understanding, never lose the wonder. Be willing to be undone by the glory of the Mysterious One. After all, the psalms tell us to worship the Lord 'in the splendor of his holiness', not in the splendour of our intellect (Ps. 29:2; 96:9). Here on earth, we will always have questions unanswered. We do well to make peace with the mystery and worship Him regardless.

So, we can consider the 10 plagues of Egypt and ask the specific meaning behind each of those acts or we can pay attention to what it tells us about our Father's nature and praise Him for His unparalleled power. We can argue the symbolic significance of Jesus' turning water into wine or we can give thanks for a Saviour of unspeakable generosity. We can question what was implied when Holy Spirit came as wind or fire, or as a dove, and in a shaking, or we can simply say 'wow' and believe Him for more:

> LORD, I have heard of your fame; I stand in awe of your deeds, LORD. Repeat them in our day, in our time make them known … Jesus Christ is the same yesterday and today and forever. (Hab. 3:2; Heb. 13:8)

SUMMARY REMARKS—STEP 3

Time to sum up Step 3, by returning to where we first began—Nehemiah, Chapter 8:

> They read out of the book of the law of God, translating and giving the meaning so that the people could understand what was read. Nehemiah the governor, Ezra the priest and scribe, and the Levites who were instructing the people said to all of them, 'This day is holy to the Lord your God. Do not mourn or weep.' (Neh. 8:8–9 CSB)

As Ezra and his Levite companions stood before those gathered by the water gate in Jerusalem, they read the Scriptures to the people and explained its meaning. In response, the assembly began to mourn and weep until the leaders stepped in and stopped them. Somehow, they had missed the point. 'Do not grieve', said Nehemiah, 'because **the joy** of the LORD is your strength' (Neh. 8:10 CSB).

As demonstrated in this story, correctly handling the Word of Truth, rightly dividing God's Word, involves addressing three critical questions of the text: *What does it say? What does it mean? What does it matter?* As you undertake this third and final step in the process of healthy hermeneutics give careful attention to the five *cutting considerations* presented earlier and recall the apostle Paul's exhortation to 'cut straight!' Finally, I encourage you to heed Nehemiah's advice: find 'JOY' in biblical revelation—the truth it makes known about *Jesus, others* and *yourself.*

Yep. One final acronym. I couldn't resist.

[My dear Timothy and Tammy]: Follow the
pattern of the sound words that you have heard
from me, in the faith and love that are in Christ
Jesus. By the Holy Spirit who dwells within us,
guard the good deposit entrusted to you …
The Lord be with your spirit. Grace be with you.
(2 Tim. 1:13–14; 4:22 ESV)

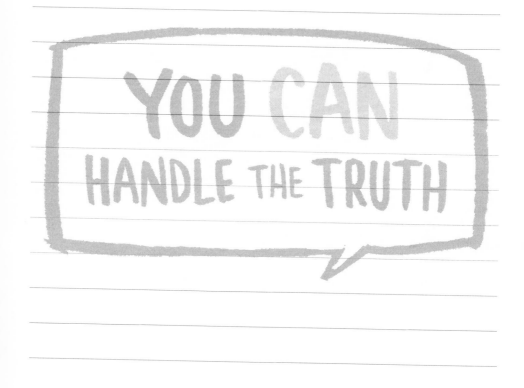

LAST BUT NOT LEAST

I close with a word of thanks.

Dad, first and foremost, this is for You. You have promised to guide me always and, time and again, have proven Yourself faithful. I am eternally grateful for all You are, all You have done, and all You have said. Great Book, by the way. You're one heck of an author.

Babe, it's here … finally! As with anything worth doing, there has been a price to pay in the development of this work, and you have been willing to invest more than anyone may ever realise to see it come together. Thanks so much. Love you loads.

To my group of keen-eyed critics who read through early drafts and provided invaluable feedback regards the content and direction of this project—including Andrew, Barry, Bette, Bruce, Catherine, Chris and David; Don, Duncan, Emma, Ilona and John; Margot, Mike, Paul, Phil, Rob, Ryan and Tony; plus Feline Graphics for layout, Louis for art, Robyn for the edit, and Chris regards publishing—many thanks to each of you for your time and input. This book is far better as a result of your labours of love. What erors remain, I claim as my own.

To my local church family who have served as a sounding board for the ideas here presented, and, more importantly, a model of what it is to live these principles out: 'For your very lives are our "letters of recommendation," permanently engraved on our hearts, recognized and read by everybody ... living letters written by Christ' (2 Cor. 3:2–3 TPT). Thanks for allowing me a place to develop my thoughts and the space to share them with others. The eternal fruit produced from this book will be credited also to you.

Finally, to the many establishments over the years, both local and beyond, who accommodated me during my lengthy writing process: from hotels and holiday homes, to parks, cafes, libraries and pubs—as I've read back through this book, memories of my time with you have often come to mind. Consider yourself an unwitting partner in the spread of God's Gospel.

Step 4

Pupil to Preacher

...me to this special bonus feature of *You Can Handle the Truth*. Here, ...r a brief glance at the art of biblical proclamation, where the student ...es a teacher and the pupil a preacher.

...He came to Nazareth, where he had been brought up. As usual, ...e entered the synagogue on the Sabbath day and stood up to ...ead. The scroll of the prophet Isaiah was given to him, and ...nrolling the scroll, he found the place where it was written: **The Spirit of the Lord is on me, because he has anointed me to preach good news to the poor.** He has sent me to proclaim ...elease to the captives and recovery of sight to the blind, to set ...ree the oppressed, to proclaim the year of the Lord's favor. He ...hen rolled up the scroll, gave it back to the attendant, and sat ...lown. And the eyes of everyone in the synagogue were fixed ...on him. He began by saying to them, "Today as you listen, this ...Scripture has been fulfilled." (Luke 4:16–21 CSB)

...ler this a fourth step in our process of correctly handling God's Word

SHARE IT WITH OTHERS

What does it say?, *What does it mean?* and *What does it matter?* have now led us to consider: *How do I share it with others?* In technical terms: hermeneutics has led us to homiletics.

Homiletics derives from the Greek *homilia* and ca[...]
'communication' or 'companionship' (1 Cor. 15:3[...]
exclusively to refer to the practice of prepar[...]
you'd expect, this is a massive subject an[...]
right. To keep things simple, we w[...]
epistles to Timothy, as we examir[...]

The Preacher in Privat[...]

The Preacher in Pu[...]

The Preache[...]

Timothy, Ta[...]

UNLOCK STEP 4
FOR FREE!

for immediate and
exclusive access to three
chapters of *bonus content*, go to:
chadmansbridge.com/step4bonus

ENDNOTES

Getting Started

1. Acts 16:9, 18, 26; 18:9.

2. Acts 15:40–41; 16:4–15; 18:1–3; Phil. 4:15–16.

3. 'Tanakh' is the Hebrew name for the Old Testament. Strictly speaking, *TaNaKh* is an acronym derived from the first letters of the three main divisions of the Hebrew Bible: Law (Torah), Prophets (Nevi'im) and Writings (Ketuvim).

4. See also John 12:14–16; 20:9.

5. It is a common misconception that Saul changed his name to Paul after his conversion; instead, he held two names simultaneously (Acts 13:9). Saul was his Hebrew/Jewish name, while Paul was his Roman name (Latin: *Paulus*).

6. You may be familiar with the suggested acronym for BIBLE: Basic Instructions Before Leaving Earth.

7. For further reading on this matter, see Gordon Fee, *Listening to the Spirit in the Text* (2000), Grand Rapids: Eerdmans; John Piper, *Reading the Bible Supernaturally: Seeing and Savoring the Glory of God in Scripture* (2017), Wheaton: Crossway Publishing.

8. Jeffrey Weima & Steven Baugh, *Zondervan Illustrated Bible Backgrounds Commentary: 1 and 2 Thessalonians, 1 and 2 Timothy, Titus* (2016), Zondervan Academic, p. 490.

9. The New Testament word for saints (Greek: *hágios*) literally means 'holy ones', an adjective used most often to describe Holy Spirit but also in reference to everyday Christian believers: those who are special, set apart and supernatural creatures by virtue of their new nature in Christ!

10. See also Acts 8:30–31.

11. For an Old Testament example, see 2 Chron. 17:7–9, in which King Jehoshaphat funds and commissions a large team of travelling Torah teachers to instruct people throughout all the towns of Judah.

12. For an extensive list of recommended resources to assist your Bible study, see Appendix 3: Building a Personal Library, in J. Duvall & J. Hays, *Grasping God's Word* (2012), Zondervan.

13. While literary interpretation may not be considered 'scientific' in the strict sense of that term, it is nevertheless widely accepted in biblical scholarship to refer to hermeneutics as both an art and a science: 'Hermeneutics, therefore, is both a science and an art. As a science, it enunciates principles, investigates the laws of thought and language, and classifies its facts and results. As an art, it teaches what application these principles should have, and establishes their soundness by showing their practical value in the elucidation of the more difficult scriptures' (Milton Terry, *Biblical Hermeneutics*, Eaton & Mains, p. 20); Also William Klein, Robert Hubbard Jr & Craig Blomberg, *Introduction to Biblical Interpretation* (2017), Zondervan, p. 5.

14. This three-part sequence mirrors the process of inductive reasoning (as opposed to deductive reasoning), and so is sometimes referred to as *inductive Bible study*. Howard Hendricks and William Hendricks employ a similar three-step structure in their excellent work *Living by the Book: The Art and Science of Reading the Bible* (2007), Moody Publishers.

Step 1: What Does it Say?

15. When dealing with literature, 'canon' refers to a body of work considered genuine or authoritative, and formally sanctioned as such by a community or group of experts in the field.

16. Recommended reading: Greg Lanier, *A Christian's Pocket Guide to: How We Got the Bible* (2018), Christian Focus Publications, UK; Jeff Lasseigne, *Unlocking the Scriptures: What the Bible Is, How We Got it, and Why We Can Trust It* (2016), Baker Books, Grand Rapids, MI.

17. For further reading on the task of translation and the history of the Bible in English, see N. T. Wright, *Scripture and the Authority of God* (2005), HarperCollins, New York, NY.

18. When recommending a Bible translation to others, consider their personal reading level and the translation-of-choice among their pastors and peers because it is often helpful to read from the same version when studying with, or learning from, those who have regular ministry input into one's life. Further reading recommendation: Gordon Fee & Mark Strauss, *How to Choose*

YOU CAN HANDLE THE TRUTH

a *Translation for All Its Worth: A Guide to Understanding and Using Bible Versions* (2007), Zondervan, Grand Rapids, MI.

19. It is not my intention to advocate for either of these translations in or of themselves, but simply to offer them as personal examples to illustrate my point.

20. It is best to understand all Bible translations as fitting on a continuum between the word-for-word approach (formal equivalency) and the thought-for-thought approach (dynamic equivalency). For further discussion on translation models/approaches, see: Dave Brunn, *One Bible, Many Versions: Are All Translations Created Equal?* (2013), IVP; Fee & Strauss, *How to Choose a Translation for All Its Worth*; J. Duvall & J. Hays, 'Bible translations' in *Grasping God's Word*.

21. For advice on choosing a translation for serious Bible study, see Michael Gorman, Chapter Two in *Elements of Biblical Exegesis: a Basic Guide for Students and Ministers* (2009), Hendrickson Publishers, Peabody, MA.

22. Jesus famously said the following regarding His parable of the sower: 'Do you not understand this parable? How then will you understand all the parables?' (Mark 4:13 ESV).

23. The word *biblia* appears in John 21:25; 2 Tim. 4:13 and Rev. 20:12.

24. Credit for the term 'Diverse Anthology' goes to Richard Shultz, *Out of Context: How to Avoid Misinterpreting the Bible* (2012), Baker Books, Grand Rapids, MI.

25. See also Zech. 7:12; 2 Tim. 3:16; 2 Peter 1:21. Referred to as the Doctrine of Inspiration, there have historically been a variety of positions explaining just how 'God-breathed' words were put to paper. Currently, the most widely held view in evangelical tradition is that of *Organic, Verbal Plenary Inspiration*, which insists that each recorded word (verbal) and all recorded words (plenary) were divinely inspired, while simultaneously fully engaging the intellect, personalities, cultural influences, lexicon and linguistic abilities of the human writer (organic). See Milton Terry, *Biblical Hermeneutics* (p. 144); Greg Lanier, *How We Got the Bible* (pp. 4–7).

26. In late 1946, nomadic shepherds stumbled upon a cave in the West Bank (a mile from the Dead Sea), housing a collection of earthenware jars filled with ancient scrolls. This chance discovery led to the unearthing of some of the oldest and best preserved manuscript copies of the Hebrew Bible. These have come to be known as the Dead Sea Scrolls.

27. See Matt. 13:1–23; Mark 4:1–20; Luke 8:4–15. The books of Matthew, Mark and Luke are known collectively as the Synoptic Gospels in that they essentially recall the same account of Jesus' life and ministry—*synoptic* means 'presenting, or taking, a common view'.

28. At the Last Supper, Judas the Betrayer called Jesus 'Rabbi/Teacher', whereas the rest of the group referred to Him as their 'Lord' (Matt. 26:20–25). It was the recognition of Christ's lordship that formed the firm foundation of the Eleven's enduring faith. A revelation, sadly, Judas refused.

29. Classic 'devotional study tools' include *My Utmost for His Highest* (Oswald Chambers), *Morning and Evening* (Charles Spurgeon) and *Every Day with Jesus* (Selwyn Hughes). There are now countless books, apps and websites devoted to this purpose.

30. For the small number of books that do *not* have a strong 'narrative' flow (Psalms and Proverbs are perhaps the most obvious examples), a chronological reading is perhaps not as vital. These can be read much like a cookbook, for example, in which the reader can simply turn to the item that most interests them. However, most Bible books are best read from start to finish, as one would with a novel or play.

31. 'The great motive of all interpretation is the acquirement of the author's thought; and the study of the book as a whole is the only scientific method of accomplishing this'. Clinton Lockhart, *Principles of Interpretation* (2nd ed, 1915), Gospel Light Publishing Company, p. 230, Delight, AR. Teaching others 'through a book' in this way (verse-by-verse or thought-by-thought) is often referred to as *expositional* teaching.

32. Recommended Reading: *How to Read a Book*, Mortimer J. Adler (1940).

33. Most noteworthy here are the contributions of Catholic Archbishop Stephen Langton (1227), Rabbi Mordecai Nathan (1448), and Robert Estienne (1555). The first Protestant Bible to include chapter and verse references throughout was the Geneva Bible of 1560, which also contained marginal notes, introductions to each book, indexes, maps, tables and more: this was the world's first 'study Bible'!

34. The desire to read through the biblical narrative 'as it happened' is not new. Second-century Christian apologist Tatian compiled the four Gospels into a chronological format in 170 AD. This Gospel harmonisation project is known as *The Diatessaron*, literally 'through the four Gospels'.

35. My *Chronological Bible-in-a-Year* reading schedule and video tutorials are available online. See www.chadmansbridge.com for details.

36. An adverb deriving from the word for 'law', *nomímōs* refers to that which is done in accordance with the rules, lawfully, rightfully or properly.

37. For some practical examples of common Scripture mishandling found in modern pulpits, see Shultz, *Out of Context: How to Avoid Misinterpreting the Bible.*

Step 2: What Does it Mean?

38. The opposite of exegesis ('drawing out' the meaning of the author) is *eisegesis* ('putting in' the meaning of the reader). Essentially, when one performs eisegesis, they make the text conform to their preferences or preconceptions: making it say what they want it to say or what they presuppose it to mean.

39. 'Exegesis is the careful, systematic study of the Scripture to discover the original, intended meaning. This is basically a historical task. It is the attempt to hear the Word as the original recipients were to have heard it, to discover *the original intent of the words of the Bible*' (Fee, *How to Read the Bible for all Its Worth*, p. 23).

40. The search for authorial intent is sometimes referred to as the grammatico-historical method of interpretation and can be aided by placing ourselves in the shoes (or 'the sandals') of the Bible's original recipients. What did they understand as they received these written or spoken words? This is often referred to as 'audience relevance'. However, we must be aware that often (particularly in the Gospels), original Bible audiences misunderstood what was being communicated. We examine several such instances in *Style of Speech*.

41. That God intended to communicate a deeper or multifaceted meaning in a text, beyond what the *human* author may have comprehended, is referred to as *sensus plenior*, a Latin term meaning 'a fuller sense'.

42. Yep, I slipped in another acronym—preacher's habit. Here is an alternate option you may prefer: Seek to discover HIM, the 'Historical Intended Meaning' of the text.

43. For my younger readers (who may have missed it), 'Who's on first?' is a reference to a classic comedy sketch by Abbott and Costello, circa 1953. Do yourself a favour and look it up.

44. At times, the title refers to neither the author nor the audience, but instead indicates its leading characters (Judges, Nehemiah and Ruth), overall theme (Lamentations and Acts) or literary genre (Proverbs and Psalms).

45. Said Stephen: '[Moses] received living words *to pass on to us*' (Acts 7:38). Clearly, God's intent was that His words spoken at Sinai to the original Hebrew hearers were to be handed down to future adherents. Stephen's contemporaries, living many centuries after Moses, were still the intended audience of God's Word given to the original exodus generation.

46. For the most part, Moses (Israel's first national prophet and leader) is attributed as the primary author of the Torah; Genesis, Exodus, Leviticus, Numbers and Deuteronomy, which some suggest was collated into a single literary work during the Babylonian exile (see Mark 12:26; Luke 24:27, 44; Acts 28:23).

47. It is helpful to note that while the Bible often speaks of the '12 tribes of Israel', there were in fact 13 once Joseph's two sons became heirs alongside the 11 brothers (Gen. 48–49). Only 12 of the tribes were allocated land in Canaan, with the tribe of Levi receiving the priesthood (Deut. 18:1–2).

48. See Col. 2:16–17; Heb. 8:5; 9:1–10:1. In fact, some instructions were made redundant many centuries before Christ because they pertained specifically to Israel's years in the wilderness. After establishing themselves in the promised land, and especially once the temple was built, laws relating to worship in the tabernacle were no longer applicable. What it *said* and what it *meant* had not changed, only how it *mattered* to future generations of worshippers.

49. The word commonly used to describe Israel's festivals as holy 'assemblies' or 'convocations' (Hebrew: *miqra*), may also speak of a public rehearsal (Lev. 23:2). In other words, the Feasts of Passover, Unleavened Bread, Firstfruits, Weeks, Trumpets, Day of Atonement and Tabernacles

were all dress rehearsals leading to the main event: the ministry of Christ!

50. The book of Proverb's final words and *Wife of Noble Character* epilogue are introduced as: 'The sayings of King Lemuel—an inspired utterance his mother taught him' (Prov. 31:1). *Strong's Exhaustive Concordance* defines the Hebrew word *Lemuel* (H3927) as 'a symbolic name of Solomon'. This idea is supported by Jewish rabbinical tradition as indicated in the Babylonian Talmud (Tractate Avot), Chapter 5. *Lemuel* may be an affectionate nickname given to Solomon from his birth mother, Bathsheba.

51. A prophet (Hebrew: *nabi*) was one called to speak on behalf of a deity, whereas a seer (Hebrew: *ro'eh*) described one who had visions. Similar in some respects, but distinct, both words are used side-by-side in 1 Sam. 9:9.

52. Prophets who operated most notably in this capacity include John of Revelation, Ezekiel and Daniel. See also Micaiah's vision (1 Kings 22:19–28) and Isaiah's courtroom commission (Isa. 6).

53. As Israel's first national prophet, leader and lawgiver; the language, themes and motifs introduced by Moses (particularly those in Deuteronomy 27–32) formed a foundation for subsequent prophets who used his words to 'testify against' the old-covenant community (2 Kings 17:13; 2 Chron. 24:19). For further study on the role of Old Testament prophets, consider Richard Pratt's online course, *He Gave Us Prophets* (2007), Third Millennium Ministries (www.thirdmill.org).

54. Hosea serves as a great example of this, beginning in third-person narrative (Hos. 1:1–6) before becoming autobiographical from 3:1; his prophecies regularly switch both author and audience. The book of Daniel is evenly split between biography in the first half (Dan. 1–6) and autobiography in the last (Dan. 7–12).

55. See Matt. 3:7–10; Luke 3:7–9. The old-covenant community had been described as a fruitless tree destined for judgment by prophets previous (e.g., Jer. 11:16–17), a motif used also for national judgments towards others (Ezek. 31; Dan. 4:23).

56. See Matt. 24–25; Luke 21:5–38. The Olivet Discourse is the name given to Jesus' lengthy prophetic teaching on the impending destruction of Jerusalem and the 'end of the age'—so called since it was spoken to His disciples while they were seated on the Mount of Olives overlooking the city's temple mount.

57. Lanier, *How we Got the Bible* (p. 92).

58. Ephesians 1:4–5 provides a good example of this with the positioning of the phrase 'in love'. Note the ESV's placement of a period: 'that we should be holy and blameless before him. In love he predestined us for adoption' with the NKJV's use of a comma in a different location: 'that we should be holy and without blame before Him in love, having predestined us to adoption'. Both renderings may work, but there is debate as to which most accurately conveys the author's intended meaning. Similar variances also appear in Eph. 1:8–9.

59. On the Damascus road, Jesus quoted a Greek proverb to Paul (Acts 26:14); while Peter quoted the ancient Mesopotamian story of Ahiqar (2 Peter 2:22). To Titus and in Athens, Paul cited Greek philosophers Epimenides and Aratus (Tit. 1:12; Acts 17:28), and to the Corinthians, Greek poet Menander (1 Cor. 15:33). 1 Enoch 1:9 is quoted directly in Jude 1:14–15. Citations from unknown sources include those found in 1 Cor. 4:6, Eph. 5:14, Phil. 2:6–11, 1 Tim. 3:16, 2 Tim. 2:11–13.

60. For more clear Corinthian quotations, see 1 Cor. 1:12 and 3:4.

61. For further reading on Paul's proposed use of a quotation-refutation device in 1 Cor. 14:34–38, see DC Arichea, 'Silence of women in the church', *The Bible Translator 46*(1), January 1995.

62. I assume the majority view that the Gospel of John, 1–3 John and Revelation share the same author, but acknowledge there is some disagreement even here.

63. The language of our New Testament, Koine Greek, relies heavily on inflections on words to alter their case, number, gender etc. Your *something-blue* Bible should provide hyperlinks to help you identify these variants, which are sometimes not as obvious in English translation.

64. For further reading on the identity of 2 John's 'chosen lady', see Donald Guthrie, *New Testament Introduction* (1990, 4th ed), InterVarsity Press, Westmont, IL, pp. 889–893.

65. The prologue of this epistle (1 John 1:1–4) constitutes a single sentence in Greek and is known to demonstrate one of the most complicated structures and styles of all John's literature.

66. For the distinctly Jewish nature of the author, audience, discourse and opponents of 1 John, and

the 'porous' boundaries of the house-churches this epistle addressed (allowing non-Christian Jews ease of access to the Jewish-Christian community), see Ben Witherington, *Letters and Homilies for Helenized Christians: Vol. 1: A Socio-Rhetorical Commentary on Titus, 1-2 Timothy and 1-3 John* (2006), InterVarsity, Grand Rapids, MI, pp. 407–409. On the point of 1:5–10 addressing the claims of non-believing heretics, those 'who reject Jesus as the incarnate Son of God', see Daniel L. Akin, '1, 2, 3 John: An exegetical and theological exposition of Holy Scripture', *The New American Commentary* 38, 2001, pp. 92–93. For Jesus specifying members of the first-century Jewish leadership and community as those who 'do not know' the Father or the Son, see John 8:13–19; 16:1–3.

67. For 'John', see Rev. 1:9; 22:8. For 'the elder', see 3 John 1:1; 2 John 1:1. For 'the disciple whom Jesus loved', see John 13:23; 19:26; 20:2; 21:7, 20, or 'the other disciple' when with Peter (John 18:15–16; 20:2–8). Interestingly, the Gospel switches from a third- to first-person narrative in the final verse (John 21:24–25), perhaps suggesting the storyteller and editor were two different people.

68. Many biblical characters in both the Old and New Testaments held multiple/dual names. Some underwent a name-change given by God (Gen. 32:28; John 1:42), some held two names for cross-cultural purposes (Gen. 41:45; Acts 13:9), and others owing to significant life events (Judg. 6:32; Ruth 1:20). Dual-name characters in the New Testament include those with foreign-language equivalents (John 21:2; Acts 13:1), those with two Jewish names (Acts 4:36) and those with family names (John 6:71; 12:4).

69. For further reading on alternate candidates to the Apostle John as the beloved disciple, see James Charlesworth, *The Beloved Disciple: Whose Witness Validates the Gospel of John?* (1995), Trinity Press International, Harrisburg, PA. For a pro-Lazarus position, see Pablo S. Muñoz, *New Insights in the Search for the Identity of the 'Beloved Disciple'* (2012), available on www.academia.edu.

70. Since God is the ultimate Author of the Scripture, the men he employed to put pen to paper are perhaps best described as His secretaries and scribes.

71. The word 'context' comes from the Latin *con* (meaning with or together) and *texere* (to weave): literally, 'to weave together'.

72. The phrase 'jot and tittle' comes from Jesus' teaching in Matt. 5:18 (KJV). A jot is the smallest letter in the Hebrew alphabet (*yod*). A tittle is smaller still, literally a fine stroke of a writer's pen, which to the astute Hebrew reader, differentiates one letter from another.

73. Ancient history includes the accounting of all human civilisations until the fall of the Roman Empire in 476 AD.

74. While I prefer the term *covenant history*, most scholars employ *redemptive* or *salvation/salvific history*.

75. Yahweh (Hebrew: *YHWH*) is the proper and distinct name for the God of Israel, as given to Moses (Exo. 3:14–15) and is used over 6,500 times in the Hebrew Bible, literally from Genesis to Malachi (Gen. 2:4; Mal. 4:5). Most English translations replace the word Yahweh with 'LORD' or simply 'God', adopting a rabbinical tradition established in the second century BC, when zealous Jews feared taking the Divine Name in vain (Ex. 20:7; Lev. 24:16).

76. See David Instone-Brewer, *Divorce and Remarriage in the Bible: The Social and Literary Context* (2002), Eedermans, pp. 15–19.

77. There is some disagreement, for example, as to whether God cut one or two covenants with Abraham. Some argue that the covenant of familial blessing (Gen. 12:1–3; 22:15–18) is separate to the covenant related to the promised land (Gen. 15:7–21). Others believe both agreements are brought together in a single covenant (Gen. 17:1–14). Regardless, the Scriptures speak of divine covenants relating to creation, Adam and Noah prior to that of Abraham (Jer. 33:20–22; Hos. 6:7; Gen. 8). Post-Sinai, further divine covenants are made with David the king, and Phinehas the priest (Num. 25:10–13; Ps. 89:3–4; Jer. 33:14–26).

78. Compare this selection of pre-Sinai and post-Sinai accounts: worshipping false gods (Josh. 24:14 and Exo. 32:7–10, 27–35), breaking Sabbath (Exo. 16:24–30 and Num. 15:32–36), murmuring against Moses' leadership (Exo. 14:11–12 and Num. 12:1–15; 16:1–50), complaining about desert conditions (Exo. 15:22–25; 16:1–14; 17:1–6 and Num. 11:1–10, 31–34; 21:4–7).

79. I encourage you to read *He Qualifies You!* for a more in-depth study of this concept, in which I clearly outline the progression of these three covenants and demonstrate the stark contrast in how

God relates to His people under each arrangement.

80. The Greek word *diathéké* can either be translated as covenant, testament or will (see Heb. 9:15–18).

81. After Christ's covenant is introduced, the apostle Paul refers to the covenant of Moses (the Sinaitic covenant) as the 'old covenant', while the book of Hebrews favours the term 'first covenant' (2 Cor. 3:14; Heb. 8–10).

82. See also Matt. 26:28; Mark 14:24; 1 Cor. 11:25; Heb. 9:13–10:18.

83. There is no coincidence that the Golden Calf story at Sinai contains the Bible's first mention of man pleading God for forgiveness (Exo. 32:30–32), that is, of requesting God to cancel a 'sin-debt'. Paul would later explain that 'sin was in the world before the law was given, but sin is not charged against anyone's account where there is no law' (Rom. 5:13). In order for forgiveness to be possible, there must first exist a debt to cancel!

84. See Matt. 5:17. These descriptors of the new covenant, in comparison to the old, are all found in the book of Hebrews, an epistle almost entirely dedicated to contrasting the two.

85. See also Heb. 8:4–5; 9:6–10; 10:1–3.

86. Nevertheless, to maintain some modicum of respect from his Jewish brothers and 'win some' over to Christ, Paul continued to observe certain rites and regulations pertaining to the old covenant, including insisting Timothy be circumcised and participating in worship at the temple and a purification rite (Acts 16:1–3; 21:20–27; 1 Cor. 9:19–20).

87. See 2 Cor. 3:7–11; Heb. 8:7–13; 9:8–11; 12:27.

88. While I do see some benefit in adjusting our terminology—describing Genesis to Malachi as the 'Hebrew Bible', and Matthew to Revelation as the 'First-Century Scriptures', for example—I'm not quite prepared to advocate for such a radical departure from the current cultural norm just yet. Let's stick with Old and New Testaments for now, so long as we are aware of the potential problems this editorial distinction may create.

89. While arguably the first ten books of the Old Testament (Genesis to Samuel) and the first five books of the New (Matthew to Acts) are presented in chronological order, for most of the Bible's 66 books, this is not the case.

90. If the three covenants reveal the different ways God has related to His people over time, the 'seven governments' describe primarily how God's people developed in their identity and relationship with one another. As per the covenantal ages, while these dispensations may be distinct, there are significant periods of overlap, as one age transitions into the next. For further reading on the metanarrative of Scripture, consider Vaughan Roberts, *God's Big Picture: Tracing the Storyline of the Bible* (2002), InterVarsity Press, Grand Rapids, MI. The author takes 'the kingdom of God' as the Bible's unifying theme and presents eight epochs to walk the reader through the unfolding narrative. See also Bruce Gore, *Historical and Chronological Context of the Bible* (2010), Trafford Publishing, Bloomington.

91. Dates provided in these headings and the corresponding article, *A Seven-Age Summary of the Biblical Chronology*, are approximate and sometimes rounded for simplicity and ease of understanding. There are various interpretative theories and approaches for dating the ancient world, and disagreements exist within biblical scholarship as to precise dates for many biblical events.

92. Creation story/stories (Gen. 1:1–2:3 and 2:4–25); ancient genealogies (Gen. 5; 10; 11:10–32).

93. Adam and Eve (Gen. 2:4–25); expulsion from the garden (Gen. 3); Cain and Abel (Gen. 4); Noah's flood and family (Gen. 6–9); Tower of Babel/Babylon (Gen. 11:1–9). While his name does not appear in Genesis, there is reason to believe that the story of Job is set during this same period of primeval history. Whether the account of Job is fictional (his name does not appear in any of Israel's genealogies) or genuinely historical is subject to debate.

94. For 'walked with God' see Enoch (Gen. 5:22–24), Noah (Gen. 6:9) and, by insinuation, Adam and Eve (Gen. 3:8).

95. From as early as the patriarchs (Gen. 22:17; 37:9–10), it is common for Hebrew authors, particularly in prophetic literature, to draw on the creation language of Genesis 1 and 2 when describing God's covenant community, their leadership, land, city and temple. In particular, see

Deut. 31:1–11; Isa. 51:15–16; 65:17–25; Jer. 4:22–28; Dan. 12:2–3. This practice is continued by New Testament authors; see Gal. 6:15–16; Phil. 2:14–16; Rev. 12:1–9.

96. For when non-Hebrews become part of Abraham's family, see Gen. 17:9–14, 27. Some believe the 'mixed multitude' who came out of Egypt in the exodus also included non-Israelites (Exo. 12:38 ESV).

97. In total, there were fifteen Hebrew judges: Moses and Joshua, twelve as described in the book of Judges, and finally Samuel, who, like the Apostle Paul, was not 'one of the Twelve' but was arguably greater than the Twelve. The other factor that makes Moses' and Joshua's ministry unique among the judges is that it is the only case in which God initiates and commands a succession from one leader to the next.

98. Prior to this, the Israelites attempted to have Gideon and his sons rule as their perpetual leaders, but he staunchly refused (Judg. 8:22–23).

99. Here, the format of our Bibles begins to deviate from what has so far been, for the most part, a pretty straightforward linear sequence. Again, I recommend you acquire a copy of a chronological Bible-reading plan, in particular to appreciate where the Psalms, books of wisdom and (later) the Prophets fit into the storyline.

100. While described as a rejection of God (1 Sam. 8:7; 10:19; 12:12) and an 'evil thing' in the eyes of the Lord (1 Sam. 12:17–20), Israel's request for a monarchy was foretold by Moses some 350 years earlier (Deut. 17:14).

101. The author of Chronicles does cite prophetic writings of such men from this era that, for whatever reason, seem to not have been preserved for us (1 Chron. 29:29; 2 Chron. 9:29; 12:15).

102. Although the tiny tribe of Benjamin is somewhat absorbed into Judah (1 Kings 11:13, 32–26; 20:12), centuries later, both Benjaminites and Levites are still identified in the return from Babylon (Ezra 1:5), and even right up to the first century, when Paul is able to claim Benjaminite ancestry (Rom. 11:1; Phil. 3:5). After the split, smatterings of other northerners also defect to Judah (2 Chron. 11:16–17; 15:9).

103. The northern kingdom's demise is succinctly summarised in 2 Kings 17. It was prophesied by the likes of Ahijah (1 Kings 14:15–16), Amos, Micah, Hosea and Isaiah and pictured in covenantal terms as both a divorce (Hos. 2:2; Jer. 3:8), and death (Hos. 6:5; 9:15–17; 13:1, 7–9), both of which were appropriate penalties for an adulterous wife, according to Torah (Lev. 20:10; Deut. 24:1–4).

104. For 'removed/thrust [from] his presence', see also 2 Kings 23:27 and 24:20 in reference to the southern kingdom, a concept Paul will allude to in 2 Thess. 1:9. In this context, Israel's destruction by Assyria, we are first introduced to the phrase 'the day of the Lord' (Amos 5:18–20), a term used subsequently by many prophetic voices, including Isaiah, Zephaniah, Joel, Malachi and the first-century apostles.

105. There would be at least three waves of Judeans taken to Babylon, with Daniel captured in the first (605 BC), Ezekiel in the second (597 BC) and Jeremiah personally witnessing the third (586 BC), when Jerusalem was virtually destroyed. While practically similar, the main difference in the fall of the two kingdoms was covenantal. Drawing on Hosea's marriage metaphor, later prophets explain that while Israel was divorced from God (Jer. 3:8), Judah would merely experience a temporary separation from Him (Isa. 54:5–8). In keeping with His promise to David, God would ensure the survival of the Judean family line (1 Chron. 17:11–14; 2 Chron. 6:16).

106. To add to the complexity, the Prophets sometimes refer to the northern Kingdom as 'Ephraim' (2 Chron. 25:7; Isa. 11:3; Ezek. 37:16; Jer. 31:6; Hos. 5:3). This is likely because the first king appointed to this kingdom, Jeroboam, hailed from this leading tribe. However, an even further look back shows us that Jacob predicted Ephraim would become a 'group of nations' (Gen. 48:19). Further, of the 12 spies sent into Canaan by Moses in Numbers 13, the two faithful ones were from the tribes of Judah (Caleb) and Ephraim (Joshua).

107. The 5Rs of Israel's restoration (return, rebuilding, resurrection, remarriage and reunification) are repeated in the pre-exilic period by Major and Minor Prophets alike. Ezekiel brings all five elements together through Chapters 36–37. See also Ezek. 11:14–20; 16:59–60; 28:25–26; 34:11–31 and Chapters 40–48.

108. Just as there were three major waves of captivity, so Ezra–Nehemiah would narrate three major waves of return and restoration: the restoration of *worship* with Zerubbabel (Ezra 1–6), restoration

of the *Word* under Ezra (Ezra 7–10), and finally, the restoration of the *walls* thanks to Nehemiah (Neh. 1–13).

109. 'Jew' literally means a man of Judah or 'Judahite' (Hebrew: *Yehudi/Yehudim*). While its first appearance is in 2 Kings 16:6, the term only comes to prominence and common usage in the narrative following Judah's fall to Babylon. See Isa. 45:1–3 for the prediction regarding Cyrus, and Jer. 25:1–14; 29:10–14 and Dan. 9:1–19 for that related to the 70-year servitude to Babylon.

110. There are differences of opinion as to when the last books of our New Testament were written, particularly so for the book of Revelation. One view is that the Apocalypse was received sometime in the mid-late-60s AD, prior to the Roman-Jewish War and the destruction of Jerusalem in the year 70. The other places the composition of Revelation in the mid-90s, making it the last book of the Bible to be written. This is the majority view among modern scholars. For further reading on the dating debate, and how it may affect our understanding of Revelation, see C Marvin Pate (ed), *Four Views on the Book of Revelation* (1998), Counterpoints Series, Zondervan, Grand Rapids, MI.

111. Jesus promises the fulfilment of everything written about Him 'in the Law of Moses, the Prophets and the Psalms' (Luke 24:44), to which Paul claims special insight into the 'mystery' of how such fulfilments were taking place (Rom. 16:25–26; Eph. 3:2–6; Col. 1:25–27). For 'end/culmination of the ages', see 1 Cor. 10:11; Heb. 9:26. For 'fullness of time/the times', see Gal. 4:4; Eph. 1:10.

112. 'The law is only a shadow of the good things that are coming—not the realities themselves ... the reality, however, is found in Christ' (Heb. 10:1; Col. 2:17). This is a major theme in the book of Hebrews particularly, which describes Israel's physical temple/tabernacle, city, mountain, altar, throne, ancestry and priesthood, together with her sacred rituals, sacrifices, customs and festivals as all superseded by spiritual equivalents in the new-covenant world.

113. The Apocalypse is another name for the book of Revelation, which John introduces as: 'The revelation [Greek: *Apokalypsis*] from Jesus Christ' (Rev. 1:1).

114. For some of Jesus' explicit predictions regarding the persecution of His followers by the old-covenant world and its leaders, see Matt. 10:16–23; 23:34; John 15:18–16:4.

115. Moses' prediction of the old-covenant community's final generation, described as 'warped, crooked and perverse' (Deut. 32:5, 20), is applied to the first-century audiences of Peter (Acts 2:40), Paul (Phil 2:15) and Jesus (Matt. 12:38–45; 16:1–4; 17:17; Mark 8:38; Luke 17:25). For 'last days/times' fulfilment, see Acts 2:14–17; Heb. 1:1–2; Jude 1:17–19.

116. As Eve was taken from the side of Adam (Gen. 2:22–24), so the church was birthed from Christ's side (John 19:34; Eph. 5:30–32). The Adam of Genesis serves 'as a pattern of the one to come' (Rom. 5:14); a pattern fulfilled in Christ, 'the last Adam' (1 Cor. 15:45).

117. For further reading on ancient cultural influence on the biblical text, see: John J Pilch, *A Cultural Handbook to the Bible* (2012), William B Eerdmans Publishing, Grand Rapids, MI; *The IVP Bible Background Commentary* (Old and New Testaments), IVP Academic, Grand Rapids, MI. See also the *Cultural Backgrounds Study Bible* by Zondervan (available in both NIV and NKJV).

118. Individualist societies are essentially the result of Western liberalism, a worldview popularised in the eighteenth-century Enlightenment era in Western Europe. Despite its obvious influence on the world, today only a minority of regions (including North America, Australia, the United Kingdom and parts of Europe) would be considered individualist. The bulk of the planet's populations live in collectivist societies.

119. This is not to say that collectivism is a more 'biblical model', in the sense that it more closely reflects God's will for the organisation of human societies; it is purely a recognition that every book in our Bible had collectivist community as part of its cultural backdrop.

120. See Acts 10; 11:14; 16:14–15, 29–34; 18:8.

121. It is worth noting that in his famous temple sermon, the apostle Peter makes clear that while Christ Jesus was sent to *all* of the Jews [plural], it was the responsibility of *each* of them [singular] to turn to Him in repentance (Acts 3:26).

122. For further reading on the collective nature of biblical societies, see E. Randolph Richards and Brandon J O'Brien, *Misreading Scripture with Western Eyes: Removing Cultural Blinders to Better Understand the Bible* (2012), IVP Books, Grand Rapids, MI.

123. The Bible's first use of the word 'nation' comes in the genealogical records of Noah's sons, aka

the table of nations, in Genesis 10. Both the New Testament and Septuagint use the Greek word *ethnos*, translated commonly as 'nations' or 'Gentiles'; from which comes the English term 'ethnicity'.

124. Acts 21:37–22:3; Rom. 9:1–5.

125. For 'set apart' language as it applied to the nation of Israel, see Ex. 8:22–23; 19:5–6; Deut. 7:7–8; 14:2; Amos 3:1–2. Centuries after Moses, God makes a covenant with David in Jerusalem, claiming that the men of Judah (i.e., the Jews) were uniquely selected from among all kingdoms of the world to bring forth God's everlasting kingdom; see 2 Sam. 7:12–16; 1 Chron. 17:11–14; 2 Chron. 6:16–17.

126. This is in keeping with Paul's claim that the Gospel 'brings salvation to everyone who believes: first to the Jew, then to the Gentile' (Rom. 1:16), a sequence clearly demonstrated in the book of Acts, as the Gospel spread from Judea to Samaria and beyond. In fact, Acts appears to break these two ethnic groups into four, whereby each receives their own outpouring of Holy Spirit: God-fearing Jews followed by half-Jews, then God-fearing Gentiles and other Gentiles (Acts 2:5; 8:14; 10:22; 19:1).

127. Interesting note: the uniquely Pauline phrase 'Grace and Peace to you', with which Paul opens every one of his epistles, appears to be a fusion of both a conventional Greek greeting (Charis!) and a Jewish greeting (Shalom!) common to the culture of the time.

128. Note how Paul uses 'brothers' to address angry Jewish mobs (Acts 22:1), the Sanhedrin and Pharisees (Acts 23:1–6) and Jewish leaders in Rome (Acts 28:17), all of whom rejected the Gospel he preached. These were not his 'Christian brothers', they were his ethnic (i.e., Jewish) brothers.

129. Gal. 2:11–21; 3:26–29; Eph. 3:1–13; Col. 1:24–27; 3:11.

130. Within the same chronological context, see Dan. 6:25 ('Then King Darius wrote to all the nations and peoples of every language in all the earth') and Ezra 1:2 ('This is what Cyrus king of Persia says: "The LORD, the God of heaven, has given me all the kingdoms of the earth"'). The earliest biblical example of this literary device is in the context of Joseph and the Egyptian famine, when it is claimed: 'And all the world came to Egypt to buy grain from Joseph, because the famine was severe everywhere' (Gen. 41:57).

131. Including the NIV, NLT and GNB. See article 'Translating Approaches' in Chapter 7.

132. Note also Peter and John's release from prison when they interpret the conspiring of local politicians as a fulfilment of Psalm 2: 'Why do the nations rage and the peoples plot in vain? The kings of the earth rise up and the rulers band together against the Lord and against his anointed one.' According to these inspired apostles, this Scripture was fulfilled by Judean rulers, not global rulers (Acts 4:25–26). For further localised meanings of 'the whole world', see Acts 17:31; 19:27; 24:5; Rom. 10:18; Rev. 3:10. For 'all the nations', see Luke 21:24; Acts 2:5. For 'the world' as referring specifically to the Jewish/old-covenant world, see John 15:18–16:3.

133. 'Scientific materialism' (or metaphysical naturalism) is the antithesis to this worldview, suggesting that natural elements are all that exist and can be entirely understood and explained by science.

134. For the five 'heavenly places' references, see Eph. 1:3, 20; 2:1–6; 3:10; 6:11–16.

135. The phrase 'gathered to their people/ancestors' is first used in the Torah when referring to the deaths of key characters such as Abraham (Gen. 15:15), Isaac (Gen. 35:29), Jacob (Gen. 49:29–33), Aaron (Num. 21:24–26) and Moses (Deut. 32:50), while the authors of Samuel, Kings and Chronicles prefer the slight variant 'rested with' (2 Sam. 7:12; 1 Kings 14:31; 15:8, 24; 2 Chron. 12:16; 14:1; 16:13). For 'land of the living' contrast, see Ps. 116:8–9; Isa. 38:10–11. For Sheol as located under/below the earth, see Gen. 37:35; Num. 16:28–33; Deut. 32:22; Job 21:13; Ps. 30:3; Prov. 15:24; Ezek. 31:14–16; for its apparent characteristics see Job 3:13–19; 10:20–22; 26:5–6; Ps. 88; 115:17; Isa. 14:9.

136. Used over 2,000 times in the Hebrew Bible, the word 'Elohim' and its derivatives can denote either a singular god or multiple gods (Ps. 82:1 contains both), much like the English terms 'sheep' or 'deer'.

137. For Yahweh as 'God of gods', see Ex. 15:11; Deut. 3:24; Ps. 86:8; 95:3; 96:4; 97:7–9; 136:2; Dan. 2:47. That a group of gods was assigned rulership over the 70 nations listed in Genesis 10, including jurisdiction over their designated lands, is supported by extra-biblical writings such as the books of Enoch, Jasher and Ecclesiastus. This idea is also acknowledged by the king of Assyria,

who insisted Yahweh be worshipped in the land of Israel to avoid ongoing spiritual misfortune (2 Kings 17:24–28).

138. For further depictions of this so-called divine council, see Gen. 11:7; 1 Kings 22:19–23; Job 1:6–12.

139. Molek (Lev. 20:1–5; 2 Kings 23:10), Baal-zebub (2 Kings 1:2–3; Mark 3:22), Gog (Ezek. 38:2–3; Rev. 20:7–8), Princes of Persia and Greece (Dan. 10:12–21) and Satan (Luke 10:17–19; Rom. 16:20; Rev. 12:7–9). That said, the Scripture contains numerous 'satans'. Indeed, the Bible's first use of the term (Hebrew: *satan*) is in reference to the angel of the Lord (Num. 22:22, 32)! In cases like these, the word is preceded by either the definite article (i.e., 'the satan', as in the book of Job) or the indefinite article (i.e., 'an accuser' or 'an adversary'). In other words, 'satan' is oftentimes used as an office, function or title. It is employed in reference to multiple characters throughout the Hebrew Bible, both human and divine (see 1 Sam. 29:4; 2 Sam.19:22; 1 Kings 5:4; 11:14, 23–25; Job 1:6–12; Ps. 109:6; Zech. 3:1–2).

140. Col. 1:15–18; Eph. 1:15–2:7. For use of *hagios* denoting divine/angelic beings, see Rev. 14:10, Jude 1:14 and Ps. 89:5–7, Dan. 4:13; 8:13 in the Greek Old Testament/Septuagint (LXX).

141. For further reading, see Michael S. Heiser, *The Unseen Realm: Recovering the Supernatural Worldview of the Bible* (2015), Lexham Press, Bellingham, WA.

142. Since the God who authored our Bible does not speak with a forked tongue, you can have confidence that, ultimately, the truths revealed in Scripture are complementary and not contradictory. By its very nature, truth is consistent.This philosophy is also what undergirds the scientific method, responsible for the technological discoveries and development of our modern world. As with the scientific method, the science of hermeneutics involves observation and correlation, or 'suggesting and testing' before conclusions are drawn.

143. Num. 35:30; Deut. 17:6; 19:15 (also John 7:51; 8:17). This 'two or three witnesses' principle is applied by Jesus when confronting a brother who has sinned and agreeing together on the verdict (Matt. 18:15–20); and by Paul when establishing his ministry authority (2 Cor. 13:1), providing guidelines for entertaining accusations against church leaders (1 Tim. 5:19), and, it seems, in dealing with divisive believers (Tit. 3:10).

144. That 'Scripture interprets Scripture' is based on the understanding that the Bible's revealed truths exist in harmony and unity, without contradiction—a principle often referred to as the 'Analogy of Faith'. See Milton Terry, *Biblical Hermeneutics* (pp. 579–581). According to the 1646 *Westminster Confession*: 'The infallible rule of interpretation of Scripture, is the Scripture itself; and therefore, when there is a question about the true and full sense of any scripture (which is not manifold, but one), it may be searched and known by other places that speak more clearly' (1:9).

145. Also Matt. 21:33–46; Mark 12:1–12.

146. Also Ps. 80:8; Jer. 2:21–22; Lam. 1:15; Isa. 5; Ezek. 15; Hos. 10:1. Jesus' teaching in Matthew 20–21 contains three vineyard-related parables, and references 'the cup' of Jesus' suffering. In prophetic literature, the cup of wine image, made from crushed and bleeding grapes, speaks of God's consuming wrath and fury (see Ps. 75:8; Isa. 51:17–22; Jer. 25:15–17; Rev. 14:9–10).

147. It is often claimed that we are to understand the Old Testament in light of the New. This may be so, but, as this vineyard example demonstrates, the inverse is equally true—the Old Testament helps us comprehend and interpret the New. In fact, almost every collective metaphor describing the identity of the Jesus community is borrowed from the Old Testament. The idea that the church is God's bride, family, army, nation, priesthood, Kingdom, body and more, has its origins in Moses and the Prophets describing God's relationship to old-covenant Israel.

148. The Greek term used by Paul in Gal. 4:13 is *astheneia*. Translation options include 'weakness' (KJV2000), 'infirmity of the flesh' (KJV, ASV), 'bodily illness' (NIV and NASB) and 'I was sick' (NLT).

149. Interestingly enough, we see a similar story play out in the life of King David. While on the run from his son Absalom, David and his entourage are pelted with stones, dirt and verbal insults from a disgruntled member of Saul's family (see 2 Sam.16:5–14). Unlike David, the apostle Paul would be embraced by his Galatian friends. Said David, 'My wounds fester and are loathsome … my back is filled with searing pain … the light has gone from my eyes. My friends and companions avoid me because of my wounds' (Ps. 38:5–12).

150. Clearly, the four Gospels share many parallel accounts, as do the histories of Samuel, Chronicles

and Kings. Many of Israel's narratives are retold in poetic form in the Psalms and Prophets, offering a new perspective on the same incidents.

151. 1 Cor. 7:25–38. In this instance, Paul specifically states that this is a rule bound to that particular time, place and situation. In the Old Testament, God issues Jeremiah a similar instruction to not marry, in light of the impending hardships to be faced by the residents of Judah and Jerusalem in the Babylonian war (Jer. 16:1–13).

152. Mary Magdalene (John 20:16–18); the Samaritan woman (John 4:28–30); Priscilla (Acts 18:24–26); other women who prophesied (Luke 2:36; Acts 2:17; 21:19; 1 Cor. 11:5).

153. Mic. 6:4; Judg. 5–6; Rom. 6:1–2, 7 (also 1 Tim. 3:11, which refers to female deacons).

154. For a comprehensive multi-tiered study on this text, see Andreas J. Köstenberger and Thomas R. Schreiner, *Women in the Church: An Analysis and Application of 1 Timothy 2:9–15* (2005), Baker Academic, Ada, MI.

155. Romans 9–11 includes direct quotations from the books of Genesis, Exodus, Leviticus, Deuteronomy, 1 Kings, Job, Psalms, Isaiah, Jeremiah, Hosea, Joel and Malachi.

156. See Hos. 2:2 and Jer. 3:6–8, in which God claims He had issued the northern kingdom a 'certificate of divorce' thereby annulling His marriage covenant with those tribes. However, He later promised to remarry her with a new covenant as one unified kingdom/bride, at some point in the future; see Jer. 31:31–32; Ezek. 16:59–62; 37:22–28; Hos. 1:11; 2:14–23.

157. Immediately after this prophecy from Caiaphas, the 'two becoming one', Jesus no longer moved about publicly among the Jews (i.e., the men of Judah), but instead withdrew north to a village called Ephraim (John 11:51–54). There is no doubt the author is drawing his audiences' attention to the promise of both Hebrew kingdoms (Judah and Ephraim) being reunited in Christ!

158. Paul's explicit references to this revealed 'mystery' (Greek: *mustérion*) of Jewish-Gentile unity in Christ include: Rom. 16:25–27; Eph. 1:9–13; 3:7–12; 5:30–32; Col. 1:25–27.

159. In Galatians, Paul explains how his Gospel convictions regarding the equal status of Jew and Gentile were confirmed by revelation from the Spirit (Gal. 1:11–12), consultation with the saints (Gal. 2:1–9) and corroboration from the Scriptures (Gal. 3:6–14).

160. See also Josh. 23:13; Ezek. 28:24.

161. See Craig S Keener, *The IVP Bible Background Commentary: New Testament* (1994, 2nd ed), IVP Academic, Grand Rapids, MI, p. 521.

162. Also Luke 12:39–40; 2 Peter 3:10; Rev. 3:3; 16:15. There are numerous parallels in the content of the Thessalonian epistles and passages in Matthew suggesting that Paul had likely acquired an early copy of this Gospel prior to his Thessalonian ministry, perhaps while visiting the apostles in Jerusalem in Acts 15. See 1 Thess. 4:15 and 1 Cor. 11:25, in which Paul cites Jesus' teachings.

163. Plague of darkness (Exo. 10:21–23); plague on firstborn and Passover (Exo. 11–12; Heb. 11:28). At the Red Sea crossing, Israel and the Egyptian armies were separated by God's glory cloud so that Israel was in light and their oppressors in darkness all night (Exo. 14:19–20). Again, the 'people of the light' and 'people of the darkness' distinction is inferred in the text.

164. See Matt. 28:1–15; Luke 24:36–44; John 20:28–29; 1 John 1:1.

165. This combination in sentence structure: raising up out from among (ek/ex) the dead ones (nekron), is employed more than a dozen times in Paul's epistles, and also by Peter (1 Peter 1:21).

166. Individuals' belonging to the collective body of Christ, and the rights and responsibilities that membership entails, is a major theme of this entire Corinthian letter: 'Don't you know that your bodies [plural] are members [plural] of Christ Himself [singular]? ... For we were all [plural] baptized by one Spirit to form one body [singular]' (1 Cor. 6:15; 12:13). See also Rom. 12:5; 1 Cor. 10:17; 12:27; Eph. 5:30.

167. The New Testament in particular contains multiple references to the eschatological 'resurrection of the dead', but perhaps the best place to begin a study on this subject is in the Prophets, particularly Hosea. After all, Paul effectively bookends his entire 1 Corinthians 15 teaching with Hosea's predictions (1 Cor. 15:4/Hos. 6:1–3; 1 Cor. 15:55/Hos. 13:12–14). To compare two very different exegetical treatments on 1 Corinthians 15, as well as the contrasting conclusions they reach, consider Samuel G Dawson, *Essays in Eschatology: An Introductory Overview of the Study of Last Things* (2017, 3rd ed), Bowie, Texas: SGP Press, pp. 147–234, and N. T. Wright, *The*

Resurrection of the Son of God: Christian Origins and the Question of God, Volume Three (2017), London: Society for Promoting Christian Knowledge, pp. 312–362. For a scholarly analysis of the corporate/collective dimension of the resurrected 'body', see Keith D Dyer, *Paul and Embodied Resurrection: Rethinking 1 Corinthians 15* (2009), Pickwick Publications, Eugene, OR, pp. 136–161 (available also at academia.edu).

168. For a comprehensive, but approachable, discussion on the importance of considering grammar, semantics and syntax, see Grant R Osborne, *The Hermeneutical Spiral: A Comprehensive Introduction to Biblical Interpretation* (2006), IVP Academic, Grand Rapids, MI, Chapters 2–4.

169. Strictly speaking—as your *something-blue* Bible will indicate—the word in John 15:2 is *airei*: the present, indicative, active, third-person singular form of *airó*. When citing Greek words, it is common practice for authors to simply reference the word in lexical form—that is, how it is listed in lexicons and dictionaries, regardless of the inflection.

170. In Ancient Israel, vine branches that trailed along the ground were later propped up by the placement of large rocks or poles underneath them. This would allow aeration of the branches to grow better grapes and ensure protection from mould and fungus produced from pre-dawn moisture on the ground. See *Zondervan Illustrated Bible Dictionary* (2011), Zondervan. Grand Rapids, MI, p. 1510; Colin Kruse, *John: An Introduction and Commentary*, TNTC Vol. 4, p. 365.

171. For a scholarly analysis of the 'lift up' translation of *airó* in John 15:2, see James Montgomery Boice, *The Gospel of John, Volume 4* (1999), Baker Book House, Grand Rapids, MI.

172. Commonly used in the field of hermeneutics, the Latin phrase *sensus literalis* means 'in the sense of the literature'.

173. For further reading on biblical literary genres, see Fee and Stuart, *How to Read the Bible for All Its Worth*, Chapters 4–13; Duvall and Hays, *Grasping God's Word*, Parts 4–5; Klein et al., *Introduction to Biblical Interpretation*, Part IV.

174. John's Gospel is unique among the others in that it contains no Parables of Jesus, in the strict sense of that term. However, this Gospel makes a point of highlighting the metaphorical nature of nearly all His teachings and preaching.

175. That said, a thorough study of the term 'three days and three nights' may indeed reveal a kind of Hebrew idiom that does not refer strictly to a 72-hour period, but rather *the best part* of a three-day period, in which even part of a day would constitute the whole. See Matt. 16:21; 27:63; Luke 24:21; John 2:19 (also 1 Sam. 30:11–13).

176. It is *possible* that Jesus' forthright assertion 'you have had five husbands, and the man you now have is not your husband' has a prophetic/non-literal meaning extending beyond this individual. After the Assyrian destruction of Samaria in 722 BC, five foreign nations emigrated to the region and worshipped their gods at five local high places. They also worshipped Yahweh, even though they were not in covenant with Him (2 Kings 17:24–41). In other words, the people of Samaria had five covenant gods (husbands) and one god to whom they were not covenanted. Jesus comes as both the perfect man and perfect God (number seven!) to remedy this situation.

177. The idea of sleep as a euphemism for death is also used by Moses (Deut. 31:16); Daniel (Dan. 12:2); Matthew (Matt. 27:52); Luke (Acts 7:60); and Paul (1 Cor. 15:6).

178. See Matt. 13:10–17; Mark 4:10–12; Luke 8:9–10. See also Matt. 16:5–12, in which the disciples miss the meaning of 'the yeast of the Pharisees and Sadducees' until Jesus provides further detail.

179. The Passion Pop Quiz—10 Statements of Jesus: Luke 22:10–12; Matt. 26:26–28; Mark 14:18; Luke 22:31; Luke 22:34; Matt. 26:39; Mark 14:61–62; Luke 23:28–31; Luke 23:43; John 19:26–27.

180. For further symbolic explanations in the Apocalypse, see Rev. 1:20; 5:8; 12:9; 17:12, 18. Old Testament prophets had many times referred to the old-covenant community with the disparaging terms 'Sodom' and 'Egypt'; John was simply borrowing this analogy from his prophetic predecessors (Deut. 28:27, 60; 29:23; Isa. 1:9–10; 3:8–9; Jer. 23:14; Lam. 4:6; Ezek. 16:44–58; Amos 4:10–11).

181. Matt. 5:29–30; 6:3; John 10:9–11; Matt. 16:23; John 6:70; Matt. 15:26; Luke 13:32; Matt. 23:24, 33.

182. Isa. 24:23; Hos. 5:7; Joel 2:31 and Gen. 37:9–10; Rev. 12:1.

183. See also Job 42:12–16. Other Old Testament passages indicate that the notion of having 'seven sons' was viewed as a sign of God's blessing and the ideal family (1 Sam. 2:5; Ruth 4:14; also Jer. 15:9).

184. References to 'forty year' reigns: Moses (Deut. 8:2); Othinel (Judg. 3:11); Deborah (Judg. 5:31); Gideon (Judg. 8:28); Eli (1 Sam. 4:18); Saul (1 Sam. 13:1; Acts 13:21); David (2 Sam. 5:5; 2 Chron. 29:27); Solomon (2 Chron. 9:30); Joash (2 Kings 12:1). For 40 years as associated with a 'generation', see Num. 14:28–35; 32:13.

185. Gen. 5:3–32. The only exception to this rule seems to be Methuselah, who is said to have lived for 969 years, a number that 'coincidentally' is augmented by 7 twice: (180 + 7) plus (775 + 7), see Gen. 5:25–27. Note also the numbers contained soon after in the flood account, and the conspicuous recurrence of 7, 40 and multiples of 10 (Gen. 7:1–24; 8:3–12; 9:28–29). See Duane L Christensen, *The Genesis Debate: Persistent Questions about Creation and the Flood* (1986), Baker, Grand Rapids, MI, p. 167.

186. For 'thousand years', see Rev. 20:1–7. For 144,000, see Rev. 7:1–8; 14:1–5. For 12 as it relates to the new Jerusalem, see Rev. 21:9–21; 22:1–2.

187. For further reading, see John J Davis, *Biblical Numerology: A Basic Study of the Use of Numbers in the Bible* (1968), Baker Academic, Grand Rapids, MI.

188. Also Ps. 18:6–17.

189. Major elements of David's Song of Deliverance (2 Sam. 22) echo those used for God's appearance at Mount Sinai: coming in a dark cloud (Exo. 19:9, 21; 24:15–16), coming 'down' (Exo. 19:11, 18, 20), thunder and lightning (Exo. 19:16; 20:18), smoke and fire (Exo. 19:18; 20:18; 24:17), earthquakes (Exo. 19:18) and a thundering voice (Exo. 19:19). Correlations also exist between the two Songs of Moses: including God blasting nostrils (Exo. 15:8), being a rock for His people (Deut. 32:4, 15, 18, 30) and spending arrows against His enemies (Deut. 32:23).

190. As with the defeat of Israel to Assyria (Amos 8:7–9); both Judah and Egypt to Babylon (Isa. 24:19–23; Ezek. 32:7–8); Babylon to the Medes (Isa. 13:10–13); and the predicted judgments against the likes of Edom, Tyre, Sidon and Philistia (Isa. 34:4–5; Joel 3:15–16).

191. This quotation comes from Jesus' Olivet Discourse, a prophecy recorded in each of the three Synoptics. Since Luke's account is specifically directed to a non-Jewish audience, a Roman called Theophilus (Luke 1:1–4), he translates some of Jesus' poetic and prophetic language into plain-speak. In this way, 'when you see the abomination of desolation spoken of by the prophet Daniel, standing in the holy place [let the reader understand]' becomes stated plainly as: 'But when you see Jerusalem surrounded by armies' (compare Matt. 24:15; Mark 13:21; Luke 21:20).

192. There are occasions in which prophetic predictions are written in what appears to be a very matter-of-fact manner, but the corresponding narrative indicates a *figurative* fulfilment! Malachi may have made it sound like the prophet Elijah was literally going to return to minister to Israel ('See, I will send the prophet Elijah to you before that great and dreadful day of the Lord comes'), but this prophecy was fulfilled by another man altogether, John the Baptiser. Not the literal Elijah, as Israel may have anticipated, but rather one who ministered 'in the spirit and power' of Elijah (Mal. 4:5; Matt. 11:13–14; 17:10–13; Luke 1:17).

193. First published in 1898, EW Bullinger's classic *Figures of Speech Used in the Bible* clarifies over 200 figures of speech used in the Bible.

194. Also Acts 14:27; 1 Cor. 16:8–9; 2 Cor. 2:12.

195. Also Deut. 9:6; 10:16; 31:27; 2 Kings 17:14; 2 Chron. 36:13; Neh. 9:17; Ps. 78:8; Jer. 7:26; Acts 7:51.

196. David Bivin and Roy Blizzard, Jr, *Understanding the Difficult Words of Jesus: New Insights from a Hebraic Perspective* (1994), Destiny Image, pp. 104–105.

197. Ellicott's *Commentary for English Readers* (1905), Matthew 5.

198. Each of these comparative examples are cited from the KJV and the NLT.

Step 3: What Does it Matter?

199. A noteworthy exception to this is Hendrick and Hendricks' *Living by the Book*, which devotes a solid portion to the modern and personal application of Scripture.

200. A composite of *orthos* (right, true or straight) and *temno* (to cut in a single line).

201. The word *ergatés* is used throughout the New Testament to describe hired hands in the context of farming (Matt. 9:37–38; 20:1–8; James 5:4), workers more generally (Acts 19:25), those who 'work evil' (Luke 13:27; 2 Cor. 11:13; Phil. 3:2) and those that labour faithfully in preaching God's Word

(Luke 10:1–7; 1 Tim. 5:8).

202. Also Luke 10:25–28.

203. As discussed previously, the Bible is primarily a book of covenant history—the tale of God's unique relationship with His covenant people. God's relationship with people, what it means to be in communion with Him, is the Bible's ultimate and overarching theme.

204. While traditionally the Lord's Prayer is a designation given to the 'Our Father in heaven' prayer from Matt. 6:9–13, this is not a prayer the Lord prayed. It is better described as the disciple's prayer. The most detailed prayer we have from Jesus personally is that in John 17, just prior to His death.

205. Now Ehud had made a *double-edged sword* about a *cubit* long, which he strapped to his *right thigh* under *his clothing* (Judg. 3:16).

206. 1 Cor. 4:1–2; Eph. 6:20; Col. 4:4. That the most vital aspects of Scripture are presented clearly is supported by the 1646 *Westminster Confession*: 'All things in Scripture are not alike plain in themselves, nor alike clear unto all; yet those things which are necessary to be known, believed, and observed for salvation, are so clearly propounded, and opened in some place of Scripture or other, that not only the learned, but the unlearned, in a due use of the ordinary means, may attain unto a sufficient understanding of them' (1:7). This idea is often referred to as *the Clarity* (or *the Perspicuity*) *of Scripture*.

207. The Greek word for 'disputable matters' in Rom. 1:14 comes from the verb *dialogizomai* (from which comes 'dialogue') and implies a back-and-forth deliberation and evaluation of ideas to reckon a matter thoroughly.

208. Including 1 Cor. 7:3–6; Eph. 5:21–33; Col. 3:18–19; Heb. 13:4; 1 Peter 3:1–7.

209. Water baptisms in Acts include Pentecost (2:38–41), Samarians (8:12–13); Ethiopian eunuch (8:36–39), Saul of Tarsus (9:18; 22:16), Cornelius and family (10:44–48), households in Philippi (16:15, 33), synagogue ruler Crispus and others in Corinth (18:8) and 12 disciples of John the Baptiser in Ephesus (19:4–7).

210. Further baptism references that potentially, although not certainly, speak of baptism *in water*, include 1 Peter 3:21 and in Paul's epistles: Rom. 6:3–4; 1 Cor. 1:13–17; 12:13; 15:29; Gal. 3:27; Eph. 4:5; Col. 2:11–12.

211. Each example comes from Mark's Gospel. See Mark 1:6; 11:12–14; 1:35; 14:37; 5:13; 16:18; 7:33; 8:23; 10:21; 6:7–9.

212. Examples of Holy Spirit outpourings, fillings and baptisms in Acts include: Acts 2:1–16; 4:31; 10:44–46; 19:6–7.

213. Stephen's comments in Acts 7:51 regarding 'uncircumcised hearts' draw on the appeals of Moses (Lev. 26:41; Deut. 10:16) and Jeremiah (Jer. 4:4; 9:26).

214. Deut. 30:6; Phil. 3:3; Col. 2:11–13.

215. Matt. 5:29–30; 18:8; Rom. 6:13.

216. This is one of the reasons I have grouped *implications* and *applications* together in this final *What does it matter?* step. Every text carries some form of implication for our learning, but not every text demands application to our lifestyle.

217. For these three covenant signs, see Gen. 17:9–14; Ex. 31:12–17; John 13:34–35; 1 John 3:23.

218. Passages that specifically speak of 'the tithe/tithes' (Hebrew: *maaser*): concerning the patriarchs (Gen. 14:17–24; 28:10–22; Heb. 7:4–10), the tabernacle (Lev. 27:30–32, Num. 18:20–29), the first temple (Deut. 12:10–11; 14:22–29; 26:12–15), the southern kingdom (2 Chron. 31:4–12), the northern kingdom (Amos 4:4–5), the second temple (Neh. 10:37–39; 12:44–47; 13:4–14; Mal. 3:7–12; Matt. 23:23, Luke 11:42; 18:12). For stewardship language 'belongs to the Lord/the Lord's portion/sacred portion' and 'present/bring', see Lev. 27:30–32; Num. 18:24–28; Deut. 26:12–14; Neh. 10:37; 13:12; Mal. 3:10.

219. Once more, it is possible that Jesus is alluding to the Song of Moses when drawing a connection between 'my church' and 'this rock'. In the Septuagint, the Greek-language version of the Old Testament, the word *ekklésia* (i.e., church), is used in Deuteronomy 31:30 when Moses speaks his prophetic song 'in the ears of all the *assembly* of Israel'. This same song describes Yahweh as Israel's 'Rock' (Deut. 32:4, 15, 18, 30).

220. The word here for 'confession' is *homologia*; from *homoú* (the same) and *légō* (to speak a conclusion). In the four other occasions it is employed in our New Testament, it is done so in the context of confessing Christ and His Gospel (2 Cor. 9:13; Heb. 3:1; 4:14; 10:23).

221. Also Matt. 27:11; Mark 15:2. A lengthier discourse between Jesus and Pilate is recorded in John 18:33–37.

222. Feeding of the 5,000 (Matt. 14:13–21; Mark 16:32–44; Luke 9:10–17; John 6:1–13); Jesus and Zacchaeus (Luke 19:1–10); Jesus and the demonised boy (Matt. 17:14–21; Mark 9:14–28; Luke 9:37–42); that Christians are created in Christs' image (Rom. 8:29; 2 Cor. 3:18; Eph. 2:10; 1 John 4:17).

223. The Greek word *logos* means 'word' or 'thought'. Although its roots stem from Ancient Greek philosophy hundreds of years before Christ, *logos* is frequently used in the New Testament to describe God's revelation. The Scriptures are referred to as God's *logos* in many places, perhaps the most significant for us being in our title text, 2 Tim. 2:15: 'correctly handles *the word* of truth'. See also 1 Tim. 4:5–6; 5:17; 2 Tim. 2:9; 4:2. For Jesus as *logos*, see John 1:1–4, 14.

224. 2 Cor. 2:4; 7:2–12; 11:2–11; 12:14–15. This issue is addressed in Hebrews: 'Have confidence in your leaders and submit to their authority' (Heb. 13:17). 'Submit' is unique here in the New Testament and means 'to not resist'. Submission in this context is not a heavy-handed command. Rather, it is a call to be open, honest and vulnerable, something that should be the most natural and normal thing to do when one has a caring leader-figure in their life. Sadly, this is not always the case.

225. For Saul's attempts on David's life, see 1 Sam. 18:10–11, 17, 25; 19:1, 9–15, 19–22; 22:17–19; 23:8–14, 24–26; 24:1–2; 26:2. For Saul's so-called repentance, see 1 Sam. 19:6; 24:16–22; 26:21–25. For Jonathan's naivety, see 1 Sam. 20:1–9; 23:15–18. For Saul's and Jonathan's death, see 1 Sam. 31:4–6; 2 Sam. 1:4–5, 17–27.

226. There is no indication that Bathsheba willingly consented to the sexual encounter with David. Instead, the text explains how the king sent palace officials to her home, in the dead of night, her husband absent, and 'took her' (2 Sam. 11:4 ESV). One may argue that David did not 'murder' Uriah, in the strict sense of that term, but he certainly used his authority to arrange this innocent man's death (2 Sam. 11:14–17). The prophet Nathan would later confront David and claim: 'You struck down Uriah the Hittite with the sword and took his wife to be your own. You killed him with the sword of the Ammonites' (2 Sam. 12:9).

227. 'There are lots of stories in the Bible, but all the stories are telling one Big Story. The Story of how God loves his children and comes to rescue them. It takes the whole Bible to tell this Story. And at the center of the Story, there is a baby. Every Story in the Bible whispers his name. He is like the missing piece in a puzzle—the piece that makes all the other pieces fit together, and suddenly you can see a beautiful picture'. Sally Lloyd-Jones, *The Jesus Storybook Bible,* Zondervan (2007) pp. 17.

228. 'Progressive revelation is a move from truth to more truth and so to full truth ... Progressive revelation is not a movement from error to truth but from truth to truth, the lesser to the greater, the provisional to the permanent, the inadequate to the perfect. Indeed, *cumulative revelation* might be a preferable term'. Alec Motyer, *6 Ways the Old Testament Speaks Today: An Interactive Guide*, Crossway (2018) pp 122–123. For more on 'progressive revelation', see Derek J. Morphew, *Biblical Interpretation 101: Historic Rules for Reading the* Bible, Vineyard International Publishing (2012) pp. 56–58.

229. Also John 1:18.

230. Theology refers to 'the study of God' and doxology to 'praise of God'. In Rom. 11:33–36, Paul famously concludes his complex theological treatment of predestination and election with a rousing expression of praise; demonstrating how deep theology leads to high praise.

REFERENCES

Adler, Mortimer, J. and Charles Van Doren. *How to Read a Book*. New York: Touchstone, 1940.

Akin, Daniel L. '1, 2, 3 John: An Exegetical and Theological Exposition of Holy Scripture'. *The New American Commentary* 38 (2001): 92–93.

Arichea, D. C. 'Silence of Women in the Church', *The Bible Translator* 46, no. 1 (1995).

Bivin, David and Roy Blizzard, Jr. *Understanding the Difficult Words of Jesus: New Insights from a Hebraic Perspective*. Shippensburg: Destiny Image, 1994.

Boice, James Montgomery. *The Gospel of John, Volume 4*. Grand Rapids: Baker Book House, 1999.

Brunn, Dave. *One Bible, Many Versions: Are All Translations Created Equal?* Downers Grove: Inter-Varsity Press, 2013.

Chambers, Oswald. *My Utmost for His Highest*, rev. ed. Grand Rapids: Discovery House, 2018.

Charlesworth, James. *The Beloved Disciple: Whose Witness Validates the Gospel of John?* Harrisburg: Trinity Press International, 1995.

Christensen, Duane L. *The Genesis Debate: Persistent Questions about Creation and the Flood*. Grand Rapids: Baker Book House, 1986.

Davis, John J. *Biblical Numerology: A Basic Study of the Use of Numbers in the Bible*. Grand Rapids: Baker Academic, 1968.

Dawson, Samuel G. *Essays in Eschatology: An Introductory Overview of the Study of Last Things*, 3rd ed. Bowie, Texas: SGD Press, 2017.

Duvall, J. and J. Hays. *Grasping God's Word*. Grand Rapids: Zondervan, 2012.

Dyer, Keith D. *Paul and Embodied Resurrection: Rethinking 1 Corinthians 15*, Eugene: Pickwick Publications, 2009.

Fee, Gordon. *Listening to the Spirit in the Text*, Grand Rapids: Eerdmans, 2000.

Fee, Gordon and Mark Strauss. *How to Choose a Translation for All Its Worth: A Guide to Understanding and Using Bible Versions*. Grand Rapids: Zondervan, 2007.

Gore, Bruce. *Historical and Chronological Context of the Bible*. Bloomington: Trafford Publishing, 2010.

Gorman, Michael. 'The Text' in *Elements of Biblical Exegesis: A Basic Guide for Students and Ministers*. Peabody: Hendrickson Publishers, 2009.

Guthrie, Donald. *New Testament Introduction*, 4th ed. Westmont: InterVarsity Press, 1990.

Heiser, Michael S. *The Unseen Realm: Recovering the Supernatural Worldview of the Bible* Bellingham: Lexham Press, 2015.

Hendricks, Howard and William Hendricks. *Living by the Book: The Art and Science of Reading the Bible*. Chicago: Moody Publishers, 2007.

Hughes, Selwyn, *Every Day with Jesus*. London: CWR, 2004.

Instone-Brewer, David. *Divorce and Remarriage in the Bible: The Social and Literary Context*. Grand Rapids: Eerdmans, 2002.

Keener, Craig S. *The IVP Bible Background Commentary: New Testament*, 2nd ed. Grand Rapids: IVP Academic, 1994.

Klein, William, Robert Hubbard Jr and Craig Blomberg. *Introduction to Biblical Interpretation*.

Grand Rapids: Zondervan, 2017.

Köstenberger, Andreas J. and Thomas R. Schreiner, *Women in the Church: An Analysis and Application of 1 Timothy 2:9–15*. Ada: Baker Academic, 2005.

Kruse, Colin. *John: An Introduction and Commentary*, Book 4. Grand Rapids: Eerdmans, 2004.

Lanier, Greg. *A Christian's Pocket Guide to: How We Got the Bible*. London: Christian Focus Publications, 2018.

Lasseigne, Jeff. *Unlocking the Scriptures: What the Bible Is, How We Got it, and Why We Can Trust It*, Grand Rapids: Baker Books, 2016.

Lloyd-Jones, Sally. *The Jesus Storybook Bible*. Grand Rapids: Zondervan, 2007.

Lockhart, Clinton. *Principles of Interpretation*, 2nd ed. Delight: Gospel Light Publishing Company, 1915.

Morphew, Derek J. *Biblical Interpretation 101: Historic Rules for Reading the Bible*. Sugar Land: Vineyard International Publishing, 2012.

Motyer, Alec. *6 Ways the Old Testament Speaks Today: An Interactive Guide*. Wheaton: Crossway, 2018.

Muñoz, Pablo S. *New Insights in the Search for the Identity of the 'Beloved Disciple'*. 2012. www.academia.edu.

Osborne, Grant R. *The Hermeneutical Spiral: A Comprehensive Introduction to Biblical Interpretation*. Grand Rapids: IVP Academic, 2006.

Pate, C. Marvin, ed. *Four Views on the Book of Revelation*. Grand Rapids: Zondervan, 1998.

Pilch, John J. *A Cultural Handbook to the Bible*. Grand Rapids: William B Eerdmans Publishing, 2012.

Piper, John. *Reading the Bible Supernaturally: Seeing and Savoring the Glory of God in Scripture*. Wheaton: Crossway Publishing, 2017.

Richards, E. Randolph and Brandon J O'Brien. *Misreading Scripture with Western Eyes: Removing Cultural Blinders to Better Understand the Bible*. Grand Rapids: IVP Books, 2012.

Roberts, Vaughan. *God's Big Picture: Tracing the Storyline of the Bible*. Grand Rapids: Inter-Varsity Press, 2002.

Shultz, Richard. *Out of Context: How to Avoid Misinterpreting the Bible*. Grand Rapids: Baker Books, 2012.

Spurgeon, Charles *Morning and Evening*. Peabody: Hendrickson Publishers, 1990.

Terry, Milton. *Biblical Hermeneutics*. Grand Rapids: Eaton & Mains, 1974.

Walton, John H., Victor H. Matthews and Mark W. Chavalas. *The IVP Bible Background Commentary (Old and New Testaments)*. Grand Rapids: IVP Academic, 2000.

Weima, Jeffrey and Steven Baugh. *Zondervan Illustrated Bible Backgrounds Commentary: 1 and 2 Thessalonians, 1 and 2 Timothy, Titus*. Grand Rapids: Zondervan Academic, 2016.

Witherington, Ben. *Letters and Homilies for Helenized Christians: Vol. 1: A Socio-Rhetorical Commentary on Titus, 1–2 Timothy and 1–3 John*. Grand Rapids: InterVarsity, 2006.

Wright, N. T. *Scripture and the Authority of God*. New York: HarperCollins, 2005.

Wright, N. T. *The Resurrection of the Son of God: Christian Origins and the Question of God, Volume Three*. London: Society for Promoting Christian Knowledge, 2017.

Zondervan Illustrated Bible Dictionary. Grand Rapids: Zondervan, 2011.

ARTICLE INDEX

TOPIC INDEX

SCRIPTURE INDEX

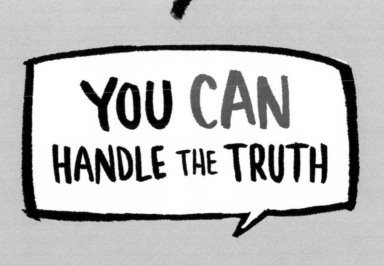

www.chadmansbridge.com/courses

Get online, and get onboard, the *You Can Handle the Truth* video mentoring program today. If you enjoyed the book—you will love this course!

Lesson One is available free, in full, and online. Check it out, at www.chadmansbridge.com/courses

AVAILABLE AS A VIDEO COURSE WITH 7 MENTORING LESSONS

... ideal for personal and small-group study!

This companion course to the book contains over five-and-a-half hours of quality content, delivered direct to camera by Chad himself, in his humorous, engaging and relaxed style.

Perfectly suited to a small-group or bible-study environment, the course is offered in *personal*, *small group* and *ministry school* editions.

He Qualifies You!

Abraham, Moses and Jesus represent the three major covenants God has offered to mankind throughout history. Each has come with the great and precious promise of God's presence and provision, and each with its own qualifying conditions. The Good News of Jesus Christ is this: *He Qualifies You!*

Clearly written and beautifully presented, this profoundly simple presentation takes its readers on a journey of discovery through the entire biblical narrative, as seen through the lenses of the divine covenants. This little book will leave you with a deeper appreciation of Jesus and His Gospel, a big-picture perspective of the Bible's overarching story, and an unshakable knowledge of the truth that, in the New Covenant, you are fully qualified to share in the blessings of God—both now, and for all eternity!

A Glorious Canvas, by Jaye Mansbridge

A Glorious Canvas: Your Gold-Filtered Life is a playbook designed to walk you through the promises of God through the full spectrum of the rainbow. Each colour, like an arrow, has the ability to strike the heart and bring new depths of glory as revelation of the love of God unfolds and cascades over your life. Arrows, which on impact, have the power to set your life alive, and on fire, with the glory of God!

LIVING
LETTERS
PUBLISHING

ABOUT THE AUTHOR
www.chadmansbridge.com

Husband to Jaye and father to four, Chad M. Mansbridge is also a
pastor, author, content creator, conference speaker,
and one of Australia's most dynamic Bible teachers—known for
his ability to communicate profound and complex truth with
clarity, simplicity, and a whole lot of fun.

A loveable Aussie larrikin with an infectious zest for life, Chad
carries an unshakable desire to see people walk in an authentic
and unhindered relationship with their Maker, and is regularly
invited to speak at churches, colleges, and conference events
throughout Australia and overseas.

Follow Chad on your favourite social media platform:
@Chad.M.Mansbridge

If you enjoyed this book, be sure to spread the word by leaving a
review at your favourite online bookseller. This helps other readers
find Chad's material and is a great way to acknowledge the impact
of his ministry on your life—giving glory to God in the process!

Made in the USA
Middletown, DE
19 November 2021

52447201R00201